Your Rights in the Workplace

FIRST EDITION

By Dan Lacey

With the Editors of Nolo Press

NOLO PRESS   BERKELEY, CALIFORNiA

Your Responsibility When Using a Self-help Law Book

We've done our best to give you useful and accurate information in this book. But laws and procedures change frequently and are subject to differing interpretations. If you want legal advice backed by a guarantee, see a lawyer. If you use this book, it's your responsibility to make sure that the facts and general advice contained in it are applicable to your situation.

Keeping UpTo Date

To keep its books up to date, Nolo Press issues new printings and new editions periodically. New printings reflect minor legal changes and technical corrections. New editions contain major legal changes, major text additions or major reorganizations. To find out if a later printing or edition of any Nolo book is available, call Nolo Press at (510) 549-1976 or check the catalog in the Nolo News, our quarterly newspaper.

To stay current, follow the "Update" service in the Nolo News. You can get the paper free by sending us the registration card in the back of the book. In another effort to help you use Nolo's latest materials, we offer a 25% discount off the purchase of any new Nolo book if you turn in any earlier printing or edition. (See the "Recycle Offer" in the back of the book.)

First Edition	DECEMBER 1991
Second Printing	April 1992
Editors	NOLO PRESS
Illustrations	MARI STEIN
Book Design	JACKIE MANCUSO
Cover Design	TONI IHARA
Index	SAYRE VAN YOUNG
Printing	DELTA LITHOGRAPH

LACEY, DAN
    Your rights in the workplace / by Dan Lacey ;
illustrations by Mari Stein. -- 1st National ed.
      p. cm.
    Includes index.
    ISBN 0-87337-159-3 : $15.95
    1. Employee rights--United States--Popular works. 2. Labor laws
and legislation--United States--Popular works. I. Title.
KF3319.6.L32 1991
344.73'012596--dc20
[347.30412596]
                                    91-32435
                                      CIP

recycled paper

To Lauren:

May you carry the flame of fairness deep into the future.

Acknowledgments

A number of people encouraged and assisted me in bringing this book to life.

My wife, Margaret, maintained her tradition of being my number-one helper and enthusiast.

Help also came from attorneys Joseph E. Kalet, associate general counsel for the Washington Metropolitan Airport Authority and author of the *Primer on Wage & Hour Laws* (BNA, 1990), who reviewed and improved my chapter on wage-and-hour law; Deborah Martin-Norcross, an employment law expert with the nationwide firm of Jackson, Lewis, Schnitzler & Krupman, who assisted me with the chapter on parents' rights even though she earns her living by batting for the opposing team; and F. Benjamin Riek III, a Cleveland-based specialist in representing workers against ex-employers, who gave me expert insights into wrongful-discharge litigation that I would not otherwise have had.

Joe Moynihan, a benefits consultant formerly with the Labor Department and my co-author in a forthcoming self-help guide to benefit programs, also contributed significantly to this book.

The staff of the Cleveland-Marshall College of Law library at Cleveland State University not only allowed me to do most of my research there, but also made the task an enjoyable one.

To all of these very generous people, I offer a heart-felt "thanks."

Table of Contents

CHAPTER 4

How to Challenge Your Job Loss

CHAPTER 5

Illegal Job Discrimination

CHAPTER 6

Sexual Harassment

CHAPTER 7

Joining and Quitting Labor Unions

CHAPTER 8

Replacing Your Income When You're Out of Work

CHAPTER 9

Healthcare Insurance, Pensions and Other Benefits

CHAPTER 10
Parents' Workplace Rights

CHAPTER 11
Keeping Your Workplace Safe

CHAPTER 12
Other Workplace Rights

CHAPTER 13
Lawyers and Legal Research

How To Use This Book

It is essential to use Chapter 1 to determine your work status before applying the rest of the information in this book to your job. As you'll see, most of the workplace laws detailed in this book apply only to employees and statutory employees, and not to people working as independent contractors or statutory nonemployees.

For the sake of simplicity, *Your Rights in the Workplace* assumes that the reader is a nonunion employee in a privately owned company. But if you're a member of a labor union, most of the laws discussed in this book still apply to you. In most circumstances, labor union members enjoy the workplace rights afforded to nonunion workers—plus some additional rights created by the contract between their employer and their union.

In general, employees of governments work under special sets of workplace laws that apply only to the level of government that employs them. However, Title VII of the Civil Rights Act of 1964 covers employees of state and local goverments. The Act also covers federal employees, but the procedures they must follow to enforce their rights under that law are different than those for other workers. (See Chapter 5.)

With the exception of Chapter 1, the information in this book can be used out of context. But, wherever possible, the many sections of this book are cross-referenced to guide you to other areas of law that may affect your employment. In a few places, footnotes are used to suggest other sources of information.

1

Determining Your Employment Status

Work comes packaged in a variety of legal forms. Only by first determining which legal category fits your work situation can you determine whether laws covering employees apply to you.

A. The IRS Makes the Rules

For the most part, America has allowed the status of being an employee to be something that just happens when you work under someone else's control and get paid for it. Being an employee has no clear legal standing of its own.

The Internal Revenue Service—because it routinely requires money be withheld from the paychecks of employees—has become the dominant judge of who is and is not an employee. The IRS does this with rules that it simply makes up. Luckily, the IRS has demonstrated uncharacteristic restraint over the years by classifying workers into only four categories.

B. Legal Categories of Work

The Internal Revenue Service recognizes four categories of employment:

1. Common-law employees

Common-law employee is the category into which most working people fit— and the one which best describes what most people think of as traditional employment: a job.

According to the IRS, the employer's right to control both the type and method of work is the basic criterion for classifying a worker as a common-law employee. The title that you or the person paying you assign to your work situation simply doesn't matter for legal purposes.

One way to decide whether you're legally an employee of a company is to find out how that company reports your income each year to the IRS. If the company you work for gives you a W-2 form at the end of each calendar year, that shows that the company considers you to be a common-law employee and intends to account to the government for you in that way. If it doesn't consider you to be a common-law employee, it will either give you an IRS Form 1099 Miscellaneous to report your income at the end of each year—or it won't report your income to the IRS at all. For the sake of simplicity, the word employee throughout the rest of this book will mean common-law employee.

BEWARE OF THE WORK-FOR-HIRE TRAP

The question of whether or not you are someone's employee can be especially important if your work involves creating intellectual properties such as song lyrics, chemical formulas, screenplays, architectural designs, book manuscripts, wallpaper patterns, computer software, poems, or paintings.

Independent contractors can negotiate which rights to their creations they are willing to sell, and on what terms, before beginning work on a project. But according to copyright and patent laws, something created by an employee within the scope of employment is a work-for-hire and, therefore, belongs to the employer.

Example: A musical composer who works as an employee of an advertising agency writes—on agency time and for an agency client—a jingle that soon sets the whole world a-humming.

The only money the composer is likely to get from that creation is a weekly paycheck. No royalties, no fame; the jingle belongs outright to the people who paid for its creation.

---

2. Independent contractors

Like the employee category, whether a worker is legally an independent contractor is determined primarily by the employer's control over the work. To be considered an independent contractor, a person must work under an arrangement in which only the outcome of the project—not the means and methods of accomplishing it—is controlled by the company or person paying for the work.

There is a second major criterion for being designated an independent contractor: You must offer your services to the public at large, not just to one company.

Example: Jeffrey does machine repairs and gets most of his income from one company that operates several factories containing hundreds of machines. When a machine breaks down, a factory manager calls him and he comes to the plant and figures out how to repair it. Sometimes, he puts the machines on his truck and takes them to his shop to be worked on there. Jeffrey also advertises his services in the local telephone directory, and through that ad he gets a few repair calls from other companies.

Because he determines how to do the repairs and also offers his work to more than one company, he is legally considered an independent contractor with every company that he works for—even the one that provides most of his income.

EMPLOYEE OR INDEPENDENT CONTRACTOR: ADDITIONAL GUIDANCE

If your work situation presents a close call as to whether you are an employee or independent contractor, consider the following factors—the same ones that the IRS looks at in determining your official status.

Instructions. An employee must comply with instructions about when, where and how to work. Even if no instructions are given, the employer control that makes you an employee exists if the employer has the right to give instructions.

Training. An employee is trained to perform services in a particular manner. Independent contractors use their own methods and receive no training from those who pay for their services.

Integration. An employee's services are integrated into the business operations because the services are important to the success or continuation of the business. This shows that the employee is subject to direction and control.

Services rendered personally. An employee renders services personally. This shows that the employer is interested in the methods by which the work is done as well as the results.

Hiring assistants. An employee works for an employer who hires, supervises and pays assistants. An independent contractor hires, supervises and pays assistants under a contract that requires him or her to provide materials and labor—and is responsible only for the result.

Continuing relationship. An employee has a continuing relationship with an employer. However, a continuing relationship may exist where work is performed frequently, although at irregular intervals. An employee who is called in to work for only a few days each month is still an employee.

Set hours of work. An employee has set hours of work established by an employer. An independent contractor establishes his or her own work schedule.

Full-time work. An employee normally works full-time for an employer. An independent contractor can work when and for whom he or she chooses. Note that this factor doesn't exclude part-time workers from being employees. (See Section C on part-time workers.) What the IRS seems to mean here is that an employee works exclusively for one employer.

Work done on premises. An employee works on the premises of an employer, or works on a route or at a location designated by an employer.

Set work duties. An employee must perform services in the order or sequence set by an employer. This shows that the employee is subject to the employer's direction and control.

Reports. An employee submits reports to an employer. This shows that the employee must account to the employer for his or her actions.

Pay. An employee is paid by the hour, week or month. An independent contractor is paid by the job or on a straight commission.

Expenses. An employee's business and travel expenses are paid by the employer, showing that the employee is subject to the employer's regulation and control.

Tools and materials. An employee is furnished with tools, materials and other equipment by an employer.

Investment. An independent contractor has a significant investment in the facilities used in performing services for someone else.

Profit or loss. An independent contractor can make a profit or suffer a loss, while an employer assumes no direct risk for the profitability of a business.

Working for more than one person or firm. An independent contractor gives services to two or more unrelated people or firms at the same time and offers services to the general public. An independent contractor makes services available to the general public.

Right to fire. An employee can be fired by an employer. An independent contractor cannot be fired as long as he or she produces a result that meets the specifications of the contract.

Right to quit. An employee can quit his or her job at any time without incurring liability. An independent contractor usually agrees to complete a specific job and is responsible for its satisfactory completion, or is legally obliged to make good for failure to complete it.

INDEPENDENT CONTRACTORS: OUTSIDE THE EMPLOYMENT LAWS

Most workplace rights guaranteed by law to employees are not guaranteed to people who work as independent contractors. Independent contractors account for only about 13% of the workforce—and this is a country, don't forget, where the majority makes the rules. In general, the relationship between independent contractors and the company or person paying for their work is covered not by the law of the workplace, but by contract law and the business codes of the states. The only substantial exceptions are where the independent contractor status is being misapplied to employees to circumvent workplace laws.

From a legal standpoint, an independent contractor is just a little one-person business and, consequently, must live by the laws that govern all businesses, large or small. For example, an independent contractor who agrees to perform a task for a specific amount of money must fulfill that contract and cannot demand to be paid time and one-half rates for spending more than 40 hours in one week completing that task.

So if you've determined that you're legitimately working as an independent contractor, you're probably feeling somewhat left out at the moment. Most of the information in this book doesn't apply to you. But it may help you to know that, although you're part of a largely unprotected minority within the workforce, the number of independent contractors is growing.

---

3. Statutory employees

This category includes groups of workers who might not seem to qualify as employees, but who have been designated by special laws as being subject to tax withholding requirements imposed upon employees. An employer's control is irrelevant here. What matters most is the specific type of work being done.

Most of the laws defining statutory employees were passed in response to special-interest political lobbying. For example, labor unions usually view independent contractors and people who work at home as threats to the work standards of unionized factories, so they have exerted political pressure to keep as many home workers as they can under the wage-and-hour laws that govern employees.

Because of such piecemeal lobbying, there is no central logic to the statutory employee category. If the law says you are one, you simply are one; there's little to be gained by trying to figure out why.

Types of workers that are statutory employees include:

- **Delivery drivers.** Drivers who deliver meat, vegetables, fruits, bakery products, or beverages other than milk; or who pick up and deliver laundry or dry cleaning, but who are legally agents of a company and are paid on commission. (An agent is someone who is authorized by another to act on his or her behalf.)

Example: A bread truck driver who sells on commission to a customer route on behalf of only one bakery would typically be an agent of that bakery—and therefore, a statutory employee of the bakery. But a restaurant supply distributor who buys bread at wholesale prices and resells it at a profit would typically be considered neither an agent nor a statutory employee of the bakery that produced the bread.

- **Insurance agents.** Insurance sales agents whose main job is selling life insurance or annuity contracts, or both, primarily for one life insurance company.

- **Home workers.** People who work at home according to a company's explicit instructions on materials or goods that are supplied by a company and which must be returned to that company or to someone designated by that company.

- **Business-to-business salespeople.** People whose main job is to sell on behalf of a company and turn in orders to that company from wholesalers, retailers, contractors, hotels, restaurants or other business establishments. The goods sold must be merchandise for resale or supplies for use in the buyer's business operation, as opposed to goods purchased for personal consumption at home.

This category applies only to those whose main job is selling business-to-business. Because the IRS sets no firm statistical standards for this type of work, the definition of "main job" is subject to differing interpretations. In general, this category is directed at traveling salespeople who might otherwise be considered independent contractors because their employers exercise so little control over their daily work activities.

Example: Mary is an on-the-road salesperson for a roofing manufacturer that supplies building contractors. Because she works primarily out of her car and an office in her home, and visits the company's headquarters only once every two weeks, the company has very little control over how and when she does her work. Nevertheless, the IRS considers her to be a statutory employee.

4. Statutory nonemployees

Like statutory employee, the category of statutory non-employee lacks a central logic. It has been specifically created through efforts by various special-interest lobby groups.

There are only two categories of statutory non-employees recognized by the IRS: licensed real estate agents and direct sellers. A direct seller is usually defined as someone who sells goods to a consumer who intends to use them personally—for example, a person who sells household vacuum cleaners through in-home demonstrations.

People working in these occupations are considered statutory non-employees if:

1. substantially all payments for their services are directly related to sales, rather than to the number of hours worked, and

2. their services are performed under a written contract providing that they will not be treated as employees for federal tax purposes.

Direct sellers must satisfy one additional requirement to qualify as statutory non-employees: They must do their selling someplace other than in an established retail store or salesroom.

WORKING FOR AN EMPLOYEE-OWNED CORPORATION

Since the late 1970s, there has been a trend within corporate America toward a great variety of financing schemes that have been lumped under the title of employee ownership. In some cases, corporations have sold entire divisions they no longer wanted to the employees of those divisions. In others, they've actually given the division to employees at no charge.

But in many cases, employee ownership programs have amounted to little more than transferring a small percentage of corporate stock to employees. Employees' retirement funds are sometimes blended with money provided by investment bankers or other investors to create an entity described as employee-owned, but to which the non-employee investors have first claim.

Consequently, hundreds of thousands of American workers are now regularly reminded by their bosses that they are part of an employee-owned company—implying that they are something other than employees. But workers whose day-to-day relationship with an employee-owned corporation fits all the IRS criteria for the category of employee are still employees of that corporation. The percentage of the corporation's stock owned or controlled by its employees simply doesn't affect their employee status.

C. Conversational Categories of Work

The following definitions cover what might be called conversational categories of work. These are tags that people and companies often give to various work relationships, but that are not really legal categories of work according to IRS rules. No matter what you, your employer or your associates call your job, it falls under one of the four official IRS categories of employment. (See Section B.)

The following explanations offer some guidance on which legal category generally best fits a work situation:

1. Consultants and subcontractors

In some areas of the United States, and within some industries, the terms consultant and subcontractor are frequently used to describe work relationships. However, the IRS doesn't recognize either one as a legal category of work. The business arrangements under which people who are really consultants and subcontractors work typically make them independent contractors.

There's nothing inherently illegal about calling yourself a consultant or subcontractor when your work situation actually makes you an employee. But some companies intentionally misuse these terms. They mislabel workers who are really employees in crude attempts to circumvent laws requiring employers to withhold taxes from employees' paychecks and to pay into programs such as unemployment insurance and workers' compensation. (See Chapter 8, Sections B and D.)

Employees who aren't familiar with workplace laws are sometimes duped by unscrupulous employers who use the titles consultant and subcontractor incorrectly. But some employees knowingly go along with such schemes because it gives them more flexibility in paying incomes taxes—or sometimes just because they think these imprecise titles sound more prestigious than employee.

However, the IRS actively enforces significant penalties for employers and employees caught using these job descriptions as an excuse for not withholding taxes—sometimes going as far as sending agents into a business to report on the conditions under which people are working. If the agents see that you're working under the control and direction of a company, but the company's records show that no taxes are being withheld from your pay, both you and your employer may soon find big bills for back income taxes plus interest in your mailboxes.

There are also other potential disadvantages—such as lack of workers' compensation coverage and ineligibility for unemployment insurance benefits—for those who work under such misdesignations.

2. Personal service contractees

Because some feel it has a flattering ring to it, people who simply work as independent contractors will say that they have a personal service contract with a company. But a personal service contract is more correctly defined as a written agreement between a company and an employee that spells out the terms of the employee's work and compensation over and above what is required by law.

For example, engineers with rare technical skills sometimes agree to leave one company for another only after their new employer promises, in a personal service contract, to employ them for several years—or to pay them the equivalent of the salary they would have received for those years if they are fired before their contract expires.

Many career advice books and articles published in recent years have recommend that you negotiate a personal service contract before taking a new job. It's a nice thought, but the truth is that very few working people have sufficient power on their side of the employment transaction to negotiate a personal service contract. If you've ever sat and waited a few weeks for the telephone to ring after sending out a couple dozen resumes, you know that when a good job offer finally does come, you're in neither a mood nor a bargaining position to do much negotiating. And for many positions, such contracts are simply impractical or unnecessary.

Consequently, personal service contracts are rare except at the highest levels of corporate management, in professional sports and other forms of commercial entertainment, and where an employee has very rare skills or is required to move to a distant country—in essence, to give up a lifestyle completely for a time—to perform a job for a limited number of years before returning home.

If you are someone's employee but also have an individual contract that specifies such things as how much you'll be paid, what hours you'll be expected to work, what bonuses you'll receive and how many years you'll be employed, you're among the lucky. Such a contract does not, however, negate the fact that you are an employee. It merely gives you some extra rights, enforceable under contract law.

If you are working under an individual employment contract but are not legally an employee or statutory employee as described in Section B, then you're either an independent contractor or statutory nonemployee, depending on the nature of the work.

3. Part-time workers

There is no single, overriding definition of what constitutes a part-time worker in workplace law. Some workplace laws specify their own definitions of full-time and part-time workers. But for the most part, it is merely contemporary American culture that defines full-time work as 40 hours of work spread over a five-day period within a given week.

Therefore, describing a job as part-time does not change a worker's legal status. A person who works substantially less than 40 hours per week, for example, and whose work situation fits the description of an employee, is an employee. And a less-than-40-hour worker whose work situation fits the description of an independent contractor is an independent contractor.

4. Job sharing

In theory, two or more people can share what used to be a high-paying job that required 40 or more hours of work per week—without having to work for the low wages traditionally paid to part-timers. But job sharing is not a legal category of work.

Workers who consider themselves to be involved in job sharing are legally employees when all other aspects of their work situation fit the definition of an employee, and legally independent contractors when all other aspects of their work situation fit the definition of an independent contractor.

5. Temporaries

On a typical day, more than one million jobs in America are filled by workers supplied to a company by services that specialize in temporary staffing.

Most people working through temporary services are legally employees of the services, not the companies to which they are assigned. The temporary service companies pay workers' wages, withhold taxes from their paychecks and contribute to programs such as Social Security and workers' compensation just as any other employer would. Many of the temporary services also offer benefit programs such as healthcare insurance to those they employ.

6. Leased employees

Employee leasing allows companies to cut costs and simplify management of workforces by paying another company that specializes in such things to properly hire and fire workers, manage benefit programs and the like. As the American workplace has grown more legally complex, employee leasing has become increasingly popular.

Like temporaries, most leased workers are legally employees of the service firm that supplies workers to the client company in which they work. The basic difference between leased workers and temporaries is that the leased employees are expected to be assigned to one job for a substantial amount of time—usually at least one year.

D. Fine Points of Being an Employee

After you've determined whether or not you are, or have been, an employee of some person or company, you'll need to know about two final details: employer ID numbers and duration of employment. Also review the title assigned to your position to make sure that you're not inviting legal trouble by using a title that does not accurately describe your job.

1. Employer identification numbers

Since we live in a world that is becoming more computerized each day, the IRS and other government agencies need a way to track employees and employers by numbers, rather than by names. There are many thousands of Smiths in America, for example, but when keyed in by their individual nine-digit Social Security numbers, computers can easily distinguish them.

You, too, have to use a government-assigned serial number if you want to be sure of your employer's identity. This may seem unnecessary. But many working people today who appear to be employed by one company are, in fact, employed by another. Look at the name badges of some service station attendants, for example. Although they're wearing uniforms done up in the colors of the oil company, their badges point out in small print that they're really working for an employee-leasing subsidiary of the oil company.

Some small, unincorporated employers use their personal Social Security numbers to identify their companies to the IRS. Larger employers, and all those that are incorporated, are assigned an Employer Identification Number (EIN) by the IRS. Each corporation is allowed to have only one EIN, so one number often is used by several divisions of a corporation that conduct business under different names.

Employment-related IRS forms such as the W-2 and the 1099-Miscellaneous include spaces in which the person or company paying you must note their identification numbers. That number is then used to track the records of the company and its employees within the IRS system.

Consequently, your employer's identification number is an important component of your employment status and history. Your true employer is the one that owns the employee identification number that appears on your records.

There are a number of reasons why a less-than-honest employer might use an identification number other than its own. One typical example would be at a hazardous waste clean-up site, where workers think they're working for a big-name company but are technically being paid by a virtually bankrupt subcontractor which is likely to go out of business about the time that it gets sued because of worker injuries.

Because of privacy laws, there is no official way to verify the validity of the employer identification number that your employer is using. Nevertheless, the IRS encourages people who suspect that their employers are using false or incorrect employer identification numbers—a tip from a disgruntled payroll office worker would be a typical reason—to report it to the criminal investigation department of their local IRS district office.

2. Duration of employment

There are no laws that specifically define when employment begins and ends. You become employed when an employer offers you a job and you begin performing it. You cease being an employee when you quit the job, or are dismissed from it by your employer and you stop performing the work.

Certainly, providing your employer with advance notice when quitting a job is a considerate way of leaving—and the one that is the most likely to provide you with a history of goodwill with previous employers. But the practice of providing an employer with two weeks of notice when resigning from a job is merely a tradition, not a legal requirement.

As an employee, you need not provide your employer with any advance notice; you can quit whenever you like.

Likewise, most employers with the exception of those covered by the plant-closing laws (discussed in Chapter 4, Section D), owe you no advance notice of dismissal.

3. Incorrect job titles

Most people would admit that they would like to be just a little more important than they already are. But that natural yearning for prestige can sometimes grow dangerously out of control in the workplace.

The craving for importance is particularly strong in the United States, where the culture generally regards people bearing corporate titles to be more credible, important and powerful—not to mention more worthy of being sent a gold MasterCard—than noncorporate folks. Try applying for a bank loan by filling in writer, dancer or musician in the blank that asks for your current employment, and you'll quickly understand why, at the peak of his career, Edgar Allen Poe once had to survive for nine days on dandelion leaves.

The most common response to the need for work status is an inflated job title. It can seem harmless to puff up a title just a wee bit. And some defend that putting a big title on a business card might even enhance chances of landing new business accounts. But pretending to have authority that you do not can create legal problems.

For example, an employee who holds the commonly inflated title of Vice President may be sued in a personal injury lawsuit against the company, as evidenced by the growing number of cases in which corporate officers are held personally responsible for the actions of the corporation. That same employee, doing the same job, would be much less likely to be sued while working under a title such as Customer Service Representative.

CHAPTER

2

Wages, Hours, Tips and Commissions

The French writer Voltaire once pointed out that work spares us from three great evils: boredom, vice and need. Most of us can tolerate a little boredom, and some may even enjoy a small helping of vice. But need is something we'd all rather avoid.

So getting paid for our work is really what employment is all about. Although we'd all like our jobs to be fun and fulfilling, we must be paid for our work—fairly and on time—so that we can enjoy the other aspects of our lives.

A. The Fair Labor Standards Act

The most important law affecting a worker's right to be paid fairly is the federal Fair Labor Standards Act or FLSA, passed in 1938 in reaction to a national job shortage and the horrible work conditions that developed during the Great Depression. It is the FLSA that supplies the legal foundation for basic employment concepts such as the federal minimum wage, restrictions on child labor, the 40-hour workweek and extra pay for working overtime. If you hear someone mention wage-and-hour law, they probably mean the FLSA.

The FLSA establishes minimums for fair pay and hours. But an employer must also comply with other local, state or federal workplace laws that set higher standards. So once you determine whether you are being paid properly under the FLSA, you may still need to check the other laws that apply to your situation.

The FLSA is one of the most complex laws of the workplace. It has been amended many times, so it's full of exceptions and exemptions. The easiest way to understand the FLSA is to look first at who it covers.

Officially, the FLSA applies only to employers whose annual sales total is $500,000 or more or who are engaged in interstate commerce. You might think that this would restrict the FLSA to covering only employees in large companies, but in reality it covers nearly all workplaces. This is because the term interstate commerce has been broadly interpreted by the courts to include, for example, any company that regularly uses the U.S. mail to send or receive letters to and from other states. It would be hard to imagine one that doesn't.

Even the fact that its employees use company telephones to place or accept interstate business calls has been interpreted by courts and federal agencies to place an employer under the FLSA.

1. Exempt employers

Farms that use less than 500 person-days of paid labor in a calendar quarter are specifically exempt from the FLSA, and there are some other very specific employer exemptions.[1] However, FLSA exemptions for employers change so often that you should double-check any exemption your employer claims by calling your local Labor Department Wage and Hour Division office, listed in the federal government section of your telephone directory.

2. Exempt employees

Some employees are exempt from the FLSA even though their employers are covered. Here are the most common categories of employees exempt from all or part of the FLSA:

---

[1]If you want to research the exemptions to FLSA coverage in detail, you'll find most of them in 29 U.S.C. §213. The most direct way to become familiar with these exemptions is to read about them in an annotated edition of the code, which is what your local library is most likely to have.

The annotated editions contain summaries of court decisions that will help you to understand the courts' rulings about this complex law. So many different arguments about the FLSA have been made in court by employers and workers with many different perspectives that reading these summaries can, believe it or not, be entertaining as well as legally useful.

- **Executive, administrative and professional workers.** Most of us know people who worked for a bank or similar nonmanufacturing company, received a promotion to a position with a executive-sounding title, and then found out that they were no longer eligible for overtime pay for all those hours they put in after the company locks its front door each night. What makes that little trick legally possible for the bank is the FLSA's exemption for workers in executive, administrative and professional positions.

It is quite easy for a company to avoid the wage-and-hour law by using such exemptions. To qualify as an exempt executive, for example, the employee must:

- exercise discretion in performing job duties

- regularly direct the work of two or more people

- have the authority to hire and fire other employees, or to order such hiring and firing

- be primarily responsible for managing others, and

- devote no more than 20% of work time to other duties that are not managerial. For certain retail and service companies, 40% of nonmanagerial time is allowed.

The definitions of administrative and professional employees are similar, but contain minor differences such as requiring that employees categorized as professionals perform work that is primarily intellectual. These definitions also change with the employee's salary level. For example, if the weekly salary of the executive, administrative or professional employee exceeds $250, fewer factors are required to qualify for the white-collar exemption.

- **Employees in training.** The Department of Labor issues special certificates to employers who demonstrate that some or all of their employees are exempt from the FLSA's minimum wage rules because they qualify as learners, apprentices or students. To be exempt under this category, the training must be for the benefit of the employee—not the employer—and must be similar to trade school instruction. The work must also satisfy several other criteria:

—The trainee must work under close supervision, and not displace employees who are not part of the training program.

—The employer must not get any immediate advantage—such as lower overall labor costs—from using the exemption.

—Both the trainee and the employer must clearly understand that the employer needn't pay wages during the training period.

—The trainee must not have a guaranteed job with the employer at the end of the training period.

- **Transportation industry workers.** Some truck drivers, taxicab drivers and others employed in the transportation industry are exempt from the FLSA. Their wages and hours are controlled instead by the Interstate Commerce Act, which is administered and enforced by the Department of Transportation.

- **Employees who work out of the country.** Most employees stationed outside of the United States are excluded from FLSA protections. However, the FLSA does cover workers in Puerto Rico, the U.S. Virgin Islands, American Samoa, Guam, Wake Island, Eniwetok Atoll, Kwajalein Atoll, Johnston Island and the Outer Continental Shelf lands.

- **Special situations.** People with severe physical handicaps employed in special workshops, volunteers in nonprofit organizations, mental patients or patient-workers at rehabilitation facilities, and prison laborers are also exempt from the FLSA. The employer should be able to show documentation of permission from the Department of Labor to employ people under special FLSA exemptions. If your employer claims that you're working under such a special situation but can't produce any such documentation, check the validity of your employer's contention with the local Wage and Hour Division Office of the Labor Department.

- **Personal companions and casual babysitters.** The answer to the question of whether a particular employment situation falls under this category typically depends on the circumstances of the individual case. For example, if you are a teenager who babysits only an evening or two each month for the neighbors, you probably can't claim coverage under the FLSA—whereas an employee of a commercial child day care center probably can.

Officially, domestic workers—housekeepers, professional babysitters, chauffeurs, gardeners—are covered by the FLSA if they are paid at least $50 in cash wages per calendar quarter by their employer, or if they work eight hours or more in a week for one or several employers.

In real life, the issues of which domestic workers are covered by the FLSA and whether their rights under that law are practical to enforce vary greatly with the circumstances of each employment situation. The best way to determine whether the FLSA applies to a particular domestic job is to call the local office of the Labor Department's Wage and Hour Division.

INDEPENDENT CONTRACTORS ARE EXEMPT

The FLSA covers only employees, not independent contractors (discussed in Chapter 1, Section B). However, whether a person is an employee for purposes of the FLSA generally turns on how dependent that worker is upon one employer, not on the Internal Revenue Service definition of an independent contractor.

If your personal financial situation makes you almost totally dependent upon being paid by one company, a court would probably rule that you are an employee of that company for purposes of the FLSA, regardless of whether other details of your work-life would appear to make you an independent contractor.

Example: A group of fishpackers worked on terms that, under Internal Revenue Service rules, would probably qualify them as independent contractors. They were free to work for other companies, they supplied their own tools, they set their own hours and they were paid by piece rates. The company that employed them argued that they were not employees but independent contractors and, consequently, need not be paid the minimum wage required by the FLSA.

However, a federal court ruled that the FLSA did govern the terms of their employment. The court reasoned that the FLSA was intended to prevent abusive work conditions, and that to exempt those fishpackers from its coverage would make them vulnerable to such conditions (*McLaughlin v. Seafood Inc.*, 867 F.2d 875 (1989)).

B. Your Rights Under the FLSA

There are a number of key rights that you are granted by the FLSA if your job is covered by the law.

1. The minimum wage

Employers must pay all covered employees not less than the minimum wage—$4.25 per hour as of April 1, 1991. The only significant exception to this minimum for covered workers is the training wage for younger workers (discussed below).

Remember, some states have established a minimum wage that is higher than the federal one, in which case the higher state standard is the rate to which you're entitled.

The FLSA doesn't require any specific system of paying the minimum wage, so employers may pay on the basis of time at work, piece rates, or according to some other measurement. In all cases, however, an employee's pay divided by the hours worked during the pay period must equal or exceed the minimum wage requirement.

Weekly wage example: A parts department employee at an auto dealership is paid $250 per week for working 40 hours each week. Even though she doesn't work by the hour, her pay is $6.25 per hour ($250 divided by 40).

Piece-rate example: A roofing worker is paid $3 for each bundle of shingles he installs. He never installs less than 100 bundles in any 40-hour week, so his pay is at least $7.50 per hour (100 bundles X $3 each, divided by 40).

Under the FLSA, the pay you receive must be in the form of cash or something that can be readily converted into cash, or other legal forms of compensation such as food and lodging. Your employer cannot, for example, pay you with a coupon or token that can only be spent at a store run by the employer. Employee discounts granted by employers cannot be counted toward the minimum wage requirement.

No pay required for time off. Neither the minimum wage section nor any other part of the FLSA requires employers to pay employees for time off, such as vacation, holidays or sick days. Although some such paid time off each year has become the standard for full-time workers in most industries, the FLSA covers payment only for time on the job.

Tips. When employees routinely receive at least $30 per month in tips as part of their job, their employers are allowed to credit a percentage of those tips against the minimum-wage requirements. On April 1, 1991, the percentage of the minimum wage that may be displaced by tips rose to 50%.

Example: Alfonse is employed as a waiter and averages $10 per hour in tips. The restaurant's owner may use a portion of those tips to displace one-half of the minimum wage requirement, but is still required to pay Alfonse at least $2.125 per hour on top of his tips for the first 40 hours worked in each week, and more for any overtime hours.

Commissions. When people are paid commissions for sales, those commissions may take the place of wages for purposes of the FLSA. However, if the commissions fail to equal the minimum wage, the employer must make up the difference.

Example: Julia, a salesperson in an electronics store, is paid a percentage of the dollar volume of the sales she completes. During one slow week she averaged only $2 in commissions per hour. Under the FLSA, her employer must pay her an additional $2.25 for each hour she worked through the first 40 hours of that week, and more for any overtime hours.

The sub-minimum training wage. Until March 31, 1993, workers ages 16 through 19 who are undergoing job training must be paid a special minimum wage of $3.35 per hour. However, those being trained must be moved up to at least the standard minimum wage as soon as they've been employed for 90 days—or in some special circumstances specified in the FLSA, 180 days—at the lower training wage.

It is illegal for an employer to fire workers who are not employees in training and then replace them with others at the training wage. It is also illegal to pay the training wage to someone whose total workhours exceed 25% of all the hours worked by all the employees in a company during a given period.

2. Equal pay for equal work

Men and women who do the same job, or jobs that require equal skill and responsibility, must be compensated with equal wages and benefits under an amendment to the FLSA called the Equal Pay Act. But because the Equal Pay Act is enforced along with other anti-discrimination laws by the Equal Employment Opportunity Commission, illegal wage discrimination based on gender is discussed in detail in Chapter 5, Section E.

3. Pay for overtime

The FLSA does not limit the number of hours a covered employee may work in a week—except through some of the child labor rules discussed in Section B4. But it does require that any worker covered (that is, any worker not exempt from the Act under the rules set out in Section A) who works more than 40 hours in one week must be paid at least one and one-half times their regular rate of pay for all hours worked in excess of 40.

> **Example:** If you work 45 hours in one week and your normal wage rate is $8 per hour, you must be paid $12 per hour for the last five hours you worked that week.

There is no legal requirement under the FLSA that you be paid at an overtime rate simply because you worked more than eight hours in one day. Nor is there anything that says you must be paid on the spot for overtime. Under this law, your employer is allowed to calculate and pay overtime by the week—which can be any 168-hour period made up of seven consecutive 24-hour periods. There are some special exceptions that allow employers with necessarily odd work schedules—such as some healthcare institutions and nursing homes—to pay employees according to multiple-week standards.

There's also nothing in the FLSA that says a workweek begins on Sunday or Monday. However, consistency is required: Your employer cannot manipulate the start of the workweek to avoid paying overtime. (For more on overtime pay, see Section C2.)

EXEMPTION FOR SKILLS TRAINING

Up to 10 hours per week of otherwise payable time is exempt from the overtime rules from wage-and-hour law if those hours are used to provide employees who never graduated from high school or otherwise demonstrated that they have attained at least an eighth-grade level education with general training in reading and other basic skills. To qualify for this exemption, the training cannot be specific to the worker's current job. It must cover skills that could be used in virtually any job.

4. Restrictions on child labor

The FLSA says a person must be at least 14 years old to be employed in a job that involves neither manufacturing nor mining—which the labor department generally regards as hazardous work situations not appropriate for child workers—providing that the job doesn't have a bad effect on the young employee's schooling or health.

For workers ages 14 and 15, the law restricts when and for how many hours they may be employed:

- They may work no more than three hours on a school day and no more than 18 hours in a school week.

- They may work no more than eight hours on a nonschool day and no more than 40 hours in a nonschool week.

- During the period that starts with the day after Labor Day and ends at midnight May 31, their workday may not begin earlier than 7 a.m. or end later than 7 p.m.

- From June 1 through Labor Day, their workday may not begin earlier than 7 a.m., but it can end as late as 9 p.m.

For other kinds of nonhazardous jobs, the employee must be at least 16 years old. To work in occupations that the Department of Labor deems to be hazardous, the employee must be at least 18 years old. To determine which types of jobs are currently considered hazardous for the purposes of the FLSA, call your local office of the Labor Department's Wage and Hour Division.

Some industries have obtained special exemptions from the legal restrictions on child labor. Youths of any age may deliver newspapers, for example, or perform in television, movie or theatrical productions.

The farming industry has been fighting the child labor restrictions as well as the rest of the FLSA ever since the law was first proposed in the 1930s, so less strict rules apply to child farm workers. (See Section E3.)

5. Pay for compensatory time

Some employers offer employees compensatory time off from work in place of cash payments for overtime. This usually occurs where an employee works for a fixed salary but isn't exempt from the FLSA's minimum wage requirement. It is legal to use compensatory time in place of cash for overtime payments, but the compensatory time must be awarded at the rate of one and one-half times the overtime hours worked, and that the comp time must be taken during the same pay period that the overtime hours were worked.

> **Example:** John is paid a fixed salary every two weeks and his standard workweek is made up of five shifts, each eight hours long. During the first week of a pay period, he works 44 hours, earning four hours of overtime pay. During the second week of that pay period he can take six hours off as comp time (4 hours X one and one-half). In the second week of the pay period, he works only 34 hours but is paid his full salary as though he had worked the full 40 hours.

Many employers and employees routinely violate the rules governing the use of compensatory time in place of cash overtime wages. However, such violations are risky for both employees, who can find themselves unable to collect money due them if a company goes out of business or they're fired, and for employers, who can end up owing large amounts of overtime pay to employees as the result of a Labor Department investigation and prosecution of compensatory time violations.

THE FACTORY WORK SCHEDULE V. THE FUN WORK SCHEDULE

Most Americans consider a normal workweek to be 40 hours, spread over a five-day period that begins each Monday, with each day's work starting in the morning and ending as evening approaches. But, in fact, that kind of schedule is a leftover from the decades when factories dominated the American economy.

Production-line manufacturing techniques made it necessary for all workers to gather around a factory's machines at the same time. The lack of strong artificial light in the early factories made the daylight hours the best time to run the production line. Biblical warnings against working on Sundays inspired the factory tradition of closing for one day at each week's end.

In the 1930s, the Fair Labor Standards Act restricted the normal factory work week to 40 hours so that fewer people would be worked to physical exhaustion—and so that industry would be forced to spread work among more employees, rescuing some un-employed people from the financial humiliation of the Great Depression. Consequently, the typical factory employee's weekend break from work grew to include Saturdays.

Today, the factory-style work schedule has faded in popularity. Companies are slowly beginning to acknowledge that most people's work no longer requires them to gather in the same place, at the same time, around the same set of machines.

In 1991, for example, The Bechtel Group engineering company in San Francisco began scheduling its employees for nine days of work in every two-week period. Each of the work days that falls on Monday through Thursday is nine hours long. On Friday, only one-half of the staff works, and the shift is only eight hours long.

The Bechtel employees still work the equivalent of 40 hours per week. But, because their employer is one of the rare ones that realizes it isn't running a factory, they do it by a schedule that gives them each the enviable total of 26 three-day weekends per year.

C. Calculating Your Regular Rate of Pay

To resolve most questions or disputes involving the FLSA, you must first know your regular rate of pay under wage-and-hour law.

Whether you work for hourly wages, salary, commissions or a piece rate, the courts have ruled that your regular rate of pay typically includes your base pay plus any shift premiums, hazardous duty premiums, cost-of-living allowances, bonuses used to make otherwise undesirable worksites attractive, and the fair value of such things as food and lodging that your employer routinely provides as part of your pay.

Obviously, there is much room here too for individual interpretation and arbitrary decisions. But the overriding concept is that everything that you logically consider to be a routine part of your hourly pay for a routine day is a part of your regular rate of pay.

The courts have often ruled that the regular rate of pay does not include contributions that an employer makes to benefit plans, paid vacation and holiday benefits, premiums paid for working on holidays or weekends, and discretionary bonuses. Some employee manuals clarify what is included in your regular rate of pay by specifying that some benefit programs are regarded by the company to be extra compensation that isn't part of an employee's regular pay.

The regular rate of pay for people who work for hourly wages is their hourly rate including the factors just mentioned. For salaried workers, the hourly rate is their weekly pay divided by the number of hours in their standard workweek.

If you work on an hourly or salary basis, you can calculate how much your employer owes you for overtime hours under the FLSA by multiplying your regular hourly rate by 150% to determine the pay you're entitled to receive for each hour over 40 you work during a week. (See B3.)

1. Piece rates and commissions

People who work on piece rates and commissions instead of by the clock will find it more complicated to calculate their regular rate of pay.

For piece-rate workers, the rate may be calculated by averaging hourly piece-rate earnings for the week.

Example: Max is an assembler in a photocopier factory who is paid a piece rate of 50 cents for each copier cover he installs. One week, he worked 40 hours and installed 400 covers, so his regular rate of pay for that week was $5 per hour (400 X .50, divided by 40).

Or one of two alternatives may be used:

—Increase the piece rate by 50% during the overtime hours. For example, Max's employer could raise his piece rate to 75 cents per copier cover (150% of .50) for overtime hours.

—Estimate an average hourly wage and then use that estimated average as the basis on which to compute overtime.

Keep in mind that if the Labor Department investigates the legality of your pay rate, it may require proof that any estimates used to calculate your pay are in line with the piece-rate pay you actually earned over a substantial time, such as several months.

The methods for calculating and paying commissions vary tremendously. If you have questions about the legality of the commission system under which you're paid, call or visit the nearest office of the Labor Department's Wage and Hour Division.

2. Tips plus overtime

If you regularly work for tips, all of the tips you usually receive aren't counted as part of your regular rate of pay when calculating overtime pay. Only the wage that your employer has agreed to pay you counts, and in most cases where people work for tips, that's the federal minimum wage.

Example: Lisa works as a waitress for wages plus tips. Because she receives substantial tips, her employer is allowed to take a 50% set-off against the minimum wage requirement, paying her a wage of just $2.125 per hour. Nevertheless, her regular rate of pay for calculating overtime pay under the FLSA standards is still the minimum wage of $4.25 per hour.

One week, Lisa worked 41 hours—one hour of overtime. For that overtime hour, she must be paid $4.25, regardless of the tips she received during that hour: the $2.125 per hour that she would normally receive after the tip credit, plus one-half her regular rate of pay, which equals another $2.125.

3. Split payscales

If your job involves different types of work for which different payscales have been established by your employer, you must calculate your regular rate of pay for each category of work, and then apply the appropriate rate to any overtime hours. The payscale that applies to the type of work you did during overtime hours is the one on which you calculate the time and one-half rule.

Example: Matt works for a company that manages a large apartment complex. When he does landscaping work there, he's paid $8 per hour. When he works as a guard with the company's private security force for the complex, he gets $5 per hour. For payroll purposes, his workweek begins on Monday.

During one week in the spring, he worked eight hours a day, Monday through Friday, for a total of 40 hours with the landscaping crew. But the landscaping crew doesn't work on weekends, and Matt needed some extra money, so he worked eight hours on Saturday with the security patrol. Sunday he took off as a day to relax and regroup.

Because the FLSA's overtime pay rules take effect only after an employee works 40 hours in one week, the eight overtime hours Matt worked with the security force were at security patrol rate of $5 per hour. His overtime pay for that week is $60 ($5 X 8 X 1 1/2).

D. Calculating Your On-the-Job Time

When a work period for which you must be paid begins and ends is determined by a law called the Portal-to-Portal Pay Act (29 U.S.C. §251). It is an amendment to the FLSA and several other workplace laws. It requires that an employee be paid for any time spent that is controlled by the employer, and that benefits the employer.

There's a lot of room for interpretation and disagreement here. Consequently, this aspect of wage-and-hour law has generated a tremendous number of clashes—and cases in which the courts have attempted to sharpen that definition of payable time.

In general, the courts have ruled that on-the-job time does not include the time employees spend washing themselves or changing clothes before or after work, or meal periods during which employees are free from all work duties.

Employers are not allowed to circumvent the Portal-to-Portal Pay Act by simply "allowing" you to work on what is depicted as your own time. You must be paid for all the time you work, voluntary or not. This issue has come up frequently in recent years because some career counselors have been advising people that volunteering to work free for a company for a month or so is a good way to find a new job. Although working for free may be legal in situations where the job being sought is exempt from the FLSA (discussed in Section A1), it is not legal when the job involved is governed by the Act.

For ease of accounting, employers are allowed to round off records of work time to the nearest five-minute mark on the clock or the nearest quarter hour. But such rounding-off becomes illegal if it results in employees being paid for less time than they actually worked. In practice, this means that your employer will usually round your work time off to add a few minutes each day to the time for which you are paid.

In calculating on-the-job time, several other issues are frequently raised, such as travel time, on-call periods, sleeping on the job and multiple employers.

1. Travel time

The time you spend commuting between your home and the normal site of your job is not considered to be on-the-job time for which you must be paid. But it may be payable time if the commute is actually part of the job.

If you're a lumberjack, for example, and you have to check in at your employer's office, pick up a chainsaw, then drive 10 miles on company lands to reach the cutting site for a particular day, your workday legally begins at the time that you check in at the office.

Otherwise, just about the only instances in which you can claim that you should be paid for your time consumed in commuting to and from work are those in which you're required to go back and forth from your normal worksite at odd hours in emergency situations.

Example: Eugene normally works 9 to 5 as a computer operator and is paid hourly. One day, about two hours after he arrived home from work, he got a call from his office notifying him that the computer was malfunctioning and that he was needed there immediately to help correct the problem. It took him one-half hour to drive back to the office, two hours to get the computer back on track and one-half hour to drive home again.

The company must pay Eugene for three extra hours, two of them workhours and the third for the extra hour of commuting time required by the company's emergency.

2. On-call periods

Employers must count as payable time periods when employees are not actually working, but are required to stay on the employer's premises while waiting for a work assignment. For example, a driver for a private ambulance service who is required to sit in the ambulance garage waiting for calls must be paid for the waiting time.

But if your employer requires you to be on call but doesn't require you to stay on the company's premises, then these two rules generally apply:

- On-call time that you are allowed to control and use for your own enjoyment or benefit is not counted as payable time.

- On-call time over which you have little or no control and which you cannot use for your own enjoyment or benefit is payable time.

Example: Jack works in an office, 9 to 5, Monday through Friday, as a client services representative for a funeral director. Because of the nature of his work, his employer also requires him to be on call at all times in case a business question arises—and it furnishes him with a message beeper. Jack can spend his free time any way he wants to. All his employer requires him to do is to call the office as soon as is convenient after his beeper registers a message, so Jack's on-call time isn't payable time.

Example: Elizabeth is a rape crisis counselor with a social service agency. Because no one can predict when crimes will occur, the agency that employs her must constantly have someone with her expertise available, including weekends. During weekends when Elizabeth is the on-call counselor, she's allowed to stay at home but must remain near her telephone at all times. She can't leave her apartment except in response to a rape report, and she can't drink any alcohol. Practically speaking, she can't even throw a little dinner party because, if a call were to come in, she'd have to leave her guests immediately. Elizabeth's on-call time isn't hers to control and enjoy, so it's payable time.

DIFFERENT PAY RATES ARE ALLOWED

Unless there's an employment contract that states otherwise, employers are generally allowed to pay a different hourly rate for on-call time than they do for regular work time, and many do. The employer need only make sure that the employees are paid at least the minimum amount required under the wage-and-hour regulations.

Example: A hospital emergency room has established a policy of paying medical technicians a high hourly rate when they're actually working on a patient, and just the minimum wage when they're merely racking up on-call time on the hospital's premises. If such a technician were to record 20 hours active time and 20 hours on-call time in one week, the FLSA requires only that he or she receive the minimum wage for the 20 on-call hours.

The courts have generally approved such split-rate pay plans for the purposes of both the minimum wage and overtime requirements if there are marked differences in the types of work performed and the employer has clearly informed employees that different wages are paid for different types of work. (See Section C3 on split payscales.)

---

3. Sleeping on the job

If you're required to be on duty at your place of employment for less than 24 hours at a time, the Labor Department allows you to count as payable any time that you're allowed to sleep during your shift of duty. If you're required to be at work for more than 24 hours at a time, you and your employer may agree to exclude up to eight hours per day from your payable time as sleep and meal periods.

However, if the conditions are such that you can't get at least five hours of sleep during your eight-hour sleep-and-eat period, or if you end up working during that period, then those eight hours revert to being payable time.

Example: Bill works on an off-shore oil rig for two days at a time. At the start of each shift, the boat takes him out to the platform and doesn't come back for him until two days later. Bill and his employer have an agreement that says Bill gets an unpaid eight-hour sleep period each day, so his payable time for each 48-hour period he spends on the platform totals 32 hours. During one of Bill's shifts, a storm blew up and caused so much trouble that he has to keep working through the night. That causes one of his sleep periods to be cut down to only two hours. Bill must be paid for the sleep period that was cut short, so his payable time at the end of that shift would be 42 hours.

4. Multiple employers

No matter how many jobs you hold, the overtime pay rules apply to each of your employers individually. If in one week you work 30 hours for one employer and 30 more for another, for example, neither one owes you overtime pay.

E. Special Laws for Farm Workers

The FLSA has always treated migrant farm workers as second-class citizens, providing their employers with numerous exemptions not available to employers in other industries. But another federal law, the Agricultural Worker

Protection Act, gives migrant farm workers some special protections that ensure their rights to be paid fairly.

1. Recruitment requirements

Under that Act, each agricultural employer, farm labor contractor or agricultural association that recruits migrant agricultural workers must disclose in writing to each worker recruited:

- the place of employment

- the wage rates to be paid

- the crops and kinds of activities on which the worker may be employed

- the period of employment

- the transportation, housing and any other employee benefits available—and whether there is a charge for each of them

- whether there is currently any strike or other concerted work stoppage, slowdown, or interruption of operations by employees at the place of employment

- whether anyone has an agreement with the employer that would allow them or the employer to profit from selling goods or services to the migrant worker. For example, if a grocery store owner had an agreement to pay a farm's owner a commission of 10% of all sales to migrant workers employed on that farm, that agreement must be disclosed to the workers.

2. Paycheck requirements

Employers of migrant farm workers are required to include with each worker's pay an itemized, written statement that includes:

- the basis on which the wages are paid

- the number of piecework units earned, if paid on a piecework basis

- the number of hours worked
- the total pay period earnings
- the specific sums withheld and the purpose of each sum withheld
- the net pay.

Employers must keep a copy of these records for at least three years. They must also pay workers their wages when due according to the terms under which they were hired, and may not force the workers to purchase any goods or services exclusively from the employer.

3. Child labor restrictions

The following less-stringent child labor restrictions apply only to farm work:

- workers who are 16 and older may perform any farm job, hazardous or not, for unlimited hours
- workers who are 14 and 15 years old may perform any nonhazardous farm job outside school hours
- workers who are 12 and 13 years old may perform any nonhazardous farm job outside of school hours if they have their parents' written consent or are employed on the same farm as their parents
- children under 12 years old may perform jobs on farms owned or operated by their parents or, with their parents' written consent, outside of school hours and in nonhazardous positions on farms that use less than 500 person-days of paid labor in a calendar quarter.

The Agricultural Workers Protection Act is enforced by the Labor Department. In some situations, the Labor Department requires that various types of postings and notices to farm workers be in the workers' native language. The best way to enforce your rights under the Agricultural Workers Protection Act is to call or visit the nearest office of the Labor Department's Wage and Hour Division, listed in your local telephone under the federal government section.

F. State and Local Wage Laws

All but a few states have laws that also set wage-and-hour standards. Some of these laws are virtually meaningless because the standards they set are below those set by federal law. On the other hand, some state wage rates are significantly higher than those set by federal law.

Alaska is a good example. Its minimum wage rose to $4.75 per hour on April 1, 1991, and must remain 50 cents higher than the federal minimum should the federal law change. What's more, Alaska is one of the few states that doesn't allow tips to be used as a credit against its minimum wage.

Whenever the FLSA sets a standard higher than one at the state or local level, the FLSA rules. When a state or local law sets standards higher than the FLSA, the state or local law is the one that applies.

Each state has its own rules for who is covered by its minimum wage law, and they are usually complex. The best way to determine whether your job is covered by a state wage-and-hour law that sets a standard higher than the FLSA is to call the local office of your state's labor department. In some states, the labor department is authorized not only to advise you on wage-and-hour laws, but also to help you collect any wages that are due you under those laws. (See Charts 2-1 and 2-2 at the end of this chapter.)

In the last few years, some counties, cities and towns have debated or passed their own wage laws. Such local wage laws are still rare and controversial, but you may want to check with the law department of the county or municipality in which you work if you have reason to think that it has passed a wage-and-hour law covering your job.

1. Pay interval laws

The question of how often you must be paid is best addressed by state wage-and-hour laws. The FLSA states only that the pay period must be no longer than once a month, but state laws controlling pay intervals often require that most employees be paid at least every two weeks or twice a month.

Like state wage-and-hour laws, state laws governing how often you must be paid are complex, usually covering only certain types of companies and employees. If you have a question about how often you must be paid under your state's laws, a call to the local office of your state's labor department should answer it.

2. Final paycheck laws

Most states also have laws that specify when the final paycheck must be issued to employees who are fired or resign, and some of those laws are quite powerful. For example, Idaho has a law requiring that an employee who is fired be paid in full within 48 hours. If not, the employee may sue for up to 30 days additional wages, plus attorney's fees (Idaho Code §45-606 (1988)). See Chart 2-1 to determine whether your state has a law that governs when final paychecks must be issued.

G. The Laws of Payroll Withholding

In the decades since the end of the Great Depression of the 1930s, the right and responsibility of employers to withhold a portion of your pay has become a virtually undisputed part of American culture. The laws that create the income tax and Social Security programs for which funds are withheld typically include the legal authorization for payroll withholding to finance those programs.

The Internal Revenue Service rules for payroll withholding and reporting vary greatly among the four legal categories of work: employee, statutory employee, statutory nonemployee and independent contractor. (See Chapter 1, Section A.) You can obtain a detailed explanation of those rules free by calling the IRS forms distribution center at 800-829-3676 and requesting Publication 937, entitled "Business Reporting." This booklet is also available at your local IRS office.

State and local payroll withholding taxes usually parallel the IRS rules, but the taxing authorities in your state and city should be able to provide you with publications outlining their payroll withholding rules.

Here are some other important legal points concerning payroll withholding:

1. Noncash compensation

Under the FLSA, employers may withhold from an employee's pay the reasonable cost or value of forms of compensation other than cash, such as food and lodging, and may use that noncash compensation to satisfy minimum wage requirements. However, employers can make such deductions only after giving the employee the choice of taking cash or other compensation.

The following additional rules apply:

- The food or facilities provided by the employer must be the kind it customarily provides, and must be for the employee's benefit. The employee must be told prior to receiving the non-cash compensation that it will be deducted from the paycheck, and must voluntarily agree to accept it.

- The employer must account for the noncash compensation at cost or its fair value, and the compensation cannot profit any person or business entity related to or otherwise affiliated with the employer. In real life, these rules are intended to prevent employers from ripping off workers by using tricky noncash compensation schemes.

Example: Bob accepted a job as a guide at a remote wilderness ski resort after being told by the employer that the job pays $10 per hour and that a room and meals come with the job. But when he got his first paycheck, Bob saw that charges for housing and meals had been deducted from his pay. And the charges were so high that he really was earning only $3 per hour, far less than the minimum wage.

Asking around among other employees at the resort, he learned that the exorbitant meal charges were billed to his payroll account by a catering service owned by the resort owner's brother-in-law. Bob's employer had violated several of the FLSA's rules governing noncash compensation, so he had the right to file a complaint with the Labor Department's Wage and Hour Division.

2. Breakage and shortages

Employers who have a policy of charging the cost of broken goods or cash register shortages to employees cannot use those charges as a credit against the minimum wage.

Example: Marie took a job at $5 an hour as a sales clerk in a busy souvenir shop near Times Square in New York City, working 40 hours a week. When she received her first weekly paycheck, the accounting stub showed that her gross pay (before taxes and other deductions) was only $160, instead of the $200 she had expected. When she asked her employer to explain the shortage, he told Marie that she's responsible for any goods that customers break while she's on duty and that he noted $40 in broken merchandise during her first week on the job.

Marie's employer violated the FLSA by using breakage charges to reduce her hourly pay rate to below the required minimum of $4.25 per hour ($160 = 40 hours X $4).

3. Loans from your employer

If your employer has loaned you money, it can withhold money from your pay to satisfy that loan. However, it is illegal to make any such deduction if it would drop your pay to below the minimum wage.

Example: Bruce works 40 hours a week at $5 per hour making deliveries for an auto parts store. He's paid each Saturday. One Monday morning, the battery in his car went dead. His employer authorized him to replace his car's battery with a new one out of the store's stock—if he agreed that the price of the new battery, $60, would be deducted from Bruce's pay.

However, it took two weeks for the store to be fully paid for the battery. Under the FLSA, Bruce's employer could legally deduct no more than $30 per week (40 hours X .75) from his gross pay to cover the battery. To deduct more would drop his pay rate of $5 per hour to below the required minimum of $4.25 per hour.

4. Withholding past-due debts

The Consumer Credit Protection Act includes a formula that limits the percentage of your wages that the courts can order to be withheld to satisfy a past-due debt—in legalese, a wage garnishment. This same law forbids your employer from firing you because you have one garnishment lodged against your wages. But if you have more than one garnishment, you lose that protection.

Some states also have laws governing garnishment of wages that set even stricter limits on how much your employer can be ordered to withhold from your wages to satisfy past-due debts.[2]

5. Child support

Under the federal Child Support Enforcement Act, employers aren't just authorized to withhold wages, they're required to. An employer who fails to with-

---

[2]For more information on wage withholdings, past-due debts and taxes, see *Money Troubles* by attorney Robin Leonard (Nolo Press).

hold wages as ordered can be made to pay the amount that should have been withheld. The amount the employer must withhold is determined by the court or other administrative body controlling the child custody case in which the employee is involved. In some states, the employer is also allowed to deduct an additional fee from your wages to cover the cost of processing your child support withholdings. A call to your state's labor department should enable you to determine the rules pertaining to child support wage withholdings that cover you.

Under the Child Support Enforcement Act, you have the right to advance notice of the start of withholding for child support, and the right to appeal such an order. Also, employers are forbidden under the Child Support Enforcement Act to discipline, fire or refuse to hire an individual because his or her pay is subject to an order for child support withholding. Employers may be fined by their state if they discriminate against you because you are the subject of a child support withholding order.

6. Back taxes

The Internal Revenue Service can require your employer to withhold extra money from your wages to cover unpaid past income taxes. Some states and municipalities also have the power to order additional withholdings from your wages to pay back taxes.

THE HISTORY OF PAYROLL WITHHOLDING

There was a time, believe it or not, when employees received all the money they had earned on payday.

The Social Security Act of 1935, a part of President Franklin D. Roosevelt's New Deal, was the first law to sink its teeth firmly into the typical paycheck. Intended only to save industrial and commercial hourly workers of the Great Depression era from poverty in old age, the original Social Security program required employers to withhold a mere 1% of workers' pay on behalf of the federal government.

Since then, the Social Security Act has been changed many times. The age of eligibility has been lowered from 65 to 62, and coverage has been extended to people unable to work because of physical disabilities, government employees, self-employed people and a number of other groups not covered by the original Act. Consequently, the amount withheld from most wages to pay for Social Security programs now is more than 7%.

The federal income tax, the other major cause of paycheck shrinkage, was created when the 16th Amendment to the U.S. Constitution was passed in 1913. The original federal income tax rates ranged from 1% to 7% of annual income above $3,000—a lot of money back then.

To pay for World War II, however, the government raised the income tax rates so dramatically that the tax on the top income level bracket hit a record of 94% in 1944 and 1945. What's more, the minimum income subject to taxation was lowered to the point that most working people were for the first time subject to at least some income tax.

The politicians soon found themselves in a bind. They knew that people would balk, to put it mildly, if they had to pay a lot of money to the government at the end of each year. So the politicians decided to lessen the trauma by making employers withhold the income tax, little by little, from workers' pay each week.

By the 1970s, employees had become so accustomed to having large sums of money withheld from their pay that most states and cities—as well as nongovernment groups such as health-insurance companies and pension-fund managers—instituted additional withholding programs.

Today, it's common for employees to have more than a third of their pay withheld by their employers on behalf of government, with still more withheld to finance private benefit plans.

H. Enforcing Your Right to Be Paid Fairly

Your first step in enforcing your right to be paid fairly should be to decide whether your complaint involves a violation of a law, or is simply a matter of disagreement or misunderstanding between you and your employer.

If, for example, your employer refused to pay you time and one-half for five hours of overtime that you worked, then the issue would be covered by the FLSA. But if you had been working under the impression that you would get a raise every year, and your employer won't give you one, then the issue is not one covered by federal wage-and-hour law.

Once you've refined your complaint, try discussing it with your employer or ex-employer before filing any official action. Some companies have formal dispute resolution programs—usually outlined in their employee manuals—that can help you resolve a pay dispute without resorting to formal legal action.

TIPS ON TALKING IT OVER WITH YOUR EMPLOYER

Most companies want to stay within the law and don't want any more legal has-sles than they already have. So the odds are that your complaint is the result of an oversight, a misunderstanding, or a lack of legal knowledge. Here are a few tips on how to present your concerns about pay to your employer or ex-employer.

Know your rights. The more you know about your right to be paid fairly, the more confident you'll be in presenting your complaint. Before you approach your employer, ask a friend or family member to compare your complaint to the rights described in this chapter.

Double-check the facts. The human memory isn't nearly as accurate as we'd like to think it is—particularly when it comes to remembering numbers. Before you approach your employer with a complaint about your pay, make sure that your math is correct. Review any written records that you have to make sure that you haven't overlooked a past event that has since slipped from your memory.

Don't let emotions take over. Discovering that your paycheck is much smaller than you expected can be very disturbing, particularly if you have pressing bills. But those bills could become even more of a problem if you lose your temper, blow up at the boss and get fired. A calm presentation of a complaint is always better than an emotional confrontation.

Treat the company with the same respect that you expect. Discussions of pay prob-lems are very personal, and should take place privately. If at all possible, don't bring up pay issues in front of co-workers. Ask for an appointment to discuss your complaint privately. Give your employer a chance to resolve your pay complaint privately, and the company will be more likely to see things your way.

If you can't reach an agreement by dealing directly with your employer, you may want to consider the option of submitting your dispute to mediation or arbitration. (See Chapter 13, Section A.) These alternatives typically are too expensive to be used to settle individual disputes involving a small dollar amount. But they can be very useful when the dispute involves a group of employees because the costs can be shared among the group's members—and the employer may even be willing to pay all or some of the costs.

I. Filing a Complaint

If your complaint involves what you believe is a violation of the FLSA, the Migrant Agricultural Worker Protections Act or another federal law, contact your local office of Wage and Hour Division of the U.S. Department of Labor, which you can find in the federal government section of most telephone directories.

If you call, write or visit your local Wage and Hour Division office, workers there will take down the information you provide and transcribe it onto a complaint form. You can request one of these forms and fill it out yourself. But since the Wage and Hour Division staff is familiar with which details are legally pertinent, they prefer to fill it out for you. Usually, they'll also ask you to provide photocopies of documents relevant to your pay dispute, such as pay stubs.

Once your complaint has been put together, Labor Department investigators will take over the job of gathering additional data which should either prove or disprove your complaint.

All complaints are confidential. If the thought of reporting your employer to the authorities frightens you, take some comfort in knowing that Labor Department investigators must keep the identities of those who file such complaints confidential. What's more, it's a crime for an employer to fire or otherwise discriminate against an employee for filing a complaint under the FLSA, or for participating in a legal proceeding related to its enforcement.

Where the federal investigators find violations of the FLSA, the action that they then take will depend upon the severity of the violations and whether or not the employer appears to have been violating the law willfully.

When the violations are severe and apparently willful, the Labor Department may ask the Justice Department to bring criminal charges against the employer. Government lawyers will handle the matter for you. If convicted, a first-time violator of the FLSA may be fined by the courts; subsequent convictions can result in both fines and imprisonment.

If the violations are not too severe, or if the Labor Department investigators feel the infractions weren't willful, one of the following steps may be taken:

- The Labor Department may set up and supervise a plan for your employer to pay back wages to you and anyone else injured by the violations.

- The Secretary of Labor may file a lawsuit asking the court to order your employer to pay you the wages due, plus an equal amount as liquidated damages. The court may also issue an injunction or order preventing your employer from continuing the illegal behavior.

- You may file your own lawsuit under the FLSA to recover the wages you're owed, plus other damages, attorney fees and court costs. You'll probably need to hire a lawyer to help with with this type of lawsuit. (See Chapter 13, Section D.)

WHEN YOU CAN'T SUE UNDER THE FLSA

You can't bring suit under the FLSA if your employer has already paid back wages to you under the supervision of the Labor Department. This amounts to an incentive system for employers: An employer who cooperates in correcting any violations discovered by the Wage and Hour Division investigators must pay only the back wages due. An employer who refuses to cooperate by paying back wages due stands the chance of having to pay double the wages, plus your attorney's fees and costs, plus the cost of its own defense.

You can't bring a lawsuit under the FLSA if the Secretary of Labor has already done so on your behalf. And if you file suit and then the Secretary of Labor files a suit over the same violations, your right to sue ends and the Labor Department takes over.

J. Violations of State and Local Laws

The laws of each state and municipality specify which branch of government is responsible for enforcing each of those laws, and what remedies—criminal, civil or both—are available. In some states, the labor department is authorized to take action on your behalf to recover unpaid wages. (See Chart 2-2 at the end of this chapter.)

What if the government agency responsible for enforcing state or local wage-and-hour laws won't take action on your behalf? Or what if the action taken by government agencies in your case doesn't bring a result that satisfies you? Because of the relatively small amounts of money typically involved, disputes over wages, commissions or other forms of compensation can often be pursued quickly and inexpensively in small claims courts without having to hire a lawyer.[3]

Chart 2-1

STATE LAWS THAT CONTROL YOUR FINAL PAYCHECK

Here's a guide to how soon your final paycheck must be given to you under the laws of the state in which you work.

Alabama

No applicable law

Alaska

Within 3 days

Arizona

If you're fired: within 3 days or next scheduled payday. If you quit: next scheduled payday

Arkansas

If you're fired: within 7 days after your demand. If you quit: no applicable law

California

If you're fired: immediately—with some special exceptions for employees of the movie, petroleum and farming industries. If you quit: within 72 hours, or immediately if you've given 72 hours notice

Colorado

If you're fired: immediately. If you quit: next scheduled payday

---

[3]For details on how to pursue your claim through small claims court, see *Everybody's Guide to Small Claims Court* by attorney Ralph Warner (Nolo Press).

Connecticut

If you're fired: next business day. If you quit: next scheduled payday

Delaware

Next scheduled payday

District of Columbia

If you're fired: next business day. If you quit: no applicable law

Florida

No applicable law

Georgia

No applicable law

Hawaii

If you're fired: next business day. If you quit: next scheduled payday

Idaho

If you're fired: within 48 hours. If you quit: no applicable law

Illinois

Next scheduled payday

Indiana

Next scheduled payday

Iowa

Next scheduled payday

Kansas

Next scheduled payday

Kentucky

If you're fired: next scheduled payday or within 14 days, whichever is later. If you quit: no applicable law

Louisiana

If you're fired: within 3 days of your demand. If you quit: no applicable law

Maine

Next scheduled payday or within two weeks after demand, whichever is earlier

Maryland

If you're fired: next scheduled payday. If you quit: no applicable law

Massachusetts

If you're fired: immediately. If you quit: next scheduled payday

Michigan

As soon as amount can be determined with due diligence

Minnesota

If you're fired: within 24 hours of demand. If you quit: within 5 days, or within 24 hours if you've given at least 5 days notice

Mississippi

No applicable law

Missouri

If you're fired: within 7 days after you make a written demand. If you quit: no applicable law

Montana

If you're fired for cause: immediately; otherwise, within 3 days. An extension of 3 additional days is given to the employer if its payroll checks come from outside the state

Nebraska

If you're fired: next scheduled payday or within 2 weeks, whichever is sooner. If you quit: no applicable law

Nevada

If you're fired: immediately. If you quit: next scheduled payday or within 7 days, whichever is earlier

New Hampshire

If you're fired: within 72 hours. If you quit: next scheduled payday; or if you give at least one pay period's notice, within 72 hours of end of work

New Jersey

If you're fired: next scheduled payday. If you quit: no applicable law

New Mexico

If you're fired: within 5 days. If you quit: no applicable law

New York

If you're fired: next scheduled payday. If you quit: no applicable law

North Carolina

Next scheduled payday

North Dakota

If you're fired: within 15 days or on the next scheduled payday, whichever comes first. If you resign: next scheduled payday

Ohio

No applicable law

Oklahoma

If you're fired: immediately. If you quit, on the next scheduled payday or within 5 days of your written demand

Oregon

If you're fired: immediately. If you quit: within 48 hours

Pennsylvania

Next scheduled payday

Rhode Island

Next scheduled payday under normal circumstances; within 24 hours if the employer is going out of business, merging or moving out of state

South Carolina

Within 48 hours or next scheduled payday, which may not be more than 30 days later

South Dakota

If you're fired: within 5 days after you've returned anything belonging to the employer. If you quit: next scheduled payday after you've returned anything belonging to the employer

Tennessee

No applicable rules

Texas

If you're fired: within six days. If you quit: no applicable law

Utah

If you're fired: within 24 hours. If you quit: within 72 hours, or immediately if you've given at least 72 hours notice

Vermont

If you're fired: within 72 hours. If you quit: next scheduled payday or, if no scheduled payday exists, the next Friday

Virginia

Next scheduled payday

Washington

Next scheduled payday

West Virginia

If you're fired: within 72 hours. If you quit: next regular payday

Wisconsin

If you're fired: within 3 days. If you quit: within 15 days

Wyoming

If you're fired: within 24 hours. If you quit: within 72 hours

Chart 2-2

STATES THAT HELP YOU COLLECT UNPAID WAGES

In the following states, you can ask the Labor Department to help you collect wages that are owed to you but haven't been paid.

They are:

Alaska	Massachusetts	Rhode Island
Arizona	Minnesota	South Carolina
Connecticut	Montana	South Dakota
Delaware	Nevada	Tennessee
Hawaii	New Hampshire	Utah
Idaho	New Jersey	Vermont
Illinois	New Mexico	Virginia
Indiana	New York	Washington
Iowa	North Dakota	West Virginia
Maine	Oregon	Wisconsin
Maryland	Pennsylvania	Wyoming

In Kansas, the state Human Resources Department will help you collect unpaid wages. In the District of Columbia, the Mayor's office will provide help.

3

Your Rights When Losing Your Job

One event in life that is almost sure to send a torrent of misinformation your way is being fired. People you used to work with, your brother-in-law, even your next-door neighbors can all be counted on to advise you, quite authoritatively, that there's a law that says you can't be fired.

No one is sure which law gives you all these unequivocal rights, of course, but everyone is positive that the law exists. Some people even believe—incorrectly—that the U.S. Constitution gives you a right to have and keep a job. Often, these well-meaning advisors will try to back up their murky legal reasoning by telling of someone they know who knows someone who got fired and became rich by suing an ex-employer.

And if, in your newly idled state, you turn on daytime television, you're likely to find on the screen the friendly face of a personal injury lawyer who, in mellow and empathic tones, urges you to inquire about your legal right to keep your job by going to your telephone and calling for a free initial consultation.

The truth is that no law gives you an automatic right to keep your job. In fact, despite the importance of job security to the majority of Americans, most of the legal principles and practices of the workplace are indisputably on the side of an employer who fires you.

A. The Doctrine of Employment-at-Will

Legally, people employed in private industry who don't belong to labor unions have no automatic legal right to their jobs.

That is because of the long-established legal doctrine of employment-at-will. That doctrine is what you're most likely to hear cited by your boss or your company's lawyers if you speak up and protest your dismissal. An employer's right to unilaterally determine whether or not you should stay on the payroll stems from a 1894 case (*Payne v. Western & Atlantic RR*, 81 Tenn. 507) in which the court ruled that employers do not need a reason to fire employees—that they may fire any or all of their workers at will. Even if the reason for dismissal is morally wrong, the court held, no legal wrong has occurred and the government has no basis to intervene.

The management of America's factories was still in the experimental stage in the 1890s when that case was decided and the business community successfully argued then and in other cases that followed that factories couldn't be operated profitably unless employers were free to hire and fire as they chose. The employment-at-will doctrine has been reinforced over and over again by subsequent court rulings—and expanded to include not only factories but also virtually all other types of private industry jobs.

The doctrine has been weakened a bit since the 1970s by rulings in wrongful-discharge suits (discussed in Chapter 4, Section A) and some new laws that are more favorable to employees. For example, some states have made it illegal to fire employees for taking time off to care for a sick child (discussed in Chapter 10, Section C) or because they are gay or lesbian (discussed in Chapter 5, Section J). And the other side of the employment-at-will logic is that employees cannot be required to remain in a job. But the employment-at-will doctrine is still staunchly defended by most of the business community, and it's still very much the dominant law of the land.

B. Why Were You Fired?

Back before any holes had been punched in the employment-at-will doctrine, companies would often refuse to give employees any reason for being fired. Since a company had the legal right to hire and fire without any justification, most opted not to invite trouble by stating a reason for firing.

Today, many companies have reversed their policies on giving reasons for dismissals. Because courts throughout the country are gradually establishing more rights for fired employees (discussed in Chapter 4), many company owners and managers—particularly those in large corporations that are attractive targets for wrongful-discharge suits—now are careful to provide at least the appearance of fair and even-handed treatment of employees who are fired. They typically do this by carefully documenting the employee's allegedly unacceptable work performance.

Then, the employer can provide the employee—and a court, should it come to that—with a very specific statement of the cause of firing, based on tangible documentation. So if you are fired, make your best effort to obtain a clear statement of the employer's reasons for doing so.

Office' or factory rumors, your suspicions or the hunches of your family just won't suffice. If you eventually decide to challenge your dismissal (discussed in Chapter 4, Section A and C), the reasons that your ex-employer stated for firing you will almost certainly become a major point in any legal battle that may develop.

LABELS MAKE NO DIFFERENCE

People tend to think that getting fired means being dismissed because you did something wrong on the job, and that when other terms are used—such as dismissal, discharge, layoff, staff cut and downsizing—it somehow means something less onerous. In hopes of preventing bad community relations and wrongful-discharge lawsuits, many companies use these gentler sounding words to describe firings.

Some companies have gone so far as to announce the process of firing large groups of employees by using sterile, institutional terms as re-organizational incentives or activity analysis and review. Still other companies have described the process of firing groups of employees as early retirement—even where the people being dismissed aren't being given anywhere near enough money to continue to live the rest of their lives without working.

Whenever you are permanently dismissed from a job without being given sufficient income to continue living without working, all these terms mean the same thing: You've been fired. (For more on true layoffs, see Section D.)

C. Documenting Your Dismissal

Even if you decide not to challenge the legality of your firing, you'll be in a much better position to enforce any of your workplace rights if you carefully document the circumstances. For example, if you apply for unemployment insurance benefits and your ex-employer challenges that application, you'll typically need to prove that you were dismissed for reasons beyond your control. (See Chapter 8, Section B.) Here are some of the best ways to document the circumstances leading to your firing:

1. Keep a daily log

Long before being fired, you may sense that something has gone wrong in the relationship between you and your employer. Perhaps your first clue will be that your pay has been stuck at one level with no raises for an unusually long time. Or you may notice that none of your work assignments extend more than a few weeks. Whatever the sign that your job may be in jeopardy, use it as a reason to begin keeping a log of your interactions with your employer.

Human memory isn't nearly as reliable as we like to think it is, and that's a truth that your employer's lawyers are likely to exploit should you end up taking legal action to challenge your firing. If you claim something happened on a Wednesday and it really happened on a Thursday, for example, the company's lawyers will try to shake you up and trample your credibility by arguing that you're unreliable and confused in general.

Record and date each work-related event such as performance reviews, commendations or reprimands, salary increases or decreases and even informal comments that your supervisor makes to you about your work. Note the date, time and location for each event; which members of management were involved; and whether or not there were witnesses. Whenever possible, back up your log with materials issued by your employer, such as copies of the employee handbook, memos, brochures and employee orientation videos.

If you are, in fact, cut from the payroll, you'll be glad you have this log of your work relationship—because your former employer is likely to have some documentation of its own.

2. Waiving your right to sue

The best documentation of your firing will be something put into writing by the company in preparation for firing you, specifying what performance the company claims is substandard.

In large companies with a human resource management staff—what used to be known as the personnel office—such documentation will most likely be handed to you as part of the firing process. You will then likely be asked to sign a statement signifying that you have read the documents and that you accept what's in them.

In most such cases, you will also be shown a check representing compensation that the company isn't required under wage-and-hour law or some contractual agreement to pay you—such as a few months' worth of extra severance pay. You will then be told that the check will be released to you immediately if you sign a waiver of any rights to take legal action against the company as a result of your dismissal. (For an example of this type of waiver, see p. 3/7-8.)

This carrot-on-the-stick method of firing can seem cruel or unfair. But it has proven effective for some companies in discouraging wrongful-discharge lawsuits.

It's not a foolproof tactic. An increasing number of employees who have signed waivers of their rights to file a lawsuit over their firing have later succeeded in having the courts throw out the waivers by arguing, for example, that the waivers were signed under duress. Whether or not signing such a waiver will prevent you from suing your ex-employer depends on the circumstances of each individual case, however, so there's no way of predicting the power of a waiver in advance.

Going along with the carrot-on-the-stick method of firing will typically give you immediate severance pay and documentation of your employer's official reasons for firing you.

However, if you have doubts about the validity of your dismissal, withhold your signature on any waiver of your right to sue while you think over the company's offer, obtain more information and perhaps hire a lawyer. (See Chapter 13.) You take the chance of not getting the money and documentation that the company waves in front of you, but you'll lower your risk of signing away essential rights.

A PREVIEW OF AN "I WON'T SUE" WAIVER

Many companies try to protect themselves against being sued over firings by asking employees who are being fired to sign a waiver, usually known as a release or a covenant not to sue, in return for something of value—such as severance pay over and above that which had been promised in the employee manual.

The element of surprise is important here in giving the employer the upper hand. Hit with the shock of being fired, you're likely to take any money that's offered while not paying too much attention to what you're signing. But if you know what these waivers typically say, you'll be in a stronger position to evaluate one that your employer may put in front of you when you're fired.

Here's the firing waiver that has been used by one large employer:

GENERAL RELEASE AND COVENANT NOT TO SUE

In consideration of the sum of $0.00, and other good and valuable consideration, John Doe, on behalf of his heirs, agents, representatives, successors and assigns hereby releases (the employer), its agents, directors, officers, employees, representatives, successors and assigns from any and all claims, demands, actions, and liabilities, (hereinafter, "claims") whatsoever, including but limited to any claims, such as those under any federal or state laws dealing with discrimination in employment on the basis of sex, race, national origin, religion, age, or handicap, which the undersigned had or now has against (the employer) its agents, directors, officers, employees, representatives, successors, and assigns by reason of any act, omission, matter, event, cause, or thing whatsoever occurring or arising prior to or on the date hereof, except that his rights, if any, in the (employer's) retirement plan are not released hereby, but survive unaffected by this instrument.

John Doe covenants with (the employer) never to institute any charges of employment discrimination with any agency, or any suit or action at law or in equity against (the employer) its agents, directors, officers, employees, representatives, successors, and assigns by reason of any claim he had or now has relating to his employment with (the employer).

In the event of rehire by (the employer) as a regular (the employer's name) employee, John Doe understands that (the employer) reserves the right to require repayment of a prorated portion of the voluntary transition payment if the time away from (the employer) is less than the number of weeks received as payment.

John Doe acknowledges that he has read and understood the foregoing and acknowledges that it is executed by him as his knowing and voluntary act.

In witness whereof, the undersigned has executed the foregoing General Release and Covenant Not to Sue at

_____

(the time)

_____

(the date)

_____

(Your signature)

_____

(Witness' signature)

BEWARE OF THE EARLY RETIREMENT WAIVER

If you're asked to sign a waiver of your right to sue in return for participation in an early retirement program offered by your ex-employer, the Older Workers Benefit Protection Act may give you the right to consider the company's offer for 45 days before you accept or reject it, and seven more days to revoke a decision to accept the company's offer. (See Chapter 5, Section G.)

---

3. Using service-letter laws

There is no federal law that requires an employer to provide you with an explanation, written or otherwise, of the reasons for your dismissal. However, at least six states have laws, commonly known as service-letter laws, that require employers to provide ex-employees with letters that describe the ex-employees' work histories. (See Chart 3-1 at the end of this chapter.)

4. State differences in service-letter laws

Service-letter laws vary greatly from state to state. Minnesota, for example, has a law that requires an employer to provide a written statement of the reasons for an employee's dismissal within five days after the employee requests such a statement in writing. Kansas also has a service-letter law, but it doesn't require an ex-employer to list a reason for your dismissal. Employers in Kansas must state only your length of employment, job classification and wage rate. If you live in a state that has a service-letter law requiring explanations of dismissals and the employer who fired you doesn't provide you with one, request one in writing.

Example:

June 10, 1992

Ellen Executive
President
Tasteless Frozen Pizzas Inc.
123 Main Street
Anywhere, MO 54321

Dear Ms. Executive:

As required by Missouri Statutes Section 290.140, I request
from you a letter stating the length of my employment with
Tasteless Frozen Pizzas Inc., the nature of my work there and
the reasons for my dismissal from employment.

Please note that this law requires you to provide me with such
a letter within 45 days of receipt of this request.

Sincerely,

Paul Smith

Paul Smith
321 Front Street
Anywhere, MO 54321
234/555-6666

Some service-letter laws specify a time limit for requesting such a letter. But if possible, it is usually wise to make your request within a day or two of your dismissal to make sure that you meet any such deadlines and to prevent the passing of time from affecting people's memories. Send your request for a service letter by certified mail so that you can prove, if necessary, that you made your request within any time limits specified.

ASK AND YOU MAY RECEIVE

If you live in a state that doesn't have a service-letter law, there is a chance that your employer won't offer you any written explanation for your firing. This is particularly likely if the company from which you're being dismissed is a small one that doesn't know much about workplace law and current legal techniques for firing employees. If no written explanation of your dismissal is given, ask the person who officially informs you of your firing for a written explanation of the company's decision to dismiss you. Be firm but polite; keep in mind that having to fire someone is an extremely stressful assignment for even the most experienced managers.

What's more, companies usually want dismissed employees to be out of their building and away from the remaining employees as quickly as possible to prevent vengeful sabotage or spreading anti-company sentiment. Therefore, a person being fired exercises a substantial amount of negotiating power by merely sitting in place in front of the person doing the firing, quietly insisting on written documentation, until the request is satisfied. Remember, however, that in some companies using your posterior as a negotiating tool can get you escorted out forcibly by the corporate security force or local police if pushed too far.

5. Letters of understanding

If you have done everything within the limits of civility but your employer still refuses to give you written documentation of its reasons for your dismissal, you may be in for a wait—and some extra work—before you get it. If your state is among the majority that have no laws requiring such documentation, there's not much else you can do to force the issue at the time of your dismissal. Later, you may obtain documentation through some of the laws granting employees access to their personnel files (discussed in Chapter 12, Section A), or by filing a wrongful-discharge lawsuit (discussed in Chapter 4, Section C), and demanding the company's internal documents concerning your employment.

But before that, you might want to write a letter of understanding to the person who fired you:

Example:

August 2, 1992

Aggie Supervisor
XYZ Company
2222 Lake Street
Anytown, CA 12345

Dear Ms. Supervisor:

I'm writing to clarify the reasons for my dismissal from
employment at XYZ Company on July 29, 1992.

My understanding is that I was dismissed because
_____.

If you feel that my understanding is incorrect, please advise
me in writing by (specify a date two or three weeks away).

Sincerely,

John Employee

John Employee

123 Any Street
Anytown, CA 12345
234/555-6666

Although you should mail your letter of understanding promptly, it's best to let it sit for a day or two after writing it. Then, read it over again to make sure you've kept it businesslike and to the point. Getting fired is a very emotional event—one that often generates more than a little anger and desire for revenge in even the most saintly people.

Correspondence between you and your former employer may eventually become the basis of future negotiations or even courtroom evidence, and you don't want its credibility to be tainted by ink from a poison pen. Send your letter of understanding by certified mail so that you'll be able to prove that the company received it. Using certified mail in this case may also help drive home to your former employer that you're serious about enforcing your rights concerning your dismissal.

If the company responds to your letter, you've obtained at least one piece of documentation of its reason for firing you. If the company fails to respond to your letter after a month or so, it's fair for you to assume that the reason stated in your letter of understanding is correct.

6. Continuing documentation

Other important forms of documentation for your firing may come your way in the weeks following your dismissal. For example, if you file a claim for unemployment compensation, your former employer will have to respond to that claim, and that response will eventually be translated into a document that the local unemployment insurance office will provide to you. Store any such documents in a file folder, shoebox, or something else of that sort so that they won't get lost or destroyed—and so that you can find and organize them easily.

D. Dealing With Temporary Job Losses

It's easy to get confused when talking about job losses because the American language still hasn't developed and adopted words that accurately describe the realities of today's workplace.

Historically, the word layoff typically was used to describe situations in which factory production workers were told not to report to work until their help was needed again on the production lines. But over time, the word has also been applied to other types of job losses—even those that obviously are permanent.

The confusion over the meaning of layoff became even worse in 1991 when some companies needed to cut costs and decided that it is more fair to make all of their employees take a week off from work without pay every once in a while than to fire a few employees. Ironically, many of these plans—which clearly fit the traditional definition of layoff—were euphemistically called job security programs.

Ignore the name that your employer assigns to a temporary loss of employment. If you become involved in an employment cut that appears to be temporary, the strategies discussed in the preceding sections of this chapter and in Chapter 4 won't be relevant. These strategies are intended for people who have lost their jobs permanently. Typically, the only legal action available to deal with a temporary loss of employment is to file an application for unemployment insurance benefits (discussed in Chapter 8, Section B) and then wait to be recalled to your job.

However, if you believe that temporary employment cuts imposed by your employer form a pattern of illegal discrimination (discussed in Chapter 5, Section B), you may want to file what is usually called an abusive layoff complaint under anti-discrimination laws. You'll probably need to hire a lawyer to help you with that kind of case. (See Chapter 13, Section D.)

Example: John is employed as a production worker at a small, nonunion steel foundry in Pittsburgh, Pennsylvania, where about two-thirds of the workers are white and one-third are black. For the past three years, business has been slow for the foundry, so some employees have been told not to report to work for six weeks at a time every few months.

The employees who are put on layoff are allowed to collect unemployment insurance benefits, which replace about one-half of the income they would receive if they were working.

But all the workers who have been put out of work temporarily, John notices, have been black. All the white workers have been employed steadily for 40 hours or more per week. Even where the black workers have been employed there longer and have more work skills, they are told to stay home while the white workers continue to work.

It appears that the foundry is treating its white workers better than those who are black, so John can take action against the abusive layoffs under Title VII of the Civil Rights Act of 1964 or under his state's anti-discrimination laws on the basis of racial discrimination.

HELP AND COMFORT FOR THE JOBLESS

Being fired from a job—particularly one that you've held for many years—can be a deep, personal trauma. So some churches responded to the needs of those who are looking for a new job. Usually, these programs are open to everyone, regardless of their personal attitudes toward organized religion, free of charge.

One of the largest of such programs is called Job Seekers. It is based at The Chapel, an independent 7,000-member congregation in Akron, Ohio. Participants meet one night each week to discuss with program leaders and each other challenges such as avoiding depression during unemployment, restructuring personal finances, preserving family morale, assessing marketable job skills and, of course, finding a new job.

If you'd like to learn more about how these programs operate, or if you'd like to start one in your community, contact Job Seekers. (See the Appendix for contact information.)

Chart 3-1

STATE SERVICE-LETTER LAWS

Six states have laws that require employers to provide ex-employees with written statements detailing their work history—usually known as service letters.

Kansas

Upon written request, an employer must provide an ex-employee with a letter stating the ex-employee's length of employment, job classification and wage rate. Kan. Stat. Ann. §44-808 (1986)

Maine

Upon written request, an employer must provide a discharged employee with a written listing of the reasons for that employee's firing. Me. Rev. Stat. Ann. 26 §630 (1988)

Minnesota

Employers must provide a discharged employee with a written listing of the reasons for the employee's dismissal. However, the ex-employee must request that listing in writing within five working days after the discharge. Minn. Stat. Ann. §181.933 (1989)

Missouri

A corporation that employs seven or more people must provide a discharged employee with a letter stating the length of the ex-employee's employment, the nature of the job the ex-employee held and the reasons for the discharge. This letter must be provided to the ex-employee within 45 days after the company receives a request for it. Mo. Ann. Stat. §290.140 (1989)

Montana

Upon request from a discharged employee, an employer must provide that employee with a written statement of the reasons for the discharge. Mont. Code Ann. §39-2-801 (1987)

Nevada

An ex-employee who held a job for 60 days or more may demand from the former employer a written statement of the reason for their departure from the job. Nev. Rev. Stat. §613.210 (1988)

4

How to Challenge Your Job Loss

The legal doctrine of employment-at-will still rules the workplace, so employers in private industry generally have the right to fire employees. (See Chapter 3, Section A.) However, if you've lost your job or think you're about to, don't despair. There are some laws that may give you leverage against being sent abruptly into the ranks of the unemployed without money or other help to ease the impact.

The odds are that you won't be able to use the legal system to completely reverse your firing and return to your job. However, the laws might help you to secure the right to be treated fairly during and after your firing, to secure a positive reference from you ex-employer to help in future job hunting, or to secure the right to continuing coverage under your ex-employer's benefit programs. You may even be able to get your former employer to pay you some compensation, or—if the damage done to you by your firing is severe enough—to win a large court judgment against your ex-employer through a wrongful-discharge lawsuit.

At the very least, understanding how and when laws may protect job security and other workplace rights should help you determine whether a lawyer who tells you that your dismissal doesn't justify legal action is telling the truth, or is merely skimming the local community of unemployed people for the cases with the highest potential for large damage awards or settlements.

BEWARE OF RECRUITERS PROMISING JOB SECURITY

In reaction to the stepped-up quest for job security, some companies have begun to use written contracts promising some form of job security as an employee recruitment tool. But some of the employment contracts being offered are more recruiting gimmicks than legitimate business agreements.

You have to look closely at the employment contracts that some recruiters are using to make sure that having one is truly to your advantage. Some key things to look for:

- Does the contract guarantee you employment for a specific period of time, such as three years, no matter what happens to the company's profits? Or does it make your employment contingent upon something such as a certain level of company-wide sales volume? In most cases, an employment contract that doesn't specify a minimum length of employment regardless of other factors is all but worthless to the employee.

- Is there any penalty to you if you leave the job before the contract is fulfilled? Some companies intimidate employees into staying in a distasteful job by having them sign a contract that requires employees to reimburse the company for training, moving or other costs if they fail to keep the job for the full length of the employment contract.

- What does the contract really cover? There is no legal definition of job security, so a company can claim that it is offering you contractual job security by merely guaranteeing only one aspect of employment. For example, a disclaimer stating that the contract guarantees only the level of pay during a three-year period—but not the continuation of employment for all three years—could leave you with no way to take action against the employer under contract law if you're fired just a few months after the contract was signed.

- If the contract contains a renewal option, what is the timetable for negotiating a renewal? You'll typically need at least three months to conduct a thorough search for a good new job, so an employment contract that leaves your future with the employer hanging until the last few weeks or days of the contract's term does more to guarantee the employer a predictable workforce than it does to provide you with secure, predictable employment.

A. What Can Make a Dismissal Wrongful?

There are no hard and fast limits on what legal arguments can be used to challenge an employee's dismissal. New ways to challenge firings in court are being developed by lawyers virtually every day. In general, these actions are lumped under the label of wrongful discharge, but you should be careful in using that term. (See p. 4/8)

There are, however, five legal theories that frequently succeed in challenges to employee firings:

- violations of public policy

- breach of implied contract

- breach of good faith and fair dealing

- illegal discrimination

- defamation

In some situations, more than one of these theories may be used to challenge a firing. (See Section C2 on packaging several claims.)

The following descriptions will give you an introduction to each of these principles.

1. Violations of public policy

The most common and simple way to challenge the employment-at-will doctrine (discussed in Chapter 3, Section A) is to show that, by firing you, your ex-employer violated public policy—that is, fired you for a reason that the law specifically says employers may not use for firing, or for a reason that most citizens would find morally or ethically disgusting.

Many states have laws that take some of the guessing out of this issue by specifying employment-related actions that clearly violate public policy, such as firing an employee for serving on a jury or for reporting a crime to police. (See Chart 4-1 at the end of this chapter.)

Many states also have laws prohibiting employers from firing workers because they take leaves from work to serve in the military reserves. But these laws have been changing quickly, so the best way to determine whether your state protects reservists against dismissals on the basis of military service is to research your state's law at a local library. (See Chapter 13, Section E.)

You can also research other areas of workplace rights for laws that include rules against firing employees who use those laws. For example, it is illegal for your employer to fire you because you filed a complaint under the Fair Labor Standards Act (discussed in Chapter 2), the Occupational Safety and Health Act (discussed in Chapter 11, Section A), or Title VII of the Civil Rights Act of 1964 (discussed in Chapter 5, Section B).

Even if the reason for your dismissal isn't specifically outlawed by a public-policy law in your state or a provision within another workplace law, the reasons for firing that are outlawed as violations of public policy in other states would probably be considered morally or ethically wrong in yours.

Example: Horatio, a salesperson in a clothing store in Nevada, was fired because he reported to police that the manager of the store was buying stolen wristwatches and selling them to customers on the sly. Nevada doesn't have a law that specifically prohibits firing an employee who reports a crime. Nevertheless, Horatio might be able to argue successfully in court that his firing violated public policy because other states, such as Maine and Oregon, have laws that specifically forbid such firings.

2. Breach of an implied contract

Another relatively simple way to challenge a firing is to show that it violates an employment contract that was implied rather than intentionally written and agreed to mutually.

Disputes over employee dismissals that involve the implied-contract argument are very much like palimony suits between former live-together lovers: There is nothing in writing—such as a marriage certificate—that clearly holds the two together. One partner, the employer, wants to say, "So long, it was fun, have a nice life," while the other, the employee, is arguing: "But I thought you said it was forever." What typically evolves is an argument over whether or not any words and things of value were exchanged between the two that, in effect, created a contract governing their relationship.

In the workplace, employers often create implied contracts because a legal contract—covering employment or anything else—is created when three things occur:

- an offer is made by one party to another

- that offer is accepted

- something of value is exchanged based on the agreement.

Until legal challenges to employee dismissals began to gain popularity in the early 1980s, many employers used terms such as permanent employment in their employee manuals, on job application forms, or orally when offering a position to a prospective new employee.

So employees who challenge their firings sometimes argue that when an employer referred to permanent employment in the hiring process, it created an implied contract between the employer and employer. They claim that implied employment contract requires the company to employ the worker for life—and that anything less than lifetime employment is a breach of contract.

Example: In 1975, Marguerite took a job as an accountant with EZ Ink Printing. EZ Ink's employee manual stated that employees were not considered permanent until they completed a 90-day probationary period.

For more than 15 years, Marguerite built her life around EZ Ink—assuming that she would be able to keep her job there until she reached retirement age. However, in 1990, EZ Ink decided to completely computerize its accounting operations—and to fire Marguerite.

Marguerite would likely be able to win a lawsuit against EZ Ink on the basis of a breach of an implied contract. The three elements required to create an implied employment contract were there:

- an offer, in the form of the employee manual's implication that all employees who remained with the company more than 90 days were permanent employees

- an acceptance of that offer—Marguerite's more than 15 years of employment by the company

- an exchange of value—the wages that EZ Ink had paid Marguerite and her labor for them.

3. Breach of good faith and fair dealing

The most flexible way to challenge a job dismissal is to show that there has been a breach of good faith and fair dealing.

This type of claim is based on the legal principle that an employer has an inherent responsibility to deal with everyone fairly and in good faith. However, employers often commit breaches of good faith and fair dealing by doing things such as:

- firing or transferring employees to prevent them from collecting sales commissions

- misleading employees about their chances for future promotions and wage increases

- contriving reasons for firing an employee on the basis of on-the-job performance when, in fact, the real motivation is to replace that employee with someone who will work for lower pay

- misleading employees about the bad aspects of a particular job—such as the need to travel through dangerous neighborhoods late at night—during worker recruitment drives

- repeatedly transferring an employee to remote, dangerous or otherwise undesirable assignments to coerce him or her into quitting without collecting the severance pay and other benefits due.

The legal claim of breach of good faith and fair dealing is so broad and flexible that, no matter what other claims you use as a basis for a wrongful-discharge action, you'll probably want to include a claim of breach of good faith and fair dealing as well. (See Section C.)

DON'T CALL IT A WRONGFUL-DISCHARGE CASE

Many lawyers who specialize in representing employees avoid calling any lawsuit a wrongful-discharge case. They do this because the employment-at-will doctrine (discussed in Chapter 3, Section A) has dominated workplace law for such a long time that many judges have a knee-jerk policy of throwing out any lawsuit that they perceive as a wrongful-discharge case.

To those judges, a wrongful-discharge lawsuit is a challenge to the employment-at-will doctrine—something that, in their minds, is not a legitimate legal argument.

To try to head off such a response, lawyers representing workers who are challenging their dismissals tend to refer to wrongful-discharge cases as something else, such as a defamation case or a complaint based on illegal discrimination. This is pure legal semantics, to be sure. But you'd be wise in most cases to train yourself not to use the term wrongful discharge in discussing your job-loss challenge with a lawyer, a judge or anyone else.

---

4. Illegal discrimination

When the civil rights movement was young and America's booming corporations were expanding in the 1960s and '70s, the focus of workplace discrimination lawsuits was on giving everyone an equal chance to be hired for, or promoted to, a good job.

Ever since American corporations began shrinking their staffs dramatically in the 1980s, however, much of the energy has gone into making sure that employees aren't being dismissed on the basis of such factors as race, skin color, gender, age, national origin, religious conviction or sexual orientation.

Indeed, in 1990, the American Bar Association released a study showing that 85% of all discrimination cases pending in federal courts centered on employee dismissals, not promotions.

The laws and legal strategies used to challenge an employee dismissal because of illegal discrimination are the same as those used to fight other forms of illegal workplace discrimination. (See Chapter 5.)

Example: Patty was employed as a customer relations manager for a supermarket chain for more than 20 years. During those years, the company's president had repeatedly told her—often in the presence of others—that she was destined to become the company's vice president of customer relations as soon as the man who held that position retired.

One day, Patty and about 50 other managers employed by the supermarket chain were called in to the human resources department one-by-one and told that they were being fired. Actually, the company didn't say they were being fired, but that they had been selected as participants in a strategic restructuring.

In the week that followed, Patty talked with some of her colleagues who also had been fired, and she found that—although only 10% of the company's middle managers were women—all of the middle managers who were fired were female. Patty may be able to win a lawsuit against the supermarket chain on the basis of illegal discrimination on the basis of gender—the fact that only female middle managers were chosen for dismissal.

Keep in mind in applying anti-discrimination laws to your firing that, although federal anti-discrimination laws can often be overly bureaucratic and ineffective, state anti-discrimination laws may give you a relatively direct basis for taking legal action. (See the discussions on state anti-discrimination laws in Chapter 5, Section I and Chapter 10, Section C.)

5. Defamation

When you make or distribute false statements about people that lower their public image, or that cause other people to avoid them, you run the risk of committing defamation. There are a lot of opportunities in the typical firing process for an employer to do just that, so it is increasingly common for former employees to use defamation as the basis for challenging a firing.

A defamation claim is not a challenge to the legitimacy of an employee's dismissal as much as it is a way of getting monetary revenge on the employer who was sloppy, insensitive or downright mean in firing you or in dealing with your need for references in obtaining a new job.

But defamation is usually difficult to prove. Typically, you must show that, in the process of dismissing you from your job or subsequently providing references to potential new employers, your ex-employer significantly damaged your good name and reduced your chances for gaining new employment. This commonly entails much legal hair-splitting over what facts surrounding a firing can be considered indisputably true; to whom the employer may communicate the facts surrounding an employee dismissal, and whether or not the distribution of the damaging information was intentional and malicious—that is, meant to harm you.

In general, you must prove three things to win a defamation lawsuit against a former employer:

1. The employer distributed false information to someone who had no legitimate need to receive it. For example, a report on the number of times you were late in reporting to work would probably be a legitimate statement for your former employer to send out in response to a reference check request from a company where you had applied for a new job. But it would probably not be legitimate for your ex-employer to send that information to a company that hadn't inquired about your work history or where you had already been hired and had been working successfully for several months.

2. Distributing the damaging information was more than an honest and unavoidable accident. If extremely sloppy recordkeeping caused your former employer to send out a report that showed you working at your previous job only two weeks instead of two years, for example, you could probably prove that your ex-employer defamed you through negligence. Or if an employer for whom you had worked for more than 10 years sent out a letter that was obviously intended to falsely depict you as a job-hopper, you could probably prove that the letter was sent out with malicious intent.

3. The information concerning you was inherently damaging—known in legalese as defamation per se (rough translation: damaging just because it is seen or heard) or actually caused you damage that you can demonstrate.

For example, a false statement that you stole money from your ex-employer would probably qualify as defamation per se because most people would lower their opinions of you because of it. But a statement that you had stayed on your last job only two months would probably be defamatory only if you could prove that it damaged you, such as in preventing you from getting a new job, causing a landlord to refuse to rent an apartment to you, or otherwise causing you social embarrassment and emotional distress.

B. Blacklisting

An especially weird category of law that is related to defamation is blacklisting. As archaic and barbaric as it may seem, there are still some companies, labor unions and people working within them that are not content to merely fire you or have you quit your job. Only your death from starvation and lack of clothing and shelter, it seems, would make your job loss complete for them. So they do and say things that they hope will prevent anyone else from hiring you.

The danger of losing a defamation lawsuit doesn't seem to dissuade these vengeful employers from trying to put former employees on a list of people that no one else will hire. So some states have passed laws that expressly allow the ex-employee to take legal action—criminal, civil or both—against anyone who works hard at preventing the ex-employee from gaining new employment. (For a state-by-state synopsis of these blacklisting laws, see Chart 4-3 at the end of this chapter.)

1. Detecting blacklisting

The mere fact that you have to work hard at finding a new job usually isn't sufficient evidence to suggest blacklisting. But a strong signal would be a series of situations in which potential new employers seem to be on the verge of hiring you, then suddenly lose all interest. This indicates that, when a prospective employer checks your references just before hiring you, the blacklister is tipped off to where you've applied for work and is able to ding you.

You can hire a lawyer or a private detective to investigate whether or not you're being blacklisted. But it's easier and cheaper to conduct your own investigation by establishing an imaginary business and using that business to inquire about your own employment record with former employers. You can create your imaginary business through the creative use of inexpensive quick-print services, private postal boxes and telephone answering services—and enlisting a little help from your friends.

2. Conducting your own investigation

Typically, you can create for a few months the illusion of a business that has classy letterhead stationery, a suite number for a mailing address and a business telephone line. Even large corporations now use voice mail and other answering systems, making telephone receptionists nearly obsolete. So it's virtually impossible for anyone to tell from any distance how large and established any company really is unless they spend a lot of time and money checking corporate credit reports.

Pretend that you've applied for a job at the imaginary company that you create, and have it go through the ritual of checking your work history with previous employers by mail. Ask a friend to use his or her name and signature to sign the reference—checking letters as your imaginary company's human resources manager.

What comes back in the mail may give you all the evidence you need to prove blacklisting. But some people who do this type of thing are actually smart enough not to write down the defamatory information that they're spreading. So if the written materials that are sent to your imaginary company don't jibe with the reactions you've been getting from potential new employers, ask your friend the human resources manager to telephone your ex-employers to discuss your work history. But always make sure that another friend is listening and taking notes on an extension telephone during the call so that they can serve as a witness to any defamation that is being directed toward you.

If you uncover evidence that you are, in fact, being blacklisted, you'll probably need to get some advice on the problem from a lawyer. (See Chapter 13, Section D.)

Using defamatory information to take away someone's means of earning a living is a very serious and evil thing. You may be able to have the blacklister arrested and prosecuted—and then be able to win a large judgment based on the blacklisting. In Iowa, for example, a company that authorizes blacklisting an ex-employee can be sued for three times the damages done by that black-listing. (See Chart 4-1 at the end of this chapter.)

C. Taking Action Against Your Dismissal

Once you become familiar with how employee dismissals are successfully challenged, compare those legal strategies to your firing and decide:

- which legal principle used to challenge a job loss best fits your situation

- whether you're willing to expend the effort, money and time it usually takes to fight a firing

- whether or not you'll need a lawyer to help you challenge your firing.

If you were fired for reasons that appear to be a violation of public policy (as discussed in Section A), you may be able to get government help in challenging your dismissal. For example, if you were fired for filing a complaint under the Fair Labor Standards Act, you can ask the Labor Department to help you fight that dismissal.

If you decide to challenge your firing on any other basis—or on the basis of a violation of public policy combined with another cause of action—you'll probably need to hire a lawyer. (See Chapter 13, Section D.)

1. What to consider before taking action

Here's a list of things you should think through before you decide to launch a challenge to your firing and begin your search for the right lawyer to help you challenge your dismissal:

Winning is usually an uphill battle. Unfair though it may be, the employment-at-will doctrine is still dominates the relationship between private employers and the people who work for them. (See Chapter 3, Section A.) At best, recent changes in workplace case law have restricted your employer to firing you only if it can come up with a good reason for the firing—something that most employers and their lawyers can easily do if they put their minds to it—and gives you a chance to explain yourself before being fired.

So to successfully challenge your dismissal in a lawsuit, you'll need to convince a court that something about your firing overpowers nearly 100 years of legal decisions generally supporting employment-at-will.

It's likely to be expensive. Because many challenges to employee dismissals are legal longshots, lawyers who specialize in this type of case often refuse to handle them on a straight contingency basis. (See Chapter 13, Section D.) If you hire a lawyer with expertise in wrongful-discharge lawsuits and your case is less than a sure win, you can expect to have to put $3,000 to $5,000 on deposit to pay for the lawyer's time if your lawsuit fails, plus an additional $1,000 to $2,000 to cover other costs. If you can't or won't put up the deposit, expect the lawyer to refuse to handle your case.

Arm yourself with knowledge. You can save yourself some time and possibly some grief by using this book to objectively analyze your job loss before you begin talking with a lawyer about handling your case.

Most Americans believe—incorrectly—that they have automatic legal rights to their jobs. As a consequence, many lawyers have spent substantial amounts of time in recent years in conversations with people who have been fired and who believe—also incorrectly—that they have a basis for filing a wrongful-discharge lawsuit against their former employers.

If you understand the employment-at-will doctrine and the ways of challenging it that may apply to your case before you contact a lawyer, you'll be more likely to get serious consideration when you need it.

Keep good documentation. The success of your lawsuit is likely to depend, to a great extent, upon how well you documented the circumstances surrounding your dismissal. (See Chapter 3, Section C.)

Before you discuss your case with a lawyer, look closely at your documentation of your job loss and try to separate the aspects of your firing that you can prove from those that you merely suspect. Assessing your case on the basis of facts that you can prove through documentation will almost always be wisest.

Your privacy rights are limited. There is very little that an employer or potential employer can't find out about you if it really wants to. (See Chapter 12.) This is particularly true in small cities, where most of the executives, business owners and lawyers typically belong to a few clubs and talk with each other often—a powerful form of business networking sometimes known as the whisper circuit.

So if you're hoping to find a new job in the same small city where you were fired, you'll run a high risk of scaring away potential new employers if you file a lawsuit against your last one.

2. Consider packaging several claims

Packaging two or more claims is desirable in most wrongful-discharge cases because contract law and many of the laws prohibiting employee dismissals as violations of public policy offer little chance of winning a large judgment.

For example, damages awarded in a lawsuit based only on a breach of an implied employment contract would typically be limited to:

- reinstatement to the job—not a desirable thing, in many cases, because there are often bad feelings between the employee and employer.

- lost wages, which often don't amount to much—particularly if you find a new job soon after being fired.

In contrast, a breach of good faith and fair dealing is a tort—an intentional or careless act of a person or institution that directly harms another person or institution. And in tort actions, you typically can ask for actual damages based on such things as emotional suffering, and for punitive damages—an amount of money that the defendant is ordered to pay as a form of punishment and as a deterrent to repeating the behavior that gave birth to the lawsuit.

Punitive damages are usually based not on the size of the injury, but on the court's estimate of how large a financial penalty would be needed to make the defendant feel the sting. In the case of many large corporations, the size of the penalty needed to make the company hurt can be quite large.

For example, a study by the Rand Corporation, a Los Angeles-based think tank, showed that of 120 wrongful-discharge suits brought in California between 1980 and 1986 (the latest years studied), 40 involved awarding punitive tort damages—and that the average total award in those cases was $520,000. It was cases of this type—based on both contract and tort law—that gave birth to the legends concerning financial windfalls to employees resulting from their dismissal from a job.

Example: Elmer was a salesperson for a building supply company whose employee manual stated that employees were considered permanent after completing a 90-day probation period. Elmer had been employed by the company for 14 years, and was about to qualify for more than $50,000 in commissions from accounts he had sold years before.

He was fired just a week before qualifying for those commissions—but he found an equivalent new job just a few weeks later. Elmer sued the company that had fired him for breach of implied contract (the employee manual's statement on permanent employment) and breach of good faith and fair dealing (the company's use of dismissal as a way to avoid having him qualify contractually for the commissions).

On the breach of implied contract count, the court awarded him only the wages he lost while unemployed—which, because he quickly found a replacement job, totaled less than $10,000. But on the breach of good faith and fair dealing claim, the court awarded Elmer the $50,000 in commissions that he would have qualified for had he not been fired, $250,000 for the emotional stress he suffered because of the ordeal of being fired and another $250,000 in punitive damages to deter his ex-employer from using that commission-avoidance trick again.

D. Plant-Closing Laws

The statutes typically known as plant-closing laws apply only to mass dismissals of employees. They are the poor cousins of wrongful-discharge lawsuits.

These laws sometimes offer a way to challenge a job loss that is much quicker, easier and less expensive than filing a lawsuit. But the amount of money and other relief that workers can seek under plant-closing laws typically is miniscule compared to the remedies available via the wrongful-discharge lawsuit route.

Although many of the corporate staff cuts in recent years have actually taken place among managerial workers who have never seen the inside of a factory, our national tradition of picturing ourselves as a country of hard-working production-line folks who march in and out of an industrial plant at the start and end of each work day caused this relatively young category of legislation to be lumped incorrectly under the name plant-closing laws.

Ignore that name if your job loss appears to be covered by one of these laws but your job wasn't in a factory. You needn't have been employed in a plant to be covered by the plant-closing laws.

1. Closings aren't outlawed

Neither the federal plant-closing law nor the state and local laws in the same category actually forbid closing worksites and dismissing the people who work there.

All those laws really do is to give employees a little advance notice that their jobs are going to go away, like it or not. In fact, statistics compiled by *Workplace Trends*, a newsletter published in Rocky River, Ohio, show that the number of corporations making mass cuts in 1990 was more than four times the number doing so in 1989, the year the federal plant-closing law took effect.

At most, plant-closing laws can provide some income between jobs for employees of companies that fail to provide a warning that they're going to make a mass staff cut—and some punishments that might persuade a company that doesn't comply with the advance-notice requirements of the plant-closing laws not to repeat that behavior.

2. The federal plant-closing law

The federal plant-closing law requires employers with 100 or more full-time employees to provide 60 days' advance written notice that they're going to lose their jobs before closing a facility or operating unit, and before putting into effect any other mass staff reduction that will last six months or more.

The employer is also required to provide 60 days' notice of the staff reduction to the chief elected official, such as the mayor or council chairperson, of the local government of the community in which the cut will take place, and to the Dislocated Worker Unit of the state in which the cut will occur. The agency designated as the Dislocated Worker Unit varies from state to state, but your state's labor department should be able to direct you to the agency responsible for assisting workers who lose their jobs in mass dismissals.

3. Exceptions to the federal plant-closing law

The federal plant-closing law does not apply if:

- less than 50 workers are cut from the payroll.

- the cut takes away the jobs of less than 500 workers and represents less than one-third of the employer's workforce.

- the workers affected are part-time. This law defines part-time workers as those who average less than 20 hours of work per week, or who have been employed by the company for less than six of the 12 months preceding the staff cut.

- the employees left voluntarily or were discharged for good cause, such as performance that doesn't meet the company's standards.

- the staff cut is the result of a natural disaster.

- the employees affected were working on a project that was considered temporary and were told that it was when they were hired.

- waiting 60 days to let the workers go would put the company in danger of going out of business.

- the employer could not have foreseen the circumstances that make the staff cut necessary.

- the employer offers the workers being cut new jobs at another site within reasonable commuting distance, and the new jobs start within six months of when the old ones ended, or the workers being cut are offered new jobs at another site anywhere and they agree to the transfers within 30 days of when the employer offers them.

- the employer voluntarily offers severance pay, not required under any contract or other agreement, that is equal to or greater than the number of days that the company is short on the 60-day notice requirement. For example, if the company gives you 30 days' notice of a mass dismissal, it can avoid breaking the law by also voluntarily giving you 30 days' severance pay.

- more than 90 days pass between two mass dismissals which would require advance notice if added together but which fall under the minimum size rules when counted separately.

4. Employer penalties for violations

Obviously, this law has almost as many holes as fabric. But employers who manage to violate it despite all the exceptions can be made to pay the following penalties:

- backpay to each employee affected by the violation, up to a maximum of 60 days' pay

- reimbursement of the employees' benefit costs that would have been paid by the company had the illegal staff cut not occurred

- a fine of up to $500 per day for each day of the violation, up to a maximum of $30,000

- any attorneys' fees incurred.

This last penalty—requiring that legal fees be paid—is important because, if you're the victim of a mass firing that violates the federal plant-closing law and the government doesn't go to bat for you, you and your co-workers will probably have no recourse but to file a lawsuit to enforce your rights.

HELP FROM THE GOVERNMENT

Before you hire a lawyer to take action under the federal plant-closing law, you may want to write or call the highest elected official of the municipality where the staff cut took place and ask him or her to pursue your complaint. The federal plant-closing law specifies that a unit of the local government aggrieved may sue the employer involved in the federal district court when the incident occurred, or in any district where the employer does business.

In general, governmental bodies aren't very aggressive in pursuing complaints against businesses. But because corporate staff cutting may be a high profile political issue, your local mayor may surprise you by suddenly becoming your legal advocate.

---

5. State and local plant-closing laws

At least nine states have their own plant-closing laws. (See Chart 4-2 at the end of this chapter.) Even a few cities, such as Vacaville, California, and Philadelphia, Pennsylvania, have laws restricting companies that order mass dismissals. Most of these laws merely add a minor restriction or two to the rules of the federal plant-closing law, such as requiring that the corporation planning a mass staff cut notify another level of government of its plans in advance.

However, some of the state plant-closing laws do provide substantial benefits for the workers they cover. For example, Hawaii's version requires an employer to make up the difference between a worker's regular pay and the unemployment compensation the worker will receive for up to four weeks after the staff cut, under certain conditions.

Each of these laws specifies different restrictions, penalties and methods of enforcement. You can usually learn the details of any state or local law governing mass dismissals by calling your state's labor department or the law department of the community in which you work.

E. Understanding Outplacement

If asked to name a major industry that grew up in the 1980s, most people would probably guess computers. But, in fact, the industry known as outplacement—services that smooth the movement of employees off of corporate payrolls—expanded with similar vigor during that decade.

Until corporate staff cutting became an epidemic during the early 1980s, the outplacement profession was economically insignificant. Today, the American outplacement industry bills its clients more than $350 million each year—and more than 2,000 people are employed as outplacement professionals.

Each year, many thousands of workers are permanently dismissed by corporations that are shrinking or dying. Most management experts agree that long-term job security is obsolete. Yet the outplacement industry continues to be regarded much as the funeral industry is: Most people avoid taking the time to understand how it works until they find themselves participating in it under duress.

Outplacement services are not employment agencies. They are not executive search firms. They are not employee leasing companies. They do not find a new job for you, but they do help and encourage you in finding one for yourself.

Although some outplacement firms offer packages of services that can be purchased by individuals, outplacement counselors are most often brought in and paid for by employers who want to diminish their risks of being sued for wrongful discharge. Outplacement benefits have even been negotiated into union contracts.

The theory underlying the popularity of outplacement in the corporate world is that fired employees who move quickly and smoothly into a new job typically don't sustain grudges against the company that fired them, nor do they experience the kind of financial problems that can inspire job-related lawsuits. In cases where a person goes through outplacement, still can't find a replacement job and decides to file a wrongful-discharge lawsuit, the company can show a court that it has done all it can to limit the damage done to the employee by the firing.

1. An overview of outplacement programs

An outplacement program typically begins with classes or individual counseling on how to take an inventory of your marketable job skills. Then, you're assigned a furnished office space from which to launch your search for a new employer. These offices are usually equipped with a telephone and an extensive library of business directories, and they have a central typing service that will pump out resumes and letters for you.

Many outplacement firms even provide the people passing through them with business cards that carry only the person's name and a daytime telephone number—but no business title—and a switchboard operator to answer their telephone calls in a corporate style—but without indicating any company affiliation. These props typically get a lot of use because in many outplacement agencies, the participants are required to turn in daily or weekly logs of potential employers they've contacted to inquire about possible job openings.

Periodic counseling and encouragement sessions with the outplacement firm's staff continue until you've found a new job, or until your ex-employer's willingness to pay for the outplacement services runs out. There is no standard duration for outplacement services. Some people spend only a few days in outplacement, but some stay for a year or more.

Because some people have a difficult time finding a new job even with the support of an outplacement firm, some of these firms now offer programs that teach new work-related skills.

2. Advantages of participation

An employer cannot force you to participate in an outplacement program. However, most large employers will continue to pay your salary and benefits for at least a few weeks or months after you're fired on the condition that you actively participate in the outplacement services provided. Drop out—and you're on your own financially.

Refusal to participate in an outplacement program might also weaken any lawsuit you might later file against your former employer because you could be depicted as contributing to your loss of employment income. Active and enthusiastic participation in outplacement would, on the other hand, provide additional verification that you were competent and professional while in the job from which you were fired.

Chart 4-1

STATE LAWS ON PUBLIC POLICY AND THE WORKPLACE

This is a synopsis of state laws that specifically protect employees in private industry from being fired or otherwise punished for doing what public policy demands of them.

Alabama

Employees may not be fired for serving on a jury. Ala. Code §12-16-8.1 (1975)

Alaska

Employees may not be fired or otherwise disciplined for serving on a jury. Alaska Stat. §09.20.015 (1988)

Employers may not discriminate against employees because they have filed complaints about, or participated in investigations of, violations of state workplace safety laws. Alaska Stat. §18.60.089 (1986)

Arizona

Employees may not be fired or otherwise punished for serving on a jury. Ariz. Rev. Stat. Ann. §21-236 (1988)

Arkansas

Employees may not be fired or otherwise punished for serving on a jury. Ark. Stat. Ann. §16-31-106 (1987)

California

Employees may not be fired or otherwise punished for serving on a jury, but must give the employer reasonable notice that a leave for jury duty will be needed. Cal. Lab. Code §230 (1989)

Connecticut

Employees may not be fired or otherwise punished for serving on a jury. Conn. Gen. Stat. §51-2472 (1988)

Employers may not discriminate against employees because they have filed a complaint about, or participated in investigations of, violations of any law. Conn. Gen. Stat. §31-51m (1988)

Delaware

Employees may not be fired, intimidated, threatened or coerced in connection with serving on a jury. Del. Code Ann. 10 §4515 (1988)

District of Columbia

Employees may not be fired for serving on a jury. D.C. Code Ann. §11-1913 (1981)

Florida

Employees may not be fired or threatened with firing in connection with serving on a jury. Fla. Stat. §40.271 (1988)

It is illegal to use a threat of firing to compel an employee to trade with, or refuse to trade with, a specific company, person or class of persons. Fla. Stat. §448.03 (1989)

Georgia

An employer may not discriminate against an employee for responding to a summons for jury duty, a court order or process, or a subpoena. Ga. Code Ann. §34-1-3 (1988)

Hawaii

An employer may not fire, threaten, or coerce an employee in connection with serving on a jury. Hawaii Rev. Stat. §612-25 (1985)

Employers may not discriminate against employees because they have filed complaints about, or participated in investigations of, violations of, any law. Hawaii Rev. Stat. §378-61 (1987)

Idaho

Employees may not be fired, threatened or coerced in connection with serving on a jury. Idaho Code §2-218 (1988)

Illinois

Employees may not be fired in connection with serving on a jury, but employers must be given reasonable notice of the need for jury duty leave. Ill. Ann. Stat. Ch. 78 §§4.1 (1990) and 33.1 (1990)

Indiana

Employees may not be fired or threatened with firing for serving on a jury. Ind. Code Ann. §35-44-3-10 (1985)

Iowa

Employees may not be discriminated against for serving on a jury. Iowa Code Ann. §607A.45 (1988)

Kentucky

Employees may not be fired for serving on a jury. Ky. Rev. Stat. Ann. §29A.160 (1985)

Employers may not discriminate against an employee for reporting a violation of state workplace safety laws. Ky. Rev. Stat. Ann. §338.121 (1988)

Louisiana

Employees may not be fired for serving on a jury. La. Rev. Stat. Ann. §23:965 (1985)

Employers may not discriminate against employees who report violations of state environmental laws. La. Rev. Stat. Ann. §30:2027 (1989)

Maine

Employees may not be fired for serving on a jury. Me. Rev. Stat. Ann. 26 §1218 (1988)

Employers may not discriminate against or otherwise punish employees who report or participate in investigations of violations of federal, state or local laws. Whistleblower Protection Act, Me. Rev. Stat. Ann. 26 §833 (1987)

Maryland

Employees may not be fired for serving on a jury. Md. Cts. & Jud. Proc. Code Ann. §8-105 (1984)

Massachusetts

Employees may not be fired for serving on a jury. Mass. Gen. Laws Ann. Ch. 268 §14A (1970)

Michigan

Employees may not be fired or otherwise punished for serving on a jury. Mich. Comp. Laws Ann. §600.1348 (1988)

Employers may not discriminate against employees because they have reported violations of any law. Mich Comp. Laws Ann. §15.361 (1981)

Minnesota

Employees may not be fired, threatened or coerced for serving on a jury. Minn. Stat. Ann. §593.50 (1988)

Employers may not discriminate against an employee for reporting a violation of a federal or state law, participating in an investigation of a crime, or refusing to participate in an activity the employee believes is illegal. Minn. Stat. Ann. §181.932 (1989)

Mississippi

Employers may not intimidate, threaten or otherwise persuade employees to avoid jury duty. Miss. Code Ann. §13-5-23 (1988)

Montana

Employees may not be fired for refusing to violate public policy, or for reporting violations of public policy. Mont. Code Ann. §39-2-904 (1987)

Nebraska

Employees may not be fired for serving on a jury, but must give the employer reasonable notice that a leave for jury duty will be needed. Neb. Rev. Stat. §25-1640 (1985)

Companies that employ 15 or more people may not discriminate against an employee for opposing or refusing to participate in any illegal act. Neb. Rev. Stat. §§48-1102 and 1114 (1986)

Nevada

Employees may not be fired or otherwise threatened for serving on a jury. Nev. Rev. Stat. §6.190 (1988)

New Hampshire

Employees may not be fired, threatened or coerced for serving on a jury. N.H. Rev. Stat. Ann §500-A:14 (1983)

Employers may not fire or otherwise discriminate against employees who report violations of law to the proper authorities or participate in the investigation of illegal actions. However, the employees must first report the violations to their supervisor. N.H. Rev. Stat. Ann. §275-E (1988)

New Jersey

Employers may not fire or otherwise retaliate against employees who report violations of law to the proper authorities or participate in the investigation of illegal actions. However, the employees must first report the violations to their supervisor—except in situations where the employees know that the supervisor is already aware of the violations, or where the employees fear physical harm as a result of their actions. N.J. Stat. Ann §34:19-3 (1989)

New Mexico

Employees may not be fired, threatened or coerced for serving on a jury. N.M. Stat. Ann. §38-5-18 (1987)

New York

Employees may not be fired or otherwise punished for serving on a jury. N.Y. Jud. Law §519 (1989)

Employers may not fire or otherwise retaliate against an employee who reports a legal violation by the employer that threatens public health or safety, participates in the investigation of a legal violation by the employer, or refuses to participate in the violation of a law. N.Y. Lab. Law §740 (1988)

North Carolina

Employees may not be fired or demoted for serving on a jury. N.C. Gen. Stat. §9-32 (1988)

North Dakota

Employees may not be fired, threatened or coerced for serving on a jury or testifying under subpoena. N.D. Cent. Code §27-09.1-17.1 (1987)

Ohio

Employees may not be fired or threatened with firing for serving on a jury, but the employer must be given reasonable notice that a leave for jury service will be needed. Ohio Rev. Code Ann. §2313.18 (1988)

Employees may not be fired or otherwise punished for reporting violations of federal, state or local law to the proper authorities. Ohio Rev. Code §4113.51 (1988)

Oklahoma

Employers may not discriminate against employees who file complaints about, or participate in investigations of, violations of certain work-related state laws. Okla. Stat. Ann. 40 §199 (1990)

Oregon

Employees may not be fired for serving on a jury. Or. Rev. Stat. §10.090 (1985)

Employers may not fire employees because they have reported certain types of legal violations, participated in investigations of certain violations, or opposed actions that would violate certain laws regarding to workplace safety. Or. Rev. Stat. §§659.270 (1967), 653.060 (1967), 659.035 (1989), 654.062 (1989)

Pennsylvania

Retailing and service companies that employ 15 or more people, and manufacturing companies that employ 40 or more people, may not fire or otherwise discriminate against employees for serving on a jury. 42 Pa. Cons. Stat. Ann. §4563 (1989)

Employers may not retaliate against employees who are victims of, or witnesses to, crimes. 18 Pa. Cons. Stat. Ann. §4957 (1989)

Rhode Island

Employees may not be fired or otherwise discriminated against for serving on a jury. R.I. Gen. Laws §9-9-28 (1985)

Employers may not fire, threaten or otherwise discriminate against an employee who reported, or participated in the investigation of, a violation of a law. R.I. Gen. Laws §36-15-1,3 (1988)

South Carolina

Employees may not be fired or demoted for serving on a jury. S.C. Code Ann. §41-1-70 (1988)

South Dakota

Employees may not be fired or otherwise discriminated against for serving on a jury. S.D. Codified Laws Ann. §16-13-41.1 (1987)

Tennessee

Employees may not be fired or otherwise discriminated against for serving on a jury. However, an employee receiving a summons to serve on a jury must show the summon to his supervisor on the next day of work to be covered by this law. Tenn. Code Ann. §22-4-108 (1988)

Utah

Employees may not be fired, threatened or coerced for serving on a jury. Utah Code Ann. §78-46-21 (1987)

Vermont

Employees may not be fired or otherwise punished for serving on a jury or as a witness. Vt. Stat. Ann. 21 §499 (1987)

Employers may not fire or otherwise discriminate against employees for filing complaints about,or participating in investigations of,violations of the state's workplace safety laws. Vt. Stat. Ann. 21 §231 (1987)

Virginia

Employers may not fire or otherwise discriminate against employees for filing complaints about or participating in investigations of violations of the state's workplace safety laws. Va. Code §40.1-51.2:1 (1986)

Washington

Employees must be given a leave of absence from work to serve as a juror. Wash. Rev. Code §2.36.165 (1989)

Employers may not fire or otherwise discriminate against employees for filing complaints about, or participating in investigations of, violations of state human rights laws. Wash. Rev. Code §§49.12.130 (1962) and 49.60.210 (1985)

Wisconsin

Employers must grant an employee a leave of absence from work to serve on a jury, and may not fire or otherwise punish an employee for serving on a jury. Wis. Stat. §756.25 (1988)

Wyoming

An employee may not be fired, intimidated or coerced for serving on a jury. Wyo. Stat. §1-11-401 (1983)

An employer may not fire an employee for filing a complaint about, or participating in investigations of, violations of the state's workplace safety laws. Wyo. Stat. §27-11-109 (1990)

Chart 4-2

STATE PLANT-CLOSING LAWS

This is a synopsis of state laws governing mass dismissals and relocations of worksites by private industry.

Connecticut

Whenever a business facility employing 100 or more workers closes or relocates, the employer must continue to pay for each worker's healthcare insurance for 120 days after the closing or relocation, or until the employee becomes eligible for replacement group coverage, whichever comes first. Conn. Gen. Stat. §31-150 (1988)

Hawaii

Companies employing 50 or more workers much give employees who will lose their jobs in business relocation or mass dismissal at least 45 days notice of their impending job loss in writing. Hawaii Rev. Stat. §394B-9 (1987)

Kansas

The Secretary of Human Resources must give prior approval to mass dismissals within certain industries such as public utilities and public transportation companies. Kan. Stat. Ann. §44-616 (1988)

Maine

Any company employing 100 or more workers must give workers who will lose their jobs in a mass dismissal or relocation of a plant to outside the state at least 60 days' notice of that dismissal or relocation. Me. Rev. Stat. Ann. tit. 26, §625-B (1988)

Maryland

Voluntary guidelines covering issues such as advance notice to employees have been established for companies planning a mass dismissal or business relocation. Md. Ann. Code Art. 83A, §§3-301 through 3-304 (1988)

Massachusetts

Employers who receive assistance from certain state agencies are, in certain circumstances, required to give employees who will lose their jobs in a mass dismissal 90 days' notice of that dismissal. Mass. Gen. Laws Ann. Ch. 149 §182 (1989)

Under certain circumstances, employers are required to continue paying for group healthcare insurance coverage for employees who lose their jobs in a mass dismissal or business relocation for up to 90 days after those employees are put out of work. Mass. Gen. Laws Ann. Ch. 175 §110D (1987)

Minnesota

The state's Commissioner of Jobs and Training must encourage employers to provide advance notice of substantial staff cuts. Minn. Stat. Ann. §268.971 (1989)

Tennessee

Companies employing 50 or more full-time workers within the state must notify state labor officials of a mass dismissal after notifying the employees who will lose their jobs in the dismissal. Tenn. Code Ann. §50-1-602 (1988)

Wisconsin

Companies employing 50 or more workers within the state must give employees who will lose their jobs at least 60 days' notice of a business closing or mass dismissal in which 25 or more full-time employees will lose their jobs. Wis. Stat. §109.07 (1988)

Chart 4-3

STATE BLACKLISTING LAWS

In general, blacklisting is defined as distributing information about an ex-employee that is intended to prevent that person from getting, or continuing in, a new job. The chart below lists state statutes that make blacklisting illegal and describes some specifics of state laws.

Arizona

Employers may distribute information on former employers to prospective new employers, but are immune from lawsuits by the former employees only if the information distributed is true and not distributed with reckless disregard for its truthfulness. Ariz. Rev. Stat. §23-1361 (1988)

California

It is illegal for an employer to make a false statement to prevent a former employee from getting a new job. However, an employer may make true statements about a former employee in response to an inquiry from a prospective new employer. Cal. Lab. Code §1050 (1971), §1052 (1989), §1052 (1971) and §1054 (1971)

Florida

Fla. Stat. §448.045 (1981)

Indiana

Employers may state the correct reason for a former employee's dismissal to prospective employers. Ind. Code Ann. §22-5-3-1 (1986)

Iowa

Iowa Code Ann. §730.1 (1979)

Kansas

Kan. Stat. Ann. §44-117 (1981)

New Mexico

N.M. Stat. Ann. §30-13-3 (1984)

North Carolina

N.C. Gen. Stat. §14-355 (1986)

Virginia

Va. Code §40.1-27 (1986)

Wisconsin

Wis. Stat. §134.02 (1974)

5

Illegal Job Discrimination

It is almost always illegal for employers to discriminate against workers because of their race, skin color, gender, religious beliefs, national origin, physical handicap—or age if the employee is at least 40 years old. In some situations, it is also illegal for employers to discriminate against workers on the basis of factors such as testing positive for the HIV virus, or being pregnant, divorced, extremely overweight, gay or lesbian.

Right-to-work laws are also a type of anti-discrimination law. But since they generally make it illegal to discriminate against a worker who doesn't belong to a labor union, they're discussed in more detail in Chapter 7, Section D.

Sexual harassment is another form of illegal workplace discrimination. However, since sexual harassment has many unique complexities, it's discussed separately in Chapter 6.

A. Federal Laws Against Discrimination

The most powerful anti-discrimination law governing the workplace is Title VII of the federal Civil Rights Act of 1964. It originally outlawed discrimination based on race, skin color, religious beliefs or national origin, and it created the Equal Employment Opportunity Commission (EEOC) to administer and enforce the legal standards it set.

Today, a number of other laws are used in conjunction with Title VII to fight unfair workplace discrimination.

- The Equal Pay Act, enacted about one year before Title VII, specifically outlaws discrimination in wages on the basis of gender.

- In 1967, the Age Discrimination in Employment Act (ADEA) was passed to also outlaw workplace discrimination on the basis of age. The ADEA itself has been amended several times, and now applies only to employees who are at least 40 years old. The Older Workers Benefit Protection Act, enacted in 1990, is an amendment to the ADEA that specifically outlaws discrimination in employment benefit programs on the basis of employees' age (see Section G), and it too applies only to employees age 40 and older. It also deters employers' use of waivers in which employees sign away their rights to take legal action against age-based discrimination. (See Chapter 3, Section C for an example of such a waiver.)

- In 1972, Title VII was amended again to outlaw discrimination based on gender.

- In 1978, Congress again amended Title VII by enacting the Pregnancy Discrimination Act (PDA), which makes it illegal for an employer to refuse to hire a pregnant woman, to terminate her employment, or to compel her to take maternity leave. (For more on parental leaves, see Chapter 10, Section C.)

- The Americans with Disabilities Act (ADA), enacted in 1990, makes it illegal to discriminate against people because of their physical condition.

B. Title VII Explained

Here are the basics of how Title VII works:

1. Employees covered

Title VII applies to all companies and labor unions with 20 or more employees. It also governs employment agencies, state and local governments, and apprenticeship programs.

While the federal government also is required to conduct its employment practices by equal opportunity standards, special procedures have been established to enforce anti-discrimination laws in relation to federal employees.

Independent contractors (discussed in detail in Chapter 1, Section B) are not covered by Title VII.

2. Types of discrimination outlawed

Under Title VII, employers may not intentionally use race, skin color, age if at least 40, gender, religious beliefs or national origin as the basis for decisions on hirings, promotions, dismissals, pay raises, benefits, work assignments, leaves of absence or just about any other aspect of the employment relationship. Title VII covers everything about the employment relationship—from pre-hiring ads to working conditions, to performance reviews, to giving post-employment references.

C. Filing a Title VII Complaint With the EEOC

Compared to most other government agencies, the EEOC has very well-defined procedures for filing complaints. But the EEOC also operates through a complex hierarchy of offices and has strict time limits for filing complaints. So you'll need to pay particular attention to timing if you decide to take action against what you believe is illegal workplace discrimination.

1. Where to file

Title VII complaints can be filed at:

- **Community equal employment opportunity agency offices.** These aren't federal offices, but agencies that have been designated as representatives of the EEOC. You can usually find out if your city or town has one by calling your city hall and asking whether it has an equal employment opportunity office, or whether there is a Fair Employment Practices Agency nearby.

- **State and regional offices of the EEOC.** You can locate the one nearest you in the federal government section of your local telephone directory, or by checking your state's section in Chart 5-1 at the end of this chapter.

If you still can't find the agency you need, write or call the EEOC headquarters in Washington, D.C. (Contact information is included in the Appendix.)

If your state has its own equal employment opportunity laws, you'll typically be allowed 300 days after the act of discrimination occurred to file a complaint. But at EEOC offices, the time limit for filing a complaint is 180 days. The safest way to proceed is to assume that 180 days is the limit in your case and file your complaint as soon as possible.

In some cases, you won't be able to recognize illegal discrimination from a single action by an employer. If you discern a pattern of illegal discrimination that extends back more than 180 days, the safest way to proceed is to assume that the EEOC time limit began with the event that caused you to recognize the pattern and file a complaint as soon as possible.

Example: A woman who worked with Jan in a pharmaceutical lab was fired in January. Two months later, the lab fired another woman. In June, a third woman was fired.

When the third woman was fired, Jan began to notice that the firings seemed to have nothing to do with job performance. Although the lab employed several men with less experience and whose job performance wasn't as good as the three women who had been fired, no men had been fired.

Jan took a few weeks to gather evidence to support her belief that the company was illegally discriminating against women on the basis of gender, and then filed a complaint with the EEOC in September.

THE GENDER GAP IN WAGES

Ever since the Industrial Revolution came to America, we've had a gender gap in wages. With very few exceptions, women have been paid less than men. That gap has been narrowing since 1980, when women typically were earning only 60% of what men earned. But the gap is still there.

For example, a study released by the Census Bureau in 1990 showed that median annual earnings for women were $18,780, still only 68% of men's median annual earnings of $27,430. (Median annual earnings means that half earned more than that and half earned less.)

Only about half of the shrinkage in the gender gap in wages has been caused by rising incomes for women. The Census Bureau found that, while incomes for women who worked year-round in full-time jobs rose 1.8% in 1989, incomes for their male counterparts dropped 1.8% in that same year.

---

2. Organize your evidence

Because illegal discrimination rarely takes the form of one simple event, it's important that you organize whatever evidence of illegal discrimination you have as well as you can before contacting the EEOC to file a complaint.

Whenever possible, keep a log of the date, time, location, people involved and nature of actions that demonstrate any pattern of illegal discrimination that you detect. Keep a file of any documents that your em-

ployer gives you, such as written performance reviews or disciplinary notices.

If you present your evidence to the EEOC in an organized way—without
yielding to the temptation to vent your displeasure with your employer's
policies and practices—you'll raise the chances of your complaint getting
full attention and consideration from the investigators who handle it.

3. How the EEOC handles complaints

When you file a complaint, typically a staff lawyer or investigator will interview you and give you an opinion on whether or not your employer's actions appear to violate Title VII. If the interviewer doesn't feel that the incident warrants a complaint, he or she will tell you so and you'll have to think
about other options.

If the interviewer feels you should pursue your complaint with the EEOC,
he or she will fill out an EEOC Charge of Discrimination form describing
the incident and send it to you to edit and sign. After receiving your complaint, the EEOC is supposed to interview the employer that is the subject of
the complaint and then try to mediate a settlement of the complaint between you and that employer.

Sometimes this happens, but many complaints just sit on someone's
desk because, the EEOC claims, its budget isn't large enough to allow it to
investigate all the claims that are filed.

A congressional report conducted in 1987 showed that the EEOC failed
to fully investigate 80% of the complaints filed there. At the end of 1990, the
EEOC had a backlog of 44,000 cases—and most of the complaints that were
being pursued were being given only superficial attention just to keep the
backlog at that level. And, unfortunately, there's nothing to indicate that the
EEOC is getting any more efficient.

4. Protection from retaliation

It is illegal for your employer to retaliate against you for filing a complaint under Title VII, or for cooperating in the investigation of such a complaint. But to take advantage of this protection, you have to be able to prove that the retaliation was a result of your filing of a complaint.

More often than not, an employer that wants to retaliate against you for filing a Title VII complaint will cite substandard on-the-job performance.

Example: Hector filed a Title VII complaint because he observed that his employer never promotes anyone of his race above a certain level. To investigate Hector's complaint, the EEOC reviewed documents related to the company's hiring practices to determine whether it is, in fact, using race as the basis for hiring decisions.

Two weeks later, Hector was dismissed from his job because, the company said, his performance was below its standards. If Hector decides to file an additional complaint charging the company with illegal retaliation, he will probably have to prove that his performance satisfied or exceeded the company's standards—and that the real reason he was fired was because he filed a Title VII complaint.

JOB DISCRIMINATION AND THE ART OF JAPANESE MANAGEMENT

Many Japanese corporations with divisions based in the United States have a special kind of problem with U.S. laws that forbid employment discrimination on the basis of race or gender.

The problem is rooted in the fact that many Japanese corporations practice what is most commonly known as shadow management. It's a system under which Americans are hired as token managers, while only executives born and raised in Japan are authorized to make important business decisions. The American managers are, therefore, shadowed by their Japanese counterparts.

What's more, because of cultural traditions in their home country, Japanese corporations rarely allow women of any race to hold positions of power.

One result of these practices and policies is that at least a dozen lawsuits charging employment discrimination on the basis of race or gender have been filed by native-born Americans against Japanese firms doing business in the United States in recent years.

These cases are particularly complex, however, because in 1953, the United States and Japan signed a treaty that allows Japanese corporations to use whatever standards they wish to hire managers (4 U.S. Treaties 2067 TJAS 2863). Then, in 1982, the U.S. Supreme Court ruled that division of companies that are incorporated in the United States are subject to U.S. civil rights laws. But many of the divisions of Japanese corporations that have operations in the United States aren't incorporated here, so there's a question of whether that Supreme Court decision applies.

Nevertheless, Japanese employers operating in the United States have lost or settled at least six such discrimination suits in recent years.

D. Filing a Title VII Lawsuit

In the very likely event that the EEOC fails to act on your complaint within 180 days, you then have the right to request from the agency where you filed your complaint a right-to-sue letter that authorizes you to file a lawsuit in federal court against the offending employer. This type of suit is complex, and in cases involving an employee dismissal is usually packaged with other claims. (See Chapter 4, Section C.) So you'll probably need to hire a lawyer to help you file a lawsuit under Title VII. (See Chapter 13, Section D.)

Once you receive your right-to-sue letter, you have only 90 days to file a lawsuit, so deadlines are very important at this point of the Title VII process, as well. The EEOC has the right to file a lawsuit on your behalf, but don't expect that to happen unless your case has a very high political or publicity value. The EEOC's out-of-pocket expenses are limited by law to $5,000 per lawsuit—many thousands of dollars less than it typically costs to take an employment discrimination case to court.

1. Class actions

The most likely way for many employees to succeed in a Title VII case is to become part of a class action lawsuit. The courts allow lawsuits to be pursued as class actions when it can be shown that a number of people have been injured by the same unlawful act. Because the potential damages from a Title VII class action suit are much larger than in an individual lawsuit, some attorneys will take those cases on a contingency basis—which means that their fees will not be paid upfront but will be taken as a percentage of the amount recovered. (See Chapter 13, Section D.)

Your local office of the American Civil Liberties Union (ACLU) should be able to direct you to lawyers who specialize in civil rights class action lawsuits. (See the Appendix for details of contacting the national headquarters of the ACLU.)

2. State and local alternatives

In general, employment-related lawsuits filed under state or local laws are easier to win than those filed under Title VII. And—unlike most Title VII cases—state and local anti-discrimination laws often offer the possibility of a larger judgment in favor of the worker who files the suit. (See Section J.)

E. The Equal Pay Act

The Equal Pay Act is an anti-discrimination law that requires employers to pay all employees equally for equal work, regardless of their gender.

1. Employees covered

Nearly all employees are covered by the Equal Pay Act. The Act applies to all employees covered by the Fair Labor Standards Act (discussed in Chapter 2), which means virtually every employee is covered. But in addition, the Equal Pay Act covers professional employees, executives and managers.

In practice, this law almost always has been applied to situations where women are being paid less than men for doing similar jobs. However, the Act technically protects both women and men from gender discrimination in pay rates.

2. Exceptions to coverage

In general, pay systems that result in employees of one gender being paid less than the other gender for doing equal work are allowed under the Equal Pay Act if the pay system is actually based on a factor other than gender.

Example: In 1960, the Ace Widget Company was founded and initially hired 50 male widget makers. Many of those men are still working there. Since 1980, the company has expanded and hired 50 more widget makers, half of them male and half female. All of the widget makers at Ace are doing equal work, but because the company awards raises systematically based on seniority, or the length of a worker's employment there, many of the older male workers earn substantially more per hour than their female co-workers who are doing equal work.

Nevertheless, the pay system at Ace Widget doesn't violate the Equal Pay Act because its pay differences between genders are based on a factor other than gender.

3. Determining job equality

Jobs don't have to be identical for the courts to consider them equal. In general, the courts have ruled that two jobs are equal for the purposes of the Equal Pay Act when both require equal levels of skill, effort and responsibility—and are performed under similar conditions.

There's a lot of room for interpretation here, of course. But the general rule is that if there are only small differences in the skill, effort or responsibility required for jobs, those jobs should still be regarded as equal.

Example: Where the major difference between the jobs being done by women and men was a weight-lifting restriction placed on the women, the court ruled that the female and male employees were performing equal work because heavy lifting represented only a small part of the job (*Shultz v. Saxonburg Ceramics Inc.*, 314 F. Supp. 1139, W.D. PA (1970)).

F. Filing an Equal Pay Act Complaint

The Equal Pay Act is enforced, along with Title VII, by the EEOC, which you can locate in the federal government section of your telephone directory.

1. Combining complaints

In complaints alleging discrimination against female employees on the basis of gender, the Equal Pay Act often is applied in conjunction with Title VII.

Example: Suzanne works as a reservations agent for an airline, answering calls on the airline's toll-free telephone number. About half of the other people doing the same job in her office are men, who are typically paid $1 per hour more than Suzanne and the other female agents. What's more, the company has established a dress code for the women in that office, but none for the men who work there.

If Suzanne decides to file a discrimination complaint against her employer, the Equal Pay Act would apply to the pay difference between females and males, and Title VII would apply to both the pay difference and the fact that only the female employees in that office are held to a dress code.

In cases where both Title VII and the Equal Pay Act apply, the Equal Pay Act offers two potential advantages:

- You can file a lawsuit under the Equal Pay Act without first filing a complaint with the EEOC.

- Unlike Title VII, the Equal Pay Act doesn't require proof that the employer acted intentionally when discriminating. That can make an Equal Pay Act case much easier to win in court.

2. Equal pay v. comparable worth

When deciding whether the Equal Pay Act applies to your job, keep in mind that this law covers only situations where men and women are performing jobs that require equal skill, effort and responsibility and are performed under similar circumstances. There are, however, situations where men and women are doing different jobs. The value to their employer of the work they're doing appears to be the same, yet men and women are, in general, working at different payrates. Disputes over this are typically lumped under the term "comparable worth."

A comparable worth case typically isn't covered by the Equal Pay Act. Because they are broader in scope, Title VII or the state anti-discrimination laws (discussed in Section D), are the ones that are used to pursue comparable worth complaints.

G. The Older Workers Benefit Protection Act

The main purposes of the Older Workers Benefit Protection Act are to make it clearly illegal to use an employee's age as the basis for discrimination in benefits, and to discourage companies from targeting older workers for their staff cutting programs. The law was passed in 1990 after a controversial U.S. Supreme Court ruling (*Public Employees Retirement Sys. v. Betts*, 109 U.S.

2854 (1989)) confused the question of when and how the Age Discrimination in Employment Act applied to benefit programs.

The Older Workers Benefit Protection Act became effective April 14, 1991, for nonunion employees in private industry. For unionized employees in private industry, it is effective on June 1, 1992, or upon the expiration of their current contract—whichever comes sooner. Like the ADEA, it covers only employees who are at least 40 years old. It contains a clause specifying that it is not retroactive.

Most of the effects of this law are very difficult for anyone but an experienced benefits administrator to understand. However, the provision of the law that you're most likely to put to use yourself—the one regulating the legal waivers that employers are increasingly asking employees to sign in connection with so-called early retirement programs—is relatively clear and specific.

1. Waiving your right to sue

By signing a waiver—often called a release or covenant not to sue—an employee agrees not to take any legal action against the employer. In return for signing the waiver, the employer gives the employee an incentive, such as a severance pay package that exceeds the company's standard policy, to leave the company voluntarily. (See Chapter 3, Section C.)

By the start of the 1990s, this type of transaction had become very popular among large corporations that wanted to reduce their payroll costs. Because older workers who have been with a company a long time typically cost more to employ than younger workers—for example, company-paid life insurance premiums are higher for older workers—most staff-cutting programs were directed at older workers. But cutting only older workers constitutes illegal age discrimination, so companies typically induced the older workers to sign away their rights to take legal action against their former employers.

Before the Older Workers Benefit Protection Act was enacted, this approach to staff-cutting subjected many workers in their 50s or 60s to a cruel squeeze play technique that is known to many management insiders as Sign or Starve.

Example: Called into his supervisor's office unexpectedly, 56-year-old Jonathan was offered the option of agreeing to "retire" early in return for a severance pay package that was larger than what he would receive under the company's standard pay policy. But to accept, he would have to sign—right then and there—a waiver of his right to sue the employer for age discrimination. No waiver, no incentive payment.

The extra 26 weeks worth of pay the company offered him really wasn't enough to allow him to retire, of course, but the meager offer made his employer feel justified in telling the local newspaper that it was conducting an early retirement program—which sounds much better than a mass firing.

What's worse, the supervisor refused to give Jonathan any indication of what would happen to him if he refused to sign, or of how the offer being made to him related to offers being made to other employees targeted for the staff cut. He wasn't given a chance to think over the offer or to discuss it with family, friends or a lawyer. Isolated and intimidated by his department's supervisor and a company lawyer, he imagined himself being fired a few weeks later and then being unable to find another decent job during the nine years he still had to go before qualifying for normal retirement benefits.

Under such pressure, Jonathan did what most people would: He accepted the company's offers and signed the covenant waiving his right to sue his employer for illegal age discrimination or any other form of wrongful termination of employment.

2. Protection against waiving rights

Fortunately, the Older Workers Benefit Protection Act gives employees some power to counteract this type of staff-cutting tactic. Under the law, you must be given at least 21 days to decide whether or not to sign such a waiver if it is one that has been presented to you alone. If the waiver is presented to a group of employees, you must be given at least 45 days to decide whether or not to sign. In either case, you have seven days after agreeing to such a waiver to revoke your decision.

Here are the other key restrictions this law places on agreements not to sue:

- Your employer must make the waiver understandable to the average individual eligible for the program in which the waiver is being used.

- The waiver may not cover any rights or claims that you discover are available after you sign it, and it must specify that it covers your rights under the ADEA.

- Your employer has to offer you something of value—over and above what is already owed to you—in exchange for your signature on the waiver.

- Your employer must advise you, in writing, to consult an attorney before you sign the waiver.

- If the offer is being made to a class of employees, your employer must inform you in writing how the class of employees is defined; the job titles and ages of all the individuals to whom the offer is being made; and the ages of all the employees in the same job classification or unit of the company to whom the offer is not being made.

- You must be given a fixed period of time, such as the minimum times discussed above, in which to make a decision on whether or not to sign the waiver.

3. The power of negotiation

In addition to giving you additional legal protections, if your employer offers you the opportunity to participate in a staff-reduction program, the Older Workers Benefits Protection Act indirectly puts you in a position to try to negotiate the terms of your departure.

The fact that your employer has made such an offer tells you that the company wants you gone and is worried that you might file a lawsuit for wrongful discharge. So, although the company may say that you have only two choices—accept or reject the offer—there's nothing preventing you from making a counter-offer.

For example, after taking a week or two to think about what you want to do with the rest of your life, you might reply to your employer's offer by saying that you'll agree to leave voluntarily if the severance pay offered is doubled. There's power in numbers, so this type of negotiating is even more likely to be effective if done on behalf of a group of employees to whom the company has made a staff-cutting offer.

As in all employment transactions, it's wise to advise your employer of your decision in writing, and to keep a copy of that letter—along with copies of all documents given to you by your employer as part of the staff reduction program. If you refuse to accept such an offer and are later dismissed, you may be able to use illegal age discrimination as a basis for challenging your dismissal. (See Chapter 4, Section A.)

4. How to take action

If you believe that an employer has violated your rights under the Older Workers Benefit Protection Act, you can file a complaint with the EEOC just as you would against any other workplace discrimination prohibited by Title VII. (See Section C.) If the EEOC fails to resolve your complaint to your satisfaction, you may decide to pursue your complaint through a lawsuit. (See Section D.)

H. The Americans With Disabilities Act

The Americans with Disabilities Act (ADA) prohibits employment discrimination on the basis of workers' disabilities. It is effective in July 1992 for companies with 25 or more employees, and in July 1994 for companies with 15 or more employees.

Because it is so new, the effects of this law haven't been explored in detail in court. But the ADA generally prohibits employers from:

- discriminating on the basis of virtually any physical or mental disability

- asking job applicants questions about their past or current medical conditions

- requiring job applicants to take pre-employment medical exams

- creating or maintaining worksites that include substantial physical barriers to the movement of people with physical handicaps.

The ADA is enforced by the Civil Rights Division of the U.S. Department of Justice, which has the right in some instances to file a lawsuit for damages on behalf of victims of discriminatory practices that are illegal under the ADA. You can locate the Justice Department office nearest you in the federal government section of your local telephone directory.

The ADA is expected to improve employment opportunities for more than 40 million people currently in the U.S. workforce.

PIZZA-MAKING ROBOT LETS DISABLED GO TO WORK

No law can get people with severe physical disabilities hired for jobs that their bodies can't perform. But scientists are discovering that, by using robots, they can help some physically disabled people find a place in the workforce by using their voices in place of missing or severely injured limbs.

Researchers at Carnegie Mellon University's Center for Human Service Robotics in Pittsburgh, for example, have developed a robot that allows people with no arms or legs to work as pizza makers. Named Pizzabot, it responds to voice commands by spreading sauce, cheese, mushrooms and other delectables on a crust. Then, when its operator tells it to, the robot rotates the crust, spreads more toppings and shoves the pizza into the oven.

Pizzabot is so good at what it does, its developers say, that a limbless worker can operate a pizza shop with just one helper—to take the pizza out of the oven, slice it, box it and ring up the purchase.

I. State and Local Anti-Discrimination Laws

Nearly all state and local laws prohibiting various types of discrimination in employment are echoes of federal anti-discrimination law in that they outlaw discrimination based on race, color, gender, age, national origin and religion. But the state and local laws also tend to go into more detail, creating categories of protection against discrimination that aren't covered by federal law.

In Louisiana, for example, it is illegal to discriminate in employment matters on the basis of a worker's political activity. In Minnesota, it is illegal to discriminate against people who are collecting public assistance. And in several states, the age range for workers protected against age-based discrimination is broader than under the federal ADEA.

Many state anti-discrimination laws also provide procedures for pursuing complaints about illegal workplace discrimination without going through the EEOC process, which is usually slow and ineffective. An employee in

New Jersey, for example, may go directly into that state's superior court with a lawsuit based on age discrimination without first complaining to the EEOC.

State laws prohibiting discrimination in employment, along with agencies responsible for enforcing anti-discrimination laws in those states, are listed in Chart 5-1 at the end of this chapter. Municipal anti-discrimination laws can usually be researched at the headquarters of your community's government, such as your local city hall or county courthouse.

J. Discrimination Against Gay and Lesbian Workers

There is no federal law that specifically outlaws workplace discrimination on the basis of sexual orientation. However, laws that do outlaw discrimination on that basis have been enacted by the District of Columbia and four states—Connecticut, Hawaii, Massachusetts and Wisconsin. (See Chart 5-1 at the end of this chapter.)

In addition, at least 80 cities prohibit discrimination based on sexual orientation. They include: Tucson, Arizona; Sacramento, California; Aspen, Colorado; Hartford, Connecticut; Atlanta, Georgia; Chicago, Illinois; Iowa City, Iowa; Boston, Massachusetts; Detroit, Michigan; Minneapolis, Minnesota; Buffalo, New York; Raleigh, North Carolina; Columbus, Ohio; Portland, Oregon; Philadelphia, Pennsylvania; Austin, Texas; Seattle, Washington and Milwaukee, Wisconsin.

In states and cities that don't have laws forbidding workplace discrimination on the basis of sexual orientation, you can often take action against an employer who fires or otherwise discriminates against you because you are gay or lesbian by filing a lawsuit claiming invasion of privacy (discussed in Chapter 12, Section A); illegal discrimination under the ADA (discussed in Section H) based on a perceived fear of HIV virus infection; or one of the other wrongful-discharge strategies (discussed in Chapter 4, Section A).

Example: Raymond's employer fired him because he was quoted in a local newspaper as a spokesperson for a gay organization that was trying to raise funds for charity. Raymond was able to win a lawsuit against the employer based on invasion of privacy, because the firing amounted to the employer exerting undue control over his private life.

K. Jobs That Require Discrimination

Under Title VII and many anti-discrimination laws at lower levels of government, an employer may intentionally use gender, religious beliefs or national origin as the basis for employment decisions only if the employer can show that the job has special requirements that make such discrimination necessary.

When an employer establishes that such a special circumstance exists, it is called a bona fide occupational qualification (BFOQ).

Example: A religious denomination that employs counselors who answer telephone inquiries from those interested in becoming members of that religion would typically be allowed to limit its hiring of counselors to people who believe in that religion. Being a member of that denomination would be a BFOQ.

In general, the courts, the EEOC and state equal employment opportunity agencies prohibit the use of BFOQs except where clearly necessary. They typically require any employer using a BFOQ in employment decisions to prove conclusively that the BFOQ is essential to the successful operation of the company or other organization.

The place where you're most likely to encounter a BFOQ is on a job application. If an employer is using a BFOQ on an application, it must state on the application that the employment qualification covered by the questions would otherwise be illegal, but has been approved by the EEOC.

If questions asked on a job application make you wonder whether that application violates an anti-discrimination law, call the nearest office of the EEOC or your state's equal opportunity agency.

L. Affirmative Action

Title VII also allows for formal programs, generally known as affirmative action, which intentionally base employment decisions on otherwise illegal factors in situations where the effects of past illegal discrimination need to be erased.

For example, companies are sometimes required by court order to abide by a racial ratio for new hires—such as one black employee hired for every two white employees hired—until the company's workforce resembles the racial mix of the community.

Affirmative action programs often generate resentment among employees who aren't members of minority groups—usually Anglo males—who see the programs as blocking their path to improved employment opportunities. But since lawsuits challenging affirmative action rarely succeeded, very little of that resentment found its way into court until 1989.

What changed the prospects of such lawsuits that year was a U.S. Supreme Court decision in a case involving a court-approved affirmative action program at the Birmingham, Alabama, Fire Department. The court ruled that a person injured by an affirmative action program may file a lawsuit in federal court challenging the legality of that program (*Martin v. Wilks*, 490 U.S. 755). Since then, a number of suits challenging affirmative action programs have been filed and reopened.

Because of the complexities of these cases, you'll probably need the assistance of a lawyer if you decide to file a lawsuit challenging an affirmative action program. (See Chapter 13, Section D.)

Chart 5-1

STATE LAWS AGAINST DISCRIMINATION IN EMPLOYMENT

This is a synopsis of factors that may not be used as the basis for employment discrimination under state laws. Keep in mind that it is only a synopsis, and that each state has its own way of determining such factors as what conditions qualify as a physical handicap.

In states where no special agency has been designated to enforce anti-discrimination laws, your state's Labor Department or Attorney General's office or the closest office of the federal Equal Employment Opportunity Office should direct you to the right agency or person with whom to file a complaint over illegal discrimination in employment.

In certain states or circumstances, you may have no way to pursue your complaint over illegal discrimination other than to file a lawsuit or to hire an attorney to file one for you.

Alabama

No true anti-discrimination law, but Ala. Code §21-71-1 (1975) encourages employment of people who are blind or otherwise physically handicapped.

Enforcing agency: None

Alaska

Race, religion, color, national origin, age, physical handicap, gender, marital status, changes in marital status, pregnancy or parenthood.

Enforcing agency:
Human Rights Commission
800 A Street, Suite 204
Anchorage, AL 99501
907/274-4692

Arizona

Race, color, religion, gender, age, physical handicap (excluding current or recent alcohol or drug use), national origin, political activities, or membership in the National Guard.

Enforcing agency:
Civil Rights Division
1275 West Washington
Phoenix, AZ 85007
602/542-5263

Arkansas

Prohibits only discrimination in wages on the basis of gender.

Enforcing agency: None

California

Race, religion, color, national origin, ancestry, physical handicap, medical condition, marital status, gender, pregnancy, childbirth or related medical conditions, political activity, or arrests or detentions that did not result in a criminal conviction.

Enforcing agency:
Department of Fair Employment and Housing
2000 O Street, Suite 120
Sacramento, CA 95814
916/445-9918

Colorado

Race, religion, color, age, gender, national origin, ancestry, physical or mental handicap, denial of membership in labor unions under certain circumstances, marriage to a co-employee, arrest records or refusal by job applicants to discuss sealed criminal records.

Enforcing agency:
Civil Rights Commission
1560 Broadway, Suite 1050
Denver, CO 80202-5143
303/894-2997

Connecticut

Race, color, religion, age, gender, sexual orientation, marital status, national origin, ancestry, present or previous mental illness, mental retardation or other physical handicap.

Enforcing agency:
Commission on Human Rights and Opportunities
1229 Albany Avenue
Hartford, CT 06112
203/566-7710

Delaware

Race, color, religion, gender, national origin, marital status, refusal to grant sexual favors, age if between 40 and 70, or physical handicap as long as the cost to the employer of accommodating the employee's physical handicap doesn't exceed 5% of that employee's annual compensation.

Enforcing agency:
Department of Labor
Labor Law Enforcement Section
State Office Building, 6th floor
820 North French Street
Wilmington, DE 19801
302/577-2900

District of Columbia

Race, color, religion, national origin, age, gender, personal appearance, marital status or family responsibilities, sexual orientation, political activities, physical handicap or matriculation.

Enforcing agency:
Commission on Civil Rights Discrimination
1121 Vermont Avenue, NW
Washington, DC 20425
202/376-8513

Florida

Race, color, religion, gender, national origin, age, marital status, physical handicap, political activity or membership in a reserve unit of the armed forces.

Enforcing agency:
Commission on Human Relations
325 John Knox Road, Suite 240
Tallahassee, FL 32304
904/488-7082

Georgia

Mental or physical handicap (excluding the use of alcohol or any illegal or federally controlled drug), age if between 40 and 70. Also prohibits wage discrimination on the basis of gender.

Enforcing agency: None

Hawaii

Race, religion, color, ancestry, gender, sexual orientation, age, marital status, mental or physical handicap, pregnancy, childbirth or related medical conditions, or records of arrest or court action.

Enforcing agency:
Department of Labor and Industrial Relations
Discrimination Complaints
888 Mililani Street, 2nd floor
Honolulu, HI 96813
808/586-8640

Idaho

Race, color, religion, national origin, gender, age, or physical or mental handicap.

Enforcing agency:
Commission on Human Rights
450 West State Street
Boise, ID 83720
208/334-2873

Illinois

Race, color, gender, national origin, ancestry, age, marital status, physical or mental handicap, or unfavorable discharge from military service.

Enforcing agency:
Department of Human Rights
William Stratten Building, Room 623
Springfield, IL 62706
217/785-5100

Indiana

Race, color, national origin, ancestry, religion or physical handicap.

Enforcing agency:
Civil Rights Commission
32 East Washington, Suite 900
Indianapolis, IN 46204
317/232-2600

Iowa

Race, color, religion, age, gender, national origin or physical handicap.

Enforcing agency:
Civil Rights Commission
211 East Maple Street, 2nd floor
Des Moines, IA 50319
515/281-4121

Kansas

Race, color, religion, gender, age if over 18, national origin or ancestry, or physical handicap.

Enforcing agency:
Civil Rights Commission
Landon State Office Building
900 SW Jackson, Suite 851S
Topeka, KS 66612-1258
913/296-3206

Kentucky

Race, color, religion, national origin, gender, age if between 40 and 70, physical handicap, or results of HIV testing.

Enforcing agency:
Human Rights Commission
332 North Broadway, 7th floor
Louisville, KY 40201
502/588-4029

Louisiana

Race, color, religion, gender, national origin, age, pregnancy, political activity, participation in investigations relating to state's employment laws, sickle cell traits, or a physical handicap that can be reasonably accommodated by the employer.

Enforcing agency:
Equal Employment Opportunity Commission
701 Loyola Avenue, Suite 600
New Orleans, LA 70113
504/589-3842

Maine

Race, color, gender, religion, national origin, ancestry, age, or physical or mental handicap.

Enforcing agency:
Human Rights Commission
Statehouse, Station 51
Augusta, ME 04333
207/289-2326

Maryland

Race, color, religion, gender, national origin, age, marital status (including a prohibition of company policies forbidding marriage between two employees or setting different benefit levels for employees designated as heads of their households), past or current physical or mental illness or handicap as long as the handicap does not prevent the worker from performing the job.

Enforcing agency:
Maryland Commission on Human Relations
20 East Franklin Street
Baltimore, MD 21202
301/333-1700

Massachusetts

Race, color, religion, gender, sexual orientation, national origin, ancestry or physical handicap as long as that handicap can be reasonably accommodated by the employer.

Enforcing agency:
Commission Against Discrimination
One Ashburton Place
Boston, MA 02108
617/727-3990

Michigan

Race, color, religion, gender, national origin, height, weight, marital status, or physical handicap.

Enforcing agency:
Michigan Department of Civil Rights
333 South Capitol, Suite 290
Lansing, MI 48913
517/335-3165

Minnesota

Race, color, religion, gender, marital status, national origin, age, physical disability or receipt of public assistance.

Enforcing agency:
Department of Human Rights
Bremer Tower
7th Place and Minnesota Streets
St. Paul, MN 55101
612/296-5663

Mississippi

No anti-discrimination laws.

Enforcing agency: None

Missouri

Race, color, religion, gender, national origin, ancestry, age or physical handicap.

Enforcing agency:
Commission on Human Rights
P.O. Box 1129
Jefferson City, MO 65102
314/751-3325

Montana

Race, color, religion, gender, age, national origin, marital status, or physical or mental handicap.

Enforcing agency:
Human Rights Commission
P.O. Box 1728
Helena, MT 59624
406/444-2884

Nebraska

Race, color, religion, gender, national origin, age if between 40 and 70, marital status or disability (excluding addiction to alcohol, other drugs or gambling).

Enforcing agency:
Equal Opportunity Commission
301 Centennial Mall South
P.O. Box 94934
Lincoln, NE 68509-4934
402/471-2024

Nevada

Race, color, religion, gender, age if over 40, national origin, physical handicap or results of HIV testing.

Enforcing agency:
Nevada Equal Rights Commission
2450 Wrondel Way, Suite C
Reno, NV 89502
702/688-1288

New Hampshire

Race, color, religion, gender, age, national origin, marital status, or physical or mental handicap.

Enforcing agency:
Human Rights Commission
163 Loudon Road
Concord, NH 03301
603/271-2767

New Jersey

Race, color, religion, gender, national origin, ancestry, age if between 18 and 70, marital status, atypical hereditary cellular or blood trait, physical handicap or service in the armed forces.

Enforcing agency:
Division of Civil Rights
31 Clinton Street
Newark, NJ 07102
201/648-2700

New Mexico

Race, color, religion, gender, age, national origin, medical condition, or physical or mental handicap.

Enforcing agency:
Human Rights Commission
1596 Pacheco
Aspen Plaza
Santa Fe, NM 87502
505/827-6838

New York

Race, color, religion, gender, age, national origin, ancestry, pregnancy, marital status, physical disability, or arrest or conviction records.

Enforcing agency:
Division of Human Rights
65 West 125th Street
New York, NY 10027
212/870-8400

North Carolina

Race, color, religion, gender, national origin, sickle cell or hemoglobin C traits, physical handicap or results of HIV testing.

Enforcing agency:
Human Relations Commission
121 West Jones Street
Raleigh, NC 27603
919/733-7996

North Dakota

Race, color, religion, gender, national origin, age, or physical or mental handicap.

Enforcing agency: None

Ohio

Race, color, religion, gender, national origin, ancestry, age or physical handicap. A separate statute specifically covers discrimination cases involving persons age 40 and over.

Enforcing agency:
Civil Rights Commission
220 Parsons Avenue
Columbus, OH 43266-0543
614/466-5928

Oklahoma

Race, color, religion, gender, national origin, age or physical handicap.

Enforcing agency:
Human Rights Commission
2101 North Lincoln Boulevard
Room 480
Oklahoma City, OK 73105
405/521-2360

Oregon

Race, color, religion, gender, national origin, marital status or age (or the marital status or age of any other person with whom the worker associates), physical or mental handicap, or a juvenile criminal record that has been expunged.

Enforcing agency:
Civil Rights Division
Bureau of Labor
P.O. Box 800
Portland, OR 97207-0800
503/229-5900

Pennsylvania

Race, color, religion, gender, national origin, ancestry, age if between 40 and 70, or physical or mental handicap.

Enforcing agency:
Human Relations Commission
Uptown Shopping Plaza
2971-E North 7th Street
Harrisburg, PA   17110-2123
717/787-4410

Rhode Island

Race, color, religion, gender, ancestry, or physical handicap.

Enforcing agency:
Commission for Human Rights
10 Abbott Park Place
Providence, RI   02903-3768
401/277-2661

South Carolina

Race, color, religion, gender, age, national origin, or physical or mental handicap.

Enforcing agency:
Human Affairs Commission
P.O. Box 4490
Columbia, SC   29240
803/253-6336

South Dakota

Race, color, religion, gender, national origin, ancestry or physical handicap.

Enforcing agency:
Commission on Human Relations
224 West 9th Street
Sioux Falls, SD   57102
605/339-7039

Tennessee

Race, creed, color, religion, gender, age if over 40, national origin, or physical or mental handicap.

Enforcing agency:
Human Rights Commission
531 Henley Street, 7th floor
Knoxville, TN 37902
615/594-6500

Texas

Race, color, religion, gender, age, national origin, or physical or mental handicap, or results of HIV testing.

Enforcing agency:
Commission on Human Rights
P.O. Box 13493
Austin, TX 78711
512/837-8534

Utah

Race, color, religion, gender, age if over 40, national origin; pregnancy, child birth or related medical conditions; or physical handicap.

Enforcing agency:
Anti-Discrimination Division of the Industrial Commission
160 East 300 South, 3rd floor
Salt Lake City, UT 84111
801/530-6801

Vermont

Race, color, religion, gender, national origin, ancestry, age, place of birth, or physical handicap.

Enforcing agency:
Attorney General's Office
Civil Rights Division
109 State Street
Montpelier, VT 05609
802/828-3171

Virginia

Race, color, religion, gender, national origin, age, marital status or physical or mental handicap.

Enforcing agency:
Council on Human Rights
1100 Bank Street
Washington Building, 12th floor
Richmond, VA 23219
804/786-3988

Washington

Race, color, religion, gender, age if between 40 and 70, national origin, marital status, or physical or mental handicap.

Enforcing agency:
Human Rights Commission
1511 Third Avenue, Suite 921
Seattle, WA 98101
206/464-6500

West Virginia

Physical or mental handicap.
Enforcing agency:
Human Rights Commission
1321 Plaza East, Room 106
Charleston, WV 25301
304/348-6880

Wisconsin

Race, color, religion, gender, age, national origin, sexual orientation, marital status, arrest or conviction record, physical handicap or membership in a reserve unit of the armed forces.

Enforcing agency:
Department of Industry, Labor and Human Relations
Equal Rights Division
201 East Washington Avenue
P.O. Box 8928
Madison, WI 53708
608/266-6860

Wyoming

Race, color, religion, gender, national origin, ancestry, age if between 40 and 70, or physical handicap.

Enforcing agency:
Fair Employment Commission
Herschler Building
Second East Street
Cheyenne, WY 82002
307/777-7262

6

Sexual Harassment

The anti-discrimination laws discussed in Chapter 5 have been the legal weapons most commonly used to combat sexual harassment. But because this workplace problem is so difficult to define and combat, it needs to be looked at separately and in greater depth.

A. What is Sexual Harassment?

In a 1986 decision (*Meritor Savings Bank v. Vinson*, 477 U.S. 57), the U.S. Supreme Court ruled that sexual harassment occurs whenever any unwanted sexually oriented behavior changes an employee's working conditions and creates a hostile or abusive work environment, regardless of whether the behavior causes economic loss for the victim.

That decision has since been reinforced and refined by other courts. In general, the definition of a hostile or abusive work environment has been divided into two categories:

- those where a supervisor demands sexual favors in exchange for tangible job benefits. For example, if your boss says, "Sleep with me and I'll promote you," that would fit this category, which is often referred to as quid pro quo.

- those where there are offensive, sexually oriented words, actions or displays, but no immediate job repercussions for the victim. For example, workplaces where employees are subjected to sexually explicit photos that offend them would fit this category.

1. The reasonable man standard

Until 1991, the legal definition of a hostile or abusive workplace was governed by a principle left over from the 1800s. Known as the reasonable man standard, it held that when abusive actions or situations were being judged by a court, they should be viewed in the context of how a reasonable man would react—and man in this case literally meant a male, not just any person.

The reasonable man standard made it difficult for women to win lawsuits based on sexual harassment because what many women see as sexually insulting is seen by many men—including male judges—to be attractive, exciting or even humorous.

For example, in one recent federal sexual discrimination suit, a female secretary charged that her male boss had sexually harassed her at work by continually subjecting her to, among other things, a picture on his office wall that depicted an elephant copulating with a rhinoceros. The male judge who dismissed the complaint ruled that neither the behavior of the woman's boss nor the "wildlife poster" on his office wall had created a hostile or abusive work environment.

SEXUAL HARASSMENT LAWS PROTECT MEN, TOO

Although sexual harassment is most often committed by men against women, it's not unheard of for men to sexually harass men—or for women to sexually harass men or other women.

For example, a recent study conducted among employees of the federal government found that 15% of the male participants had been subjected to sexual harassment at work. Of that group, 22% reported that they had been sexually harassed by other males.

Since Title VII and most state anti-discrimination laws protect both genders, men who are harassed sexually at work can also file lawsuits seeking their protections.

---

2. The reasonable woman standard

In early 1991, three courts ruling in three separate cases substantially changed the reasonable man standard. Those courts agreed with arguments made by plaintiffs that women and men often react to things in different ways.

In one of those cases, for example, experts testified that 75% of males polled in a study said they would be flattered by sexual advances made toward them at work, while the same percentage of women said they would be offended by such advances.

Since such differences between typical male and female reactions were proven scientifically, the courts held, the question of whether or not a particular action or situation constitutes sexual harassment of a woman should be judged on the basis of how a reasonable woman would react. (The cases that introduced the reasonable woman standard are *Ellison v. Brady,* 924 F. 2d 871 (9th Cir., 1991); *Robinson v. Jacksonville Shipyards,* 760 F. Supp. 1486 (1991); *Radtke v. Everett,* 471 N.W. 2d 1589 (1991).

MALE BOSSES STILL DOMINATE

One reason sexual harassment at work is most often instigated by men against women may be that men, as a group, have more power to bring about such harassment.

A study released in 1991 by the consulting firm of Accountants on Call in Garden City, New Jersey, found that 66% of all employees in America report to a male supervisor. The power of men over the workplace is particularly high in manual labor occupations where, according to the study, 73% of the employees are supervised by a male.

Despite this imbalance of workplace power, the employees who participated in the study expressed little desire for change. In fact, among the female participants who expressed a preference for a boss of a specific gender, 65% said they'd rather be supervised by a male.

But those attitudes may change over time, because the preference for male supervision is highest, the study found, among older workers with little education.

B. Sexual Attraction v. Sexual Harassment

Sexual harassment and sexual attraction in the workplace aren't the same thing. In fact, sexual attraction is not a problem on its own. If two people working together find each other attractive, then there is a positive judgment going in both directions—and that can be very beneficial for both employees and their employers.

Example: Shauna and Roberto work together as a sales team for a computer software company. Often, closing a deal involves taking the prospective buyers out to dinner, after which the final sales presentation is made.

Shauna enjoys working with Roberto, finding him to be intelligent, ambitious, reliable, well mannered and always distinctively dressed when he's on the job. Roberto enjoys working with Shauna because she has the same attributes. It would be naive to deny that Shauna and Roberto find each other sexually attractive, and there's nothing inherently wrong with that. In fact, the positive feelings that exist between them keep both at a high level of enthusiasm while on the job.

But sexual attraction can become a workplace problem when one person oversteps the limits of what a co-worker considers to be a desirable level of expression of that attraction.

Example: One day, Shauna and Roberto closed their biggest sale ever. After everyone else had left the room where the sale had been made, they instinctively threw their arms around each other and hugged in a gesture of exuberance and congratulation.

All was well until Roberto tried to convert the affectionate hug into a sexual encounter by moving his right hand onto Shauna's breast and kissing her. This obviously sexual contact exceeded Shauna's personal standard for relationships with co-workers. She immediately withdrew from the embrace, telling Roberto firmly that she didn't think that his actions were appropriate.

Sexual attraction becomes sexual harassment when the boundaries established by common sense or by any of the people involved are intentionally challenged or violated by a co-worker.

Example: Roberto, his ego stung by what he felt was a negative assessment of his sexual attractiveness by Shauna, underwent a character change. He began to make sexual jokes at her expense during sales presentations. At the end of each presentation, he went out of his way to find opportunities to touch her—sometimes provocatively—while packing their presentation cases. Inside the lids of some of the presentation cases, Roberto taped photos torn from sexually explicit magazines.

Under Title VII of the Civil Rights Act of 1964, subsequent court rulings, and guidelines issued by the Equal Employment Opportunity Commission (EEOC), Shauna would likely be able to make a strong case of sexual harassment against Roberto.

C. Getting Relief Without Going to Court

If the nature and severity of the sexual harassment directed toward you hasn't been too extreme or long-lived, you may prefer to try ending it without using the courts. The actions that a person is willing and able to take vary with each individual and situation, but here are two possibilities:

- Confront your harasser and tell him that you disapprove of his actions toward you and are preparing to report him to management. In some cases, the harassment will stop right then and there.

  But the psychological drives underlying sexual harassment can be complex, so the harassment may continue or even get worse after such a confrontation.

- Use your company's internal system for stopping sexual harassment. Look in your employee manual to see if the system is detailed there. If it isn't, ask your company's human resources or personnel department to assist you in resolving your complaint. In large companies with established complaint procedures, you'll probably have to go no further.

1. Shifting responsibility to management

If the harassment doesn't end after you've tried personal confrontation or your employer's internal complaint resolution system, you may be able to stop it by shifting responsibility to the management of your company.

In general, the courts have ruled that under Title VII and the legal principle of respondeat superior (rough translation: let the master answer), companies, their executives and supervisors who control employees who commit sexual harassment can be held responsible for that harassment if the supervisors knew, or should have known, that it was being committed. Some state courts have ruled that this principle can be applied to the enforcement of state anti-discrimination laws, as well.

This principle has even been extended to situations where employees are sexually harassed by people who aren't employees but are in some way controlled or influenced by the employer.

Example: Natalie worked as a cocktail waitress in a hotel lounge where she was required to wear a skimpy outfit—and was often sexually harassed by male customers. The hotel's management was responsible for that harassment, a federal court ruled, because it had not taken action to stop it.

2. How to take action

Because of the principle of respondeat superior, one of the best ways to bring sexual harassment at work to a quick halt without going into court is to put your company's senior management on notice that you are being harassed—and that you are prepared to take legal action against both the company and the harasser. Make your complaint in writing to the company's highest-ranking executive, with a copy to your immediate supervisor.

Example:

April 25, 1992

Mr. Harvey Anyman
President, Mildew Management Corp.
123 Main Street
Swamp City, FL 98765

Dear Mr. Anyman:

I am writing to advise you that my co-worker,
_____, has been leaving sexually explicit
photos in my desk drawer, with notes attached to them
suggesting that we "get together and party" during our
lunch hours. Copies of several of these notes are
attached to this letter.

I do not welcome these sexual advances, and they are
creating a hostile and abusive work atmosphere for me. I
have clearly advised _____ of my position,
but the harassment continues.

As you are probably aware, such sexual harassment is a
violation of Title VII of the Civil Rights Act of 1964.
Please take whatever action you feel is necessary to stop
this harassment immediately, and advise me in writing of
your action. If you do not respond to this letter within
two weeks, I will file a sexual harassment complaint with
the Equal Employment Opportunity Commission.

Thank you for your assistance with this problem.

Sincerely,

Mary Jo Employee

cc: Eleanore Anywoman,
    Department Manager

Most sensible employers, upon receiving such a letter, will nearly stumble over themselves to stop the harassment quickly.

Still, it is sensible to protect your rights for the future. Keep a copy of your complaint letter in a file, along with any documents that you receive from the company in response and any evidence of the harassment that you've collected such as sexually suggestive notes or photos sent to your by the harasser.

Also keep a log of the incidents of harassment and any witnesses to them. Then, if relief doesn't arrive from your company's executive suite, you'll be well prepared to take further legal action.

Odds are that going to management directly will bring you relief from sexual harassment more quickly and painlessly than any other strategy. And while quick action on your complaint will usually get your employer and your supervisor off the hook legally, it won't prevent you from filing a lawsuit against the harasser should you later decide that such an action is necessary.

Of course, this approach isn't a good one if the harasser is the company's chief executive. In that case, your best approach is to file a complaint under Title VII. (See Section E.)

D. Federal Rules Against Sexual Harassment

At least in theory, Title VII of the Civil Rights Act of 1964 is the most powerful legal weapon against sexual harassment in the workplace. Title VII doesn't specifically mention sexual conduct. However, according to the Equal Employment Opportunity Commission (EEOC)—which is the agency responsible for enforcing Title VII—sexual harassment occurs when:

- submitting to sexually related conduct or conditions is a condition of continued employment.

Example: Denise's boss threatens to fire her if she refuses to allow him to fondle her sexually while she's taking dictation from him.

- pay raises, promotions or other aspects of employment depend upon whether or not the employee submits to sexually related conduct or conditions.

Example: Cindy is passed over for the 10% wage increase granted to everyone else in her department because she has refused her boss' repeated invitations to spend weekends with him at his beachfront condo.

- sexually oriented conduct or conditions create a hostile or abusive working environment.

Example: Ellen's boss routinely shocks and intimidates her by leaving dildos and other sex toys in the top drawer of her desk.

1. Indirect sexual harassment

Under Title VII, you do not have to be a direct, personal target of sexually oriented activity to be a victim of sexual harassment.

Example: Although she has never been sexually approached by her boss, Marita is repeatedly passed over for wage increases. Meanwhile, several female co-workers with less experience and education—but who, unlike her, seek out sexual encounters with her boss because of his reputation for trading pay raises for sex—are routinely granted raises that put them above Marita on the wage scale. Marita is a victim of indirect sexual harassment, the courts have ruled, even though nothing of a sexual nature has been forced upon her.

Another form of indirect sexual harassment occurs when the harassing activities aren't sexual, but are directed only at employees of one gender.

Example: Anka and Helene are the only females on a highway construction crew. The male members of the crew have been warned by their supervisor that harassment such as posting up sexually explicit photos or directing sexually explicit insults at Anka and Helene will not be tolerated. However, several of the men repeatedly harass the women by hiding the tools that the women are assigned to use and by sabotaging their tools so that they break under heavy use.

Anka and Helene may be able to prove they are being sexually harassed at work, even though nothing sexually explicit is being directed toward them. The legal logic here is that their gender is the basis for the harassment directed toward them.

2. Harassment by top executives

It is illegal for an employer to retaliate against an employee for taking action under Title VII. So if your harasser is one of the company's top executives, filing a Title VII complaint will give you more protection against being fired because you complained than any of the other remedies discussed in this chapter.

E. Filing a Title VII Complaint

The procedures for filing a complaint or a lawsuit under Title VII on the basis of sexual harassment are the same as for any other type of illegal workplace discrimination. (For details, see Chapter 5, Section F.) However, the odds are that the EEOC won't file a suit on your behalf. For example, during fiscal year 1990, the EEOC filed a lawsuit in only 50 of the 5,694 sexual harassment complaints filed with it.

F. Other Legal Remedies

Title VII limits the money damages you can request to punish your harasser, and you'll probably need to hire a lawyer to help you with a lawsuit charging sexual harassment under Title VII. So the cost of bringing a lawsuit under it often exceeds the amount of money that you can get as a judgment. Even if you win a Title VII case, the money you'll receive will be limited to back wages and attorney fees.

In contrast, state anti-discrimination laws (see Chart 5-1) and personal injury lawsuits based on such claims as intentional infliction of emotional harm often offer alternatives to Title VII lawsuits that can result in very large money awards. But you'll also likely need the help of an attorney if you decide to pursue your sexual harassment complaint in one of these ways. (See Chapter 13, Section D.)

G. Employment-Related Rape

The most brutal type of sexual harassment in the workplace occurs when a man traps a woman into sexual intercourse against her will by abusing his control over the location of her work assignments or by threatening her employment situation.

Although everyone knows that work-related rape happens with some frequency, our laws have been slow to acknowledge the harm in such incidents. The tradition of male producers forcing actresses to engage in sex if they want to work in the theater or movies, for example, is still referred to jokingly in many circles as the casting couch. But you won't find many actresses who think that crack is funny.

The possible situations in which a woman may be surprised, trapped and coerced into sex by a male who ranks above her at work have increased dramatically in recent years as the practice of men and women traveling together on business, or working together outside the office, has become more common and accepted. Otherwise alone in an unfamiliar location, a person can become particularly vulnerable to emotional and economic intimidation from a supervisor.

Example: Veronica, a municipal bond agent with a bank in New York City, traveled to Los Angeles on business with Jeremy, the bank's vice president in charge of municipal finance. As they checked into their hotel, Jeremy instructed Veronica to meet with him to coordinate the details of their presentation to clients scheduled for early the next morning.

When Veronica arrived at Jeremy's suite about an hour later, she was dismayed to see a half-empty bottle of vodka and a copy of a sexually explicit magazine, opened to the centerfold, on his desk. Jeremy came up to her from behind, picked her up and carried her—despite her protests—into the bedroom. Dropping her onto the bed, he positioned himself on top of her.

Throughout the ordeal, Veronica repeatedly warned Jeremy to stop, that she didn't want to have sex with him. But Jeremy countered her protests with intimidations and insults such as "Why do you think I approved your promotion last month?" and "All the senior executives are waiting to hear what you're like in bed." And most bluntly "You'll do this if you want to keep your job."

Eventually, Jeremy overwhelmed Veronica and raped her. No deadly weapon or overt violence had been used, but Veronica was able to have Jeremy prosecuted criminally for rape because California law forbids using duress to force a person into sexual intercourse.

1. Expanding definitions of rape

Until recently, such employment-related sexual assaults typically were dealt with, if they were dealt with at all, as a form of sexual harassment—a civil offense that usually must be pursued by a lengthy and expensive lawsuit and can't result in the attacker going to jail.

However, in some states the legal definitions of criminal rape, sexual battery and related crimes have been expanded in recent years to include the use of non-violent coercion to drive a victim into submission. (See Chart 6-1 at the end of this chapter.)

Although typically discussed as date rape or acquaintance rape, these broader definitions often can also be used against male supervisors who abuse their physical control over a female employee's whereabouts or use threats of adverse employment actions—or both—to coerce sexual intercourse.

Counseling organizations and some lawyers who specialize in sexual harassment cases are increasingly advising women who have been subjected to workplace rape to file criminal charges, as well as civil lawsuits, against their attackers.

Even in states where the laws still require that violent force be used before a sexual attacker can be charged with a crime, prosecutors and the courts sometimes interpret the requirement of force in rape statutes very broadly, so that attacks where no weapon was used and no physical violence occurred are included.

2. How to take action

If you have suffered an employment-related rape, there are some essential steps that you should follow if possible:

- Get medical attention and a complete medical examination as soon as possible after the rape occurs. Tell the examining physician that you've been raped so that the tests necessary to support a criminal prosecution will be conducted.

- Report the rape to the police in the locale in which it occurred as soon as possible. If you don't know what municipality you were in when the rape occurred, telephone the state police and ask what police department you should contact.

Don't be discouraged if the police treat your complaint with skepticism. Many rank-and-file police officers are ignorant of the legal concepts governing sexual assault, and others allow their personal views on these cases to cloud their application of the law. Insist on filing a written criminal complaint to protect your rights later on, and ask for a copy of that complaint for your files.

If the police officer with whom you speak seems unwilling to cooperate, ask whether there is a victim-witness counselor you can contact.

- Follow up on your police complaint as quickly as possible with a written complaint to the prosecutor who handles cases where the rape occurred. If you don't know who that is, ask someone at the police department where you filed your complaint. Keep a copy of your complaint for your personal files as well.

- Report the rape to the management of the company that employs you as soon as possible. Sending a photocopy of your police report, with a cover letter, to your company's president by certified mail would be a good way to do this.

- File a sexual harassment complaint with the EEOC. The fact that you've filed a criminal charge doesn't prevent you from also filing a civil complaint.

- Get as much support and advice on your situation as you can. Most communities have a rape crisis center, and these centers can typically connect you with a specially trained person who will counsel you on all the physical, emotional and legal issues involved.

- Consider the options of filing a workers' compensation claim based on any injury that resulted from the rape, or of filing a personal injury lawsuit as a result of those injuries. You'll probably need the help of a lawyer to fully investigate these two options.

Usually, the agencies that assist rape victims also maintain a list of attorneys who specialize in sexual assault or sexual harassment cases, or both. If you can't locate a rape crisis center near you, call the National Coalition Against Sexual Assault and ask to speak with one of their advocates. (See the Appendix for contact details.)

Chart 6-1
RAPE WITHOUT WEAPONS OR PHYSICAL VIOLENCE

This is a list of states that are frequent destinations for business and convention travel, and in which neither the use of a weapon nor physical violence is a prerequisite for a criminal charge of rape, or a similar sexual offense.

Don't let the fact that the state in which you were sexually attacked isn't on this list deter you from filing a criminal complaint. Even in states where sexual assault laws technically require that a weapon or physical violence be used before criminal charges can be brought, local prosecutors and courts sometimes interpret those requirements more broadly.

California

Rape is defined as sexual intercourse against the victim's will by means of force, violence, duress, menace or fear of immediate and unlawful bodily injury. Duress is defined as a direct or implied threat of force, violence, danger, hardship, or retribution sufficient to coerce a reasonable person to perform an act they wouldn't otherwise have performed, in light of the totality of the circumstances.

Colorado

Second-degree sexual assault is defined as sexual intrusion without force or threat of serious injury or death, but using a threat of sufficient consequence reasonably calculated to cause submission against the victim's will. Third-degree sexual assault is defined as sexual contact to which the perpetrator knows that the victim does not consent.

Florida

Sexual penetration without consent, where the force used is not likely to cause serious personal injury, is a level of sexual battery.

Hawaii

Second-degree sexual assault is defined as the knowing subjection of another to penetration by compulsion. Third-degree sexual assault is defined as the reckless subjection of another to penetration by compulsion. Fourth-degree sexual assault is defined as the knowing subjection of another to sexual contact by compulsion.

New York

Sexual misconduct is defined as intercourse without consent.

7

Joining and Quitting Labor Unions

Labor unions are organizations that deal collectively with employers on behalf of employees. Their best-known role is negotiating group employment contracts for members. But unions also often perform other workplace chores such as lobbying for legislation that benefits their members and sponsoring skill training programs.

Some labor unions also operate benefit programs such as vacation plans, healthcare insurance, pensions and programs that provide members with discounts on various types of personal needs such as eyeglasses and prescriptions drugs.

Most unions are operated by a paid staff of professional organizers, negotiators and administrators, with some help from members who volunteer their time. In general, the money to pay unions' staffs and expenses comes from dues paid by their members—which typically total about $40 per member per month.

The laws and court decisions governing labor unions and their relationships with employers are so complex and separate from the rest of workplace law that this chapter can give you only an overview.

If you're already a member of a labor union and want to continue as one, the information in this book can help you to doublecheck on the performance of your union's leaders.

If you are not represented by a union and would like to be, or if you're a member of a union and want out, this chapter will help you become familiar with the basic laws labor unions must follow and your rights in dealing with them.

A. The National Labor Relations Act

Labor unions got the legal right to represent employees in their relationships with their employers in 1935 when the National Labor Relations Act (NLRA) was passed. That federal Act also created the National Labor Relations Board (NLRB) to police the relationships among employees, their unions and their employers.

1. Legal requirements

The NLRA requires most employers and unions to negotiate fairly with each other until they agree to a contract that spells out the terms and conditions of employment for the workers who are members of the union. The NLRB enforces this requirement by using mediators, administrative law judges, investigators and others.

2. Groups excluded from the NLRA

Certain groups of employees are not covered by the NLRA. They include:

- managers, supervisors and confidential employees such as company accountants
- farm workers
- the families of employers
- government workers
- domestic servants who work in their employers' homes
- certain industry groups, such as railroad employees, whose work situations are regulated by other laws.

The NLRA also contains some special exemptions for specific groups of workers within industries that are otherwise covered. Call your local NLRB office, listed in the federal government section of the telephone directory, for more information on whether your job is covered by the NLRA.

B. The Bargaining Unit

The basic union building block under the NLRA is the bargaining unit: a group of employees who perform similar work, share a work area and who could logically be assumed to have shared interests in such issues as pay rates, hours of work and workplace conditions.

A bargaining unit may be only a part of a larger union, or it may constitute a whole union itself. And a bargaining unit isn't always limited to people who work in one building or for one company. For example, the workers in several small, independent sheet metal shops in a specific city will often be members of the same union bargaining unit.

On the other hand, a bargaining unit may include only part of a company. So it's possible—and quite common—for only a small portion of a company's workforce to be unionized, or for various departments in one company to be represented by different unions.

C. Types of Union Work Situations

If you take a job that is covered by a contract between the employer and a labor union, a representative of the union will typically approach you about membership requirements shortly after you're hired.

At that point, you'll want to determine what type of relationship exists between your job and the union. Unionized work situations generally fall into one of four categories: open shop, agency shop, union shop and closed shop.

The type of shop that exists within a unionized bargaining unit will be spelled out in the contract between the union representing that unit and the employer. Ask the union representative for a copy of the contract governing your job before you sign up for union membership.

1. The open shop

Here, a union represents the bargaining unit of which you're a member, but you're not required to join the union or pay dues to it. Open shops are most commonly found in states that have passed right-to-work laws, described in Section D.

2. The agency shop

You can make your own decision about whether or not to join the union. But, whether you join or not, you'll have to pay to the union the same dues and other fees that other members of your bargaining unit are required to pay. This type of arrangement is legal in any state that hasn't passed a right-to-work law. (See Section D.)

3. The union shop

Although you're not required to be a union member when you take the job, you'll be forced to join after a specified period of time—usually within 30 days after starting your new job—if a union shop clause is included in the contract covering your bargaining unit. Whether or not union shops are legal is a matter of controversy because the controlling law, Section 8(a)(3) of the NLRA, seems to contradict itself.

First, the Section specifies that it's legal for a contract to require an employee to join a union within 30 days of starting a job. But it also states that an employer may fire you because of your lack of union membership only if the union rejected or expelled you for failing to pay the union's regular fees and dues.

In 1963, the U.S. Supreme Court ruled that the second clause is the one that controls. (The decision that is widely considered to be the landmark on the legality of union shops is *NLRB v. General Motors*, 373 U.S. 734.)

If you take a job in a company in which the union contract calls for a union shop but you refuse to join the union, the employer and the union will usually overlook your refusal to join as long as you pay the union's fees and dues. You can, however, expect to be subjected—at the very least—to cold shoulder treatment by union officials and members if you refuse to join.

4. The closed shop

You can't work here unless you are already a member of a specific union before being hired. Closed shops are illegal throughout the United States under the NLRA. (A key decision by the U.S. Supreme Court in 1984 outlawed closed shops: *Ellis v. Brotherhood of Ry., Airline and S.S. Clerks*, 466 U.S. 435.)

D. Right-to-Work Laws

Section 14(b) of the NLRA authorizes each state to pass laws that require all unionized workplaces within their boundaries to be open shops—and 21 states have passed such laws: Alabama, Arizona, Arkansas, Florida, Georgia, Idaho, Iowa, Kansas, Louisiana, Mississippi, Nebraska, Nevada, North Carolina, North Dakota, South Carolina, South Dakota, Tennessee, Texas, Utah, Virginia and Wyoming.

In each of these states, you have the right to hold a job without joining a union or paying any money to a union, so they're usually called right-to-work laws.

One boon for employees in right-to-work states is that the NLRA requires that a union give fair and equal representation to all members of a bargaining unit, regardless of whether they are union members. If you're employed in a right-to-work state and are a member of a bargaining unit represented by a labor union, you can refuse to join the union or to pay any money to it—and the union still must represent you the same as your union co-workers.

If the union representing your bargaining unit fails or refuses to represent you in such situations, you can file an unfair labor practices charge against it with the NLRB.

UNION-FREE POLICIES MAY VIOLATE YOUR RIGHTS

In companies where the employees are not represented by unions, it's common practice for the employer to openly state its wish to remain union-free. In general, companies have the right to make such statements under Section 8(c) of the National Labor Relations Act, as well as under the freedom of speech provisions of the First Amendment to the U.S. Constitution.

However, recent rulings by the National Labor Relations Board indicate that employers must be very careful about where and how they express their wishes for a workplace free of unions. If they aren't, they run the risk of violating the employees' right to unionize under the National Labor Relations Act.

One of the most significant rulings restricting union-free statements was issued by the NLRB in 1989, after a union that hoped to organize the employees of a hotel chain filed an unfair labor practices charge against the chain.

The hotel company's management had violated the NLRA, the NLRB ruled, by its positioning of a union-free statement in the policy manual that it gave to all new employees. The page following the one on which the union-free statement appeared asked employees for their signature, verifying that they accepted the terms of employment set out in the manual.

The sequence of those pages in the employee manual, the NLRB decided, could lead employees to believe that adhering to the company's union-free policy was a condition of continued employment. And making employees believe that would violate Section 8(a) of the NLRA, which makes it illegal for an employer to coerce employees away from pursuing their right to union representation (293 NLRB No. 6, 130 LRRM 1338 (1989)).

E. Union Elections

When a union files a petition with the NLRB to be recognized as the representative of a bargaining unit, the petition includes the union's description of what group of workers it would like to have included in that bargaining unit. The employer contests these descriptions and tries to have the size of the bargaining unit trimmed down. Negotiations follow, and if the union and the employer can't agree on the exact shape and size of a bargaining unit, the NLRB decides.

Bargaining units are little democracies, in which the majority rules and the minority must comply. For example, if you work in an office and more than half of the people who work there with you vote to be represented by a union, the entire office is likely to be designated as a bargaining unit. You'll be represented by that union—even if you don't want to be.

Except in a few circumstances, the NLRB generally will conduct an election for a bargaining unit to decide whether or not it wants to be represented by a certain union whenever at least 30% of the members of that bargaining unit indicate they want an election to be held. The members of the bargaining unit may express their wishes for an election by signing a group petition—or by signing individual cards that state, in essence, the same thing—and presenting that evidence of their wishes to their local NLRB office.

1. Types of union elections

NLRB-supervised elections generally fall into three categories:

- Certification elections, in which the employees who make up a bargaining unit vote on whether to have a union begin representing them.

- De-certification elections, in which the employees who make up a bargaining unit vote on whether to end their representation by a specific union.

- Situations where the employees who make up a bargaining unit want to switch unions. The existing union must be voted out through a de-certification election and the new union voted in through a certification vote.

2. Restrictions on union elections

The courts have reached different conclusions about whether a union-related election can be held. But there are three NLRB policies on union-related elections that you can usually count on. The NLRB will not conduct an election:

- during the first year that a bargaining unit is represented by a particular union

- within a year of the last election held for that bargaining unit

- during the period covered by a union contract.

If the contract lasts more than three years, the NLRB will conduct an election at the end of the first three years of the contract if that's what the bargaining unit's members want.

F. Your Right to Unionize

Sections 7 and 8 of the National Labor Relations Act guarantee employees the right to create, join and participate in a labor union without being unfairly intimidated or punished by their employers.

1. Employees' rights

Generally, the courts have ruled that Section 7 gives employees the right to:

- discuss union membership and read and distribute literature concerning it during nonwork time in nonwork areas such as an employee lounge

- sign a card asking your employer to recognize your union and bargain with it; to sign petitions and grievances concerning employment terms and conditions; and to ask your co-workers to sign petitions and grievances

- display your pro-union sentiments by wearing message-bearing items as hats, pins and T-shirts on the job.

2. Employers' limitations

The courts have also ruled, in general, that Section 8 of the National Labor Relations Act means that an employer may not:

- grant or promise employees a promotion, pay raise, a desirable work assignment or other special favors if they oppose unionizing efforts

- dismiss, harass, reassign or otherwise punish or discipline employees— or threaten to—if they support unionization

- close down a worksite or transfer work or reduce benefits to pressure employers not to support unionization.

3. How to unionize

What typically occurs when a group of employees wish to campaign for unionization of their jobs is that they contact a union they think would be interested and propose the idea.

Unions are usually listed in the Yellow Pages of your local telephone directory under Labor Organizations. Don't let their names discourage you. It's not unusual nowadays for meatpackers to belong to the United Steel Workers, for example, or for office workers to belong to the Teamsters union that originally represented freight drivers. The only practical way to determine which unions might be interested in unionizing your workplace is to call and ask.

If the union you approach is interested, it will assign professional organizers who will guide you through the rest of the process. If it's not interested— perhaps because your employer is too small or because you work in an industry with which it isn't comfortable—that union should be able to suggest another one that would be more appropriate for you to contact. If not, contact the American Federation of Labor and Congress of Industrial Organizations (AFL-CIO). (See the Appendix for contact information.)

The National Labor Relations Act allows you to form your own, independent union to represent only the workers at your place of employment without affiliating with any established union. Such unions exist, but the complexities of labor law and the cost of running an independent union typically make them infeasible in all but the largest companies.

G. Your Right to De-Unionize

What if your bargaining unit is unionized, but you don't think union membership is serving your best interests? Just as it gives them the right to unionize, the NLRA gives employees the right to withdraw from union membership.

1. How to de-unionize

There are two basic ways to de-unionize:

1. Conduct a campaign among the members of your bargaining unit to get them to petition the NLRB to conduct a de-certification election. If you're able to bring about an election, you'll probably also have to campaign hard against the union for the votes of other members of the bargaining unit.

2. Resign your individual membership. The courts have ruled that informing your employer that you want check-off deductions for union dues and fees stopped is not sufficient to quit a union; you must advise the union in writing of your decision to quit.

In right-to-work states, such a resignation leaves you free and clear of the union altogether—no membership, no dues or fees. In other states, you may be required to continue paying fees and dues to your bargaining unit's union if the contract there calls for a union or agency shop, as described in Section C.

2. Limitations on unions

The NLRA also prohibits unions from interfering with your right to reject or change union membership. Unions may not:

- restrain or coerce employees from exercising their rights under the NLRA. This includes the violence and threats of violence that some unions use against people who reject union membership

- cause or encourage an employer to discriminate against an employee or group of employees because of their de-unionization activities.

- interfere in any way with an employee's right to freely express opinions on union membership

- fail or refuse to bargain in good faith with an employer on behalf of a bargaining unit that has designated the union as its bargaining agent, even if the union and the bargaining unit are at odds

- prevent you from going to work by using such tactics as mass picketing.

H. Religious Objections to Unions

Some employees are members of religions with beliefs that conflict with membership in a labor union. If your religion prohibits you from taking oaths, for example, having to swear allegiance to a labor union might force you to violate your religious beliefs.

In general, the courts have recognized an employee's right to refuse to join a union on religious grounds. However, you can still be required to pay union dues and fees if you work in an agency or union shop in a state that hasn't passed a right-to-work law. (See Section D.)

I. Working As a Striker Replacement

In recent years, a significant number of companies against which unions have launched strikes have decided to try to replace strikers with new employees. Although many people regard striker replacements as traitors and even call them by the traditional slur "scab," you have the legal right to take a job as a replacement for a striking employee.

There are some things you should be aware of before taking a job as a striker replacement:

- Companies that are intent upon replacing striking workers often hire specialized law firms that are just as cold and abrupt about getting rid of replacements as they are strikers, should that serve their interests.

- Striking workers who fear the permanent loss of their jobs may become quite vicious in trying to intimidate you and your family. Physical violence, threats of physical violence and various forms of harassment such as late-night telephone calls are common in such situations.

- It is not unusual for police officers, who are often union members themselves, and judges, who often fear the wrath of voters in highly unionized neighborhoods, to turn a blind eye to assaults on people who work as replacements for strikers.

If you take a job as a replacement for a striker, keep your own thorough record of that work experience in case a striking worker or the struck employer violates your rights in the course of resolving their dispute. Save any threatening letters sent to you to use as evidence in filing criminal charges, and any documents given to you by the employer such as pay stubs that might be used to prove violations of your rights under such laws as the Fair Labor Standards Act. (See Chapter 2.)

J. Deducting Union Dues From Your Pay

One thing on which labor unions and the government agree is that it's easier to get money from people who never get to touch that money in the first place. To ease their operations, many union contracts include a check-off clause.

Much like income tax withholding, the check-off clause requires your employer to withhold your union dues from your pay and then forward the money to the union. By voting to approve a contract between your union and your employer, you also signify approval of any check-off clause in that contract. So unions' practice of having employers withhold dues from a paycheck is generally legal.

K. Getting Free Help With Union Matters

It's easier to get free legal advice and help with labor union matters than on any other aspect of workplace law.

The place to start is your local office of the NLRB, listed in the federal government section of your telephone directory. If the NLRB considers your union-related problem to be a serious one, it will pay for all the costs of the investigations and hearings required to take your complaint through the legal process.

If the NLRB can't or won't help, you can turn to several other sources. If you consider yourself to be pro-union, contact AFL-CIO headquarters. If you consider yourself to be anti-union, contact the National Right-to-Work Committee. If you're unsure about what your opinion on unions is, call both.

These organizations maintain expert legal staffs to answer union-related questions. They may even provide you with free legal representation. (Contact information for both of these sources is included in the Appendix.)

You can sue unions and employers over violations of the NLRA, and many people have won such lawsuits. However, you'll probably need a lawyer's help to file a lawsuit under the NLRA. (See Chapter 13, Section D.)

8

Replacing Your Income When You're Out of Work

It's extremely important to know when and how to pursue your rights under the government programs designed to replace your regular income when you're not working. If you don't, you'll run the risk of committing the most commonly punished offense in the United States: running out of money.

The three most important income-replacement programs are unemployment insurance, workers' compensation and Social Security disability insurance.

A. Choosing the Right Program

When your employment is interrupted, it is important to act quickly to replace as much of your income as you can. Each day that passes without you earning money puts you and those who rely on you for financial support in greater risk of running into money troubles. In some states, for example, the gap between the time that a person files for unemployment insurance and the time he or she receives the first unemployment check averages six weeks. What's more, applying for the wrong income-replacement program can waste many more precious days, weeks or even months.

Here is a brief breakdown of what is covered by each of the three major income-replacement programs:

- **Unemployment insurance.** This program may provide some financial help if you lost your job, temporarily or permanently, through no fault of your own.

- **Workers' compensation.** When you can't work because of a work-related injury or illness, this is the program that is most likely to provide you with replacement income promptly. It may also pay the medical bills resulting from a workplace injury or illness; compensate workers for a permanent injury, such as the loss of a limb; and provide death benefits to the survivors of workers who die from a workplace injury or illness.

- **Social Security disability insurance.** This is intended to provide income to adults who, because of injury or illness, cannot work for at least 12 months. Unlike the workers' compensation program, it doesn't require that your disability be caused by a workplace injury or illness.

Once you've decided which of these program applies to your situation, read the more detailed description of that program below and then take the appropriate actions to obtain the benefits to which you're entitled.

DUAL PAYMENTS FOR DISABLED WORKERS

Many disabled employees qualify for benefits under both workers' compensation and Social Security disability insurance. There's nothing illegal about collecting from both at the same time if the claims you file are truthful.

However, if you qualify for benefits from both programs, the total benefits you receive from both programs cannot equal more than 80% of your average earnings prior to becoming disabled.

Some states also allow disabled workers to collect both unemployment and workers' compensation benefits at the same time. When in doubt, file truthful claims for any program for which you might logically qualify and let the system decide if you're eligible for benefits.

B. Unemployment Insurance

Unemployment insurance, often called UI or unemployment compensation, is intended to provide you with a regular paycheck after you're let go from a job—until you're either called back to that job or find a new one. Founded in 1935, the unemployment insurance program is run jointly by the federal government and the states, and is paid for primarily by a tax on employers. Under normal circumstances, unemployment insurance benefits are limited to 26 weeks. However, effective late 1991, UI benefits are extended by an additional 33 weeks for all employees whose original 26 week benefit period ran out after March 1, 1991. Except that in AL, CT, ME, MA, MI, MS, NJ, RI and WV, the extension is for 20 weeks. The laws governing unemployment insurance vary from state to state, but the rules explained below generally apply.

1. Employees covered

Unemployment insurance covers employees of all levels, including part-timers and temporaries.

To be covered, you must have worked as an employee for a substantial period and earned a minimum amount of wages before becoming unemployed. In most states, you must have been employed for at least six months during the year before your job loss. The amount you are required to have earned to qualify for unemployment insurance benefits varies by state, and is frequently changed to reflect inflation and the cost of living.

You don't need to be a U.S. citizen to be covered, but you must have the documents required by the U.S. Immigration and Naturalization Service to legally work in the United States. (See Chapter 12, Section H.)

In some cases, people treated as independent contractors by companies are ruled by the courts to be employees—and therefore eligible for unemployment insurance benefits. (See Chapter 1, Section B.)

2. Employees not covered

As with most workplace laws, the exceptions to unemployment insurance coverage are the result of decades of political lobbying by special-interest groups. So there's no central logic to the list of workers who aren't covered.

The categories of employees not covered by unemployment insurance usually include people employed by small farms, casual domestic workers and babysitters, newspaper carriers under age 18, children employed by their parents, their spouses or their children, employees of religious organizations and elected officials.

3. Eligibility for benefits

Even if you're covered by unemployment insurance, you may not be paid by the program unless you fit a few additional requirements. The two most basic rules are:

- You must be available to be recalled to your old job or to work in a similar one. For example, you may become ineligible if you take a new job or if you take a long vacation during which you can't be reached by your former employer or a new one.

- You must be physically able to perform your old job or a similar one.

The requirement that workers be physically able to work can be confusing when applied to pregnant women. In general, the courts have ruled that unemployment insurance benefits can't be denied simply because the employee is pregnant, but can be denied if the pregnancy makes the employee physically unable to perform her normal job or one similar to it.

Workers who are physically unable to perform their jobs usually have to apply for the workers' compensation or disability insurance programs. (See Sections D and F). However, a few states pay unemployment insurance benefits during periods of temporary disability. Your local unemployment insurance agency should help you determine whether your state is one of them.

4. Disqualification for benefits

Even if you're covered by unemployment insurance and otherwise eligible to receive it, there are factors that can disqualify you from receiving benefits. The reasons for disqualification vary from state to state, but the most common ones are that:

- you are unemployed because you went on strike

- you were fired from your job for misconduct

- you refused to accept a similar job without good reason

- you quit your job without a good reason.

The last reason to be shut off from benefits—quitting your job—is particularly troublesome. Disputes over unemployment insurance claims often occur when the employee believes that his or her reason for quitting a job was a good one, and the employer disagrees.

Of course, the definition of a good reason to quit a job varies with each person and each circumstance. Reasons that are usually considered good enough for you to quit your job and still be eligible for unemployment insurance include:

- Some form of fraud was involved in recruiting you for the job. For example, employers sometimes offer a certain level of wages and benefits, but then try to cut back on that offer once the employee shows up for work.

- Your life or health was being endangered by the employer's failure to maintain workplace safety.

- The nature of your work was changed dramatically from what you had originally been hired to do, or your wages and benefits were substantially reduced without your consent.

- You were being sexually harassed on the job, and your employer refused to correct the situation.

- A change in the location of your work made it impractical for you to continue in the job.

- Your spouse had to relocate to take a new job.

You can quit your job for other reasons and still file a claim for unemployment insurance benefits. But if your former employer challenges your claim, you'll need to prove through the appeal process described below that your reason was good enough.

BEWARE OF JOB LOSS INSURANCE POLICIES

As the concept of long-term job security fades, some businesses are trying to exploit employees' fears of job loss by offering insurance policies that claim to cover certain bills during periods of unemployment.

Flyers urging you to buy job-loss insurance are often included with your monthly credit card statement. The glitzy ads usually offer to make the payments on that credit card account should you lose your job. And mortgage companies frequently offer job loss insurance as a part of the process of closing the purchase of a home, arguing that your mortgage payments would be made by the insurance company should you become unemployed.

Such insurance usually isn't a wise buy for most people. Look closely at the fine print of most job-loss insurance policies and you'll see a long list of situations in which you wouldn't be eligible for benefits. Typical exceptions: you're out of work for less than several weeks, you volunteered for an early retirement program, you were fired because of something you did at work, or you're involved in a labor dispute.

Just about the only situations in which you might receive benefits from most job-loss policies would be if your employer suddenly went bankrupt, or your boss simply said to you, "Get out of here, you're fired"—something that, in today's legally complicated workplaces, is unlikely to happen anywhere except in the comic strips.

---

5. Severance pay

In most cases, severance pay benefits that you earned while working don't affect your eligibility for unemployment insurance benefits.

> **Example:** Jodie worked five years for a company whose employee benefits program credited workers with one week of severance pay for each year they were employed. So when the company fired her and several other employees in a cost-cutting move, she received severance pay equal to five weeks of her normal pay. Her severance pay didn't affect her right to collect unemployment insurance benefits because the severance pay was actually delayed payment of money that Jodie earned during the years that she was employed by that company.

However, as protection against wrongful-discharge lawsuits, employers increasingly use an offer of an unearned severance payment—usually several months' worth of the employee's normal pay—to get an employee to quit a job rather than be fired. (See Chapter 3, Section C.)

In such situations, severance pay can delay the start of unemployment insurance benefits—or even make a worker ineligible for them.

Example: Raj worked for a company that wanted to economize by cutting 500 employees. He accepted the company's offer of six months' severance pay—four months more than the two months' severance pay he had earned through the benefits program—in return for a signed statement that he had not been dismissed, but had volunteered to quit his job.

When Raj filed a claim for unemployment insurance benefits, he was shocked and disappointed when it was turned down. His ex-employer contested it— claiming that Raj had made a decision to quit voluntarily.

Raj appealed the denial of his claim, and he won because he proved that he was coerced into quitting. But the appeal office also ruled that Raj couldn't begin collecting unemployment insurance benefits until the four months covered by the unearned severance package had expired.

Regulations and rulings covering the effects that severance pay has on unemployment insurance vary greatly from state to state, and are changing rapidly. In some cases, groups of workers who have been cut from company payrolls through offers of severance packages have created enough political pressure to have the rules in their state changed in their favor.

If you quit your job in exchange for severance pay, protect your rights by filing a claim for unemployment insurance benefits. If that claim is denied, you'll then have the right to explain during the appeals process what really happened —or to benefit from any changes in your state's unemployment insurance rules covering severance pay.

C. Filing an Unemployment Insurance Claim

Claims for unemployment insurance benefits are accepted and paid by the states through thousands of offices throughout the country. The names for the agencies that handle the claims vary, but are typically something that sounds more upbeat than unemployment—such as Bureau of Employment Security, Job Service Office or State Employment Service.

Whatever your local version is called, you can locate the office closest to you by checking the state government section of your local telephone directory. Because of the varying names used and the fact that there are many other government programs relating to jobs, it's wise to call the agency that you think is the unemployment insurance office to confirm that it's the correct one before visiting it.

You can help your claim get processed quickly by bringing the proper documentation with you when you visit the local office. Bring along:

- A detailed work history covering at least a few years prior to your unemployment, including accurate names, addresses, telephone numbers and IRS employer identification numbers of your previous employers.

- Recent pay stubs and other wage records, such as the W-2 form on which your employer reports your income to the Internal Revenue Service.

- Your Social Security card, or another document that shows your Social Security number.

- Any documentation you have of why you are unemployed, such as a layoff or dismissal notice from your employer, and your employer's unemployment insurance account number, if it has been provided to you. (For more on how to document a job loss, see Chapter 3, Section C.)

Typically, your first visit to the unemployment insurance claims office will include some type of orientation—ranging from simple instructional signs hanging from the ceiling to sophisticated video productions. In any case, you'll be required to fill out forms explaining your unemployment. This is where your documentation will be especially useful.

WATCH YOUR WORDING

Unless you were clearly dismissed from your job because of something you did wrong, avoid using the word "fired" in filing out any forms or answering any interview questions at the unemployment insurance office. There are many unspecified words thrown around concerning the end of employment, but fired is the one most often taken to mean that you did something wrong and were dismissed because of it. "Laid off" is an equally vague term, but it is less likely to raise questions about the validity of your claim.

Once you've handed in your forms, the rituals that follow vary somewhat from state to state. For example, you may be interviewed that day or told to come back for an interview. If a second visit is required, be sure to take your employment document collection with you.

Whatever the ritual, the goal of the unemployment insurance claim filing process is to determine whether you're entitled to benefits, and what the amount of those benefits should be. When your first visit is over, the clerks at the unemployment insurance office will begin verifying your claim by sending inquiries to your former employers.

The employers then must respond, either verifying or disputing your version of the circumstances surrounding your unemployment, the wages you received and other relevant information. The process usually takes at least a few weeks, and sometimes more.

While you're waiting for your claim to go through this long verification process, you'll probably be required to visit the unemployment insurance office once each week or two to sign a statement affirming that you still meet all the legal requirements of the program, and that you're looking for a new job. It's important that you comply with this reporting requirement even before receiving unemployment insurance checks because, once your claim is verified, you'll usually be paid after the fact for all the weeks for which you did qualify for benefits.

1. Where to file if you move

If you become unemployed in one state and then move your residence to another, you can file your claim in your new state but your benefits will be determined by the rules used by your former state. Although your new state administers your claim, the cost of your benefits is charged back to the state in which you became unemployed. A move will also add time to processing your claim—usually increasing the delay by several weeks.

Keep in mind that even when you relocate, you still must meet all the requirements of the unemployment insurance program to qualify for benefits. Your new location must be one to which you were required to move by family circumstances, or in which it is logical for you to expect to find a new job. For example, you can't decide to move to a small seacoast town with virtually no business activity because you like the lifestyle there, quit your old job for no other reason, and then expect to be eligible for unemployment insurance when you get to your new home and can't find work.

2. Calculating your benefits

In most states, you become eligible for unemployment insurance benefits after you've been unemployed for one week.

The unemployment insurance program is supposed to provide you with half of the income you received while you were employed. However, each state has set its own minimum and maximum benefit payment, and some pay supplements for your dependents.

To calculate your benefits, the unemployment insurance office will typically use a rather complicated formula premised on the base period of your wages. The base period is set by looking at your earnings in the four quarters before the last full quarter in which you worked before the one in which you filed your claim.

For example, if you filed a claim in February of 1992 (the middle of the first quarter), most states would use your average wages for the last quarter of 1990 and the first three quarters of 1991 as the basis for determining your benefits. The quarter within that base period in which you had the highest wages is the one on which most states calculate the amount of your weekly unemployment insurance benefits.

Example: Bart worked for four years as a mechanic in an auto repair business. During the first three years, he always worked 40 hours a week at $10 per hour. His wages totaled $400 each week. At the start of his fourth year there, a new freeway was built near the shop where he worked, and the shift in traffic hurt the shop's business. Bart began averaging only 30 hours of work each week, being paid only $300 each week. At the end of the fourth year, the shop went out of business, leaving Bart unemployed.

After accepting and verifying Bart's claim, the people at the unemployment insurance office used as his base period the last quarter of the third year and the first three quarters of his fourth year at the shop. Since he was working 40 hours a week during the third year, the quarter of his base period in which his wages were highest was the last quarter of the third year. His weekly unemployment benefit is 50% of $400, or $200.

Some states also pay partial benefits to people whose work hours slip below their normal level for a substantial period. These programs vary widely, so when in doubt, it's wise to inquire at the unemployment insurance office and file a claim whenever it appears to be appropriate.

The method of paying benefits also varies among the states, but you'll typically receive your check in the mail every two weeks after your claim is verified and your benefit level is determined.

3. Continuing your benefits

Once you've qualified for unemployment insurance benefits, you can't just sit back and welcome the checks each week. You must continue to comply with the state program's rules and rituals to keep them coming.

You must visit the unemployment insurance office as frequently as your state requires it. During each visit, you'll have to verify that you remain unemployed but available for work; that you remain physically able to work, and that you are actively looking for work. The documents you sign on your visits to the unemployment insurance office will typically ask you to certify that you continue to meet these requirements, and it is usually a criminal offense to lie about any of your answers.

In some states, you'll also be required to list a minimum number of potential employers to whom you've applied for work since the last time you signed for benefits. This requirement may vary according to economic conditions. If the lines at the unemployment insurance offices get too long in your area, for example, your state may ask you to merely mail in your information every two weeks.

The unemployment insurance program can't require you to take a job that varies much from your normal field of work and your normal wage level. But these ranges are subject to interpretation, so exercise care in deciding where to apply for a new job. Apply only for jobs that are close to your normal type of work and wage levels so that you won't run the risk of having your unemployment insurance claim discontinued because you refused to accept substitute employment.

A LITTLE TALK MAY GO A LONG WAY

Keep in mind that while unemployed people frequently miss the social interaction they enjoyed on the job and need someone to talk with, the unemployment insurance office isn't a good place to strike up a conversation.

If you say the wrong thing to the clerks there, such as telling them about a little fishing trip you took because you had a lot of free time, they may use that information to disqualify you for benefits during that period, or to discontinue your claim completely.

4. Employer appeals

If your claim is approved, your ex-employer will have the right to appeal it. There are cases, of course, where some former employees begin to collect unemployment insurance benefits to which they're not legally entitled—and the employer justifiably appeals the decision.

However, some employers have an outrageous policy of appealing all unemployment insurance claims filed against them. Typically, they use tactics such as claiming that workers quit when, in fact, they were fired because business became slow.

These employers often hire lawyers or agencies that specialize in frustrating unemployment insurance claims—hired gunslingers who make a living by fighting employees' claims for so long that the employees find new jobs in the meantime and drop their claims. It's a poker game, and they're betting that you'll drop out.

If your claim is approved but your employer appeals it, you'll be notified of that appeal in writing. In general, an appeal by your ex-employer of an approved claim will be conducted in the same way as an appeal of a denied claim (discussed below).

You will be able to continue collecting your benefits until a decision is issued on your ex-employer's appeal. You may, however, be required to repay all or part of the benefits if your ex-employer wins the appeal. Typically, your ability to repay is the deciding factor in such circumstances.

5. Appealing a denied claim

If your claim is denied, you'll be notified in writing of that decision, the reason for it and the number of days you have after being notified of that decision to indicate that you want to appeal. The amount of time allowed to begin to appeal the denial of an unemployment insurance claim varies from state to state, but generally ranges from one to four weeks from the time that the notice of denial is mailed to you.

In some states, the form you need to file to begin an appeal will be included with the notice that your claim has been denied. If it isn't, call or visit the unemployment insurance office where you filed your claim to obtain a copy of the form.

The hearing will likely be scheduled within a few weeks after you advise the unemployment insurance office of your intention to appeal its decision, and you'll have the option of representing yourself or having a lawyer or someone else do it. If you don't want to represent yourself and can't afford a lawyer, check with your local Legal Aid Society or a local law school to see if someone there can represent you. If you're unemployed and without benefits, chances are good that they will help.

Your ex-employer also has the option of being represented by a lawyer or an agency that specializes in challenging unemployment insurance claims. Typically, the appeal hearing will be conducted informally before a hearing examiner, referee or administrative law judge. At the hearing, you and your ex-employer will be allowed to bring witnesses, and most of the formal rules of evidence that apply to formal courtroom proceedings won't apply or will be only loosely enforced.

6. Representing yourself

If you organize your documentation of the reasons that you're unemployed and present them in an organized manner, you can do a good job of representing yourself in all but the most complex cases. At this level, the appeal process is intended to resolve disputes rather than to take on the look of a formal court action, so don't be afraid to ask questions at the unemployment insurance office or at your hearing.

Well before the hearing is scheduled to begin, write down the reasons that you feel you're entitled to unemployment insurance benefits in as few words as possible, then practice presenting those reasons to a friend or family member. Don't give in to the human temptation to use the hearing as an opportunity to insult or get revenge on your former employer.

Do as thorough and thoughtful a job of researching, organizing, documenting and presenting your case as you can. Keep your argument as focused as possible, because it's at this level that you're most likely to win a decision that will quickly start your benefit checks flowing. (For details of how to document your job loss, see Chapter 3, Section C.)

If you win this appeal, you'll soon begin receiving benefits, typically including back payments from the date on which you first became eligible.

Both you and your ex-employer will have the option of appealing the ruling on your appeal to the state courts. However, only a tiny percentage of unemployment insurance cases continue up into the state courts or higher.

Those that do typically require help from a lawyer. (See Chapter 13, Section D.)

7. Expanding eligibility limits

In general, the limits of eligibility for unemployment insurance benefits have been expanding. For example, in 1991, a Minnesota appeals court ruled that a woman who had been fired because her baby's poor health had forced her to take about two months off from work during a five-month period was entitled to collect unemployment benefits.

Her original claim for unemployment insurance benefits was turned down because her employer had considered her absence from work to be misconduct. But the appeals court disagreed, ruling that taking time off from work because of child care responsibilities wasn't misconduct (*McCourtney v. Imprimis Technology, Inc.*, 465 N.W. 2d 721).

It's important to note, however, that the ruling doesn't mean that anyone can take time off from work to take care of any child and qualify for unemployment benefits. One of the decisive factors in that case was the fact that the employee had tried very hard to find a daycare program for her baby, but was unable to because of its illness.

D. Workers' Compensation

The workers' compensation system provides replacement income to employees who are injured or become ill as a result of their jobs. Benefits may also extend to workers' dependents and to the survivors of workers who are killed on the job. In some circumstances, workers' compensation also protects employers from being sued for those injuries or deaths. The system is paid for primarily by insurance premiums paid by employers.

Like unemployment insurance, the workers' compensation system is national, but is administered by the states. The laws and court decisions governing it follow a pattern throughout the country, but vary significantly from state to state.

NO WORKER IS IMMUNE FROM INJURIES

Even the most refined and romantic work situations can cause human injury and loss of income. Consider, for example, the injuries that often befall church bell ringers in Great Britain.

A study published in 1990 by the *British Medical Journal* showed that the 40,000 British men and women who practice the bell-ringing profession suffer many injuries at work—the most common being torn fingernails, rope burns, accidental teeth extractions and sprained muscles.

The most dangerous aspect of the bell-ringers' job, the study found, is the high-speed lift. Such a lift occurs when a heavy church bell goes out of balance and the ringer holding its rope is pulled toward the ceiling at speeds in excess of 50 miles per hour.

The situation is sometimes worsened when the ringer's head gets caught in a loop in the rampaging bell's rope, creating an accidental near-hanging. In one case, an 80-year-old bell ringer was nearly scalped when the rope tightened around his eyebrows during a high-speed lift.

The study found that five British bell ringers died recently from injuries suffered at work.

---

1. Employees covered

In general, anyone who qualifies as an employee under the Internal Revenue Service guidelines (discussed in Chapter 1, Section B), is covered by workers' compensation insurance.

However, coverage details vary from state to state. In some states, companies with fewer than five employees aren't required to carry workers' compensation coverage, and many states exclude farm workers and domestic workers from coverage.

Many states require employers to post an explanation of workers' compensation coverage in a prominent place within the work area. So if your employer keeps such a notice on your workplace bulletin board, you're probably covered. If you're unsure whether your employer is covered, your local workers' compensation agency should tell you. Look in the state government section of your local telephone directory for contact details.

AVOIDING THE CAUSES OF REPETITIVE MOTION ILLNESS

In a typical year, more than six million work-related injuries and illnesses occur in the United States. The most rapidly growing category of workplace illness is made up of those caused by repetitive motions of the human body.

Carpal Tunnel Syndrome—which primarily afflicts the wrists, hands and forearms—is the most widely publicized type of repetitive motion illness. But, in fact, many other parts of the body are susceptible to injury from being used repeatedly to perform motions that exceed the specifications for which nature designed them. It is not unusual, for example, for people working on auto factory and meat processing production lines to suffer repetitive motion illness to their elbows, fingers, shoulders, backs, knees, ankles and feet.

Typical symptoms of repetitive motion illness include swelling and redness near bone joints; extreme sensitivity of the affected body part to movement and external touch; pain, both sharp and dull, in the overused area that may radiate into other parts of the limb, abdomen, head or back; and numbness of the affected body part or those near it.

If detected early, injuries caused by repeated motions can often be cured by a short period of rest, light medication and rehabilitative exercise. The most serious and neglected cases, however, can escalate to a lifelong physical disability.

Work-related motion injuries are typically covered by workers' compensation insurance. But the best workers' compensation claim is the one that you never have to file, so here are a few of the steps that health experts recommend to avoid becoming afflicted with a work-related repetitive motion injury:

- Take frequent, short breaks from repetitive, physically stressful work whenever possible. This allows your muscles and joints to recover a bit from unnatural tensions that may result from your work.

- Do stretching exercises at work regularly, paying particular attention to the parts of your body that are likely to be used most often. This reduces the muscle tightening that is believed to contribute to the illness.

- Stay alert for early symptoms, such as stiffness or other discomfort in heavily used body parts. Quick and complete recovery is much more likely if the symptoms are recognized early.

- Redesign your work tools or your typical work position and movements—or ask your employer to—as soon as high stress and wear on a specific part of your body become apparent. Good examples of redesigning are add-on wrist supports for use with personal computer keyboards and ergonomic lines of office furniture.

- Remember that heart-pounding physical exertion is not necessary for dangerous body stress to occur. Just as you can wake up with a sore shoulder after sleeping all night in the wrong position, you can subject yourself to the dangers of muscle and tendon injury even in jobs that involve very limited exertion. (For more on pre-venting workplace injuries, see Chapter 11, Section D.)

2. Injuries covered

To be covered by workers' compensation, the injury needn't be caused by a sudden accident such as a fall. With a few exceptions, any injury that occurs in connection with work is covered.

Officially, injuries that can be shown to have been intentionally self-inflicted by the employee, or to have been caused by substance abuse, generally are not covered. However, the courts have often sided with the injured worker when such cases are disputed, often ruling that the injury is covered as long as the employee's behavior wasn't the only thing that caused the injury.

The legal definition of when you are working for workers' compensation purposes also has expanded in recent years. For example, some employees who were injured by playing baseball or football on a company-affiliated team have been allowed to collect workers' compensation benefits for those injuries because the courts have reasoned that they were helping to adver-tise their employer's business by participating in sports it sponsored.

3. Illnesses covered

A common illness becomes an occupational illness for purposes of workers' compensation when the nature of a job increases the worker's chances of suffering from that disease. Illnesses that are the gradual result of work conditions—for example, emotional illness, repetitive motion injuries and stress-related digestive problems—increasingly are being recognized by the courts as being covered by workers' compensation insurance.

One of the most dramatic expansions of the definition of illness caused by work occurred in 1990, when a Michigan appeals court ruled that a brewery worker was eligible for workers' compensation benefits because his tendency toward alcoholism—he typically drank 15 to 20 bottles of beer at work each day, and more at home—had been made worse by the fact that his employer gave employees free beer to drink during their breaks (*Gacioch v. Stroh Brewery Co.*, 466 N.W. 2d 302).

4. Deaths covered

Dependents of workers killed on the job in front of witnesses are almost always eligible to collect workers' compensation benefits.

When an employee is found dead in the workplace, no one witnessed the death and no cause of death is obvious, the death is usually covered by workers' compensation. The possibilities of suicide or murder are usually ignored by courts unless there is strong evidence that the death qualifies as one or the other.

E. Filing a Workers' Compensation Claim

The first step in every workers' compensation claim is to inform your employer of your injury as soon as possible after getting any medical care required.

Typically, your employer will have claim forms for you to fill out and submit, or can obtain a form quickly. It then becomes your employer's responsibility to submit the paperwork to the proper insurance carrier and to your state's workers' compensation agency.

In the unlikely event that your employer refuses to cooperate with you in filing a workers' compensation claim, a call to your local workers' compensation office will usually remedy the situation. Look in the state government section of your local telephone directory for contact details.

If your claim is not disputed by your employer or its insurance carrier, it will be approved and an adjuster for the insurance company will typically contact you or your employer with instructions on how to submit your medical bills for payment.

If your injury isn't permanent and doesn't cause you to lose income, the payment of your medical bills will probably be the extent of your claim and there won't be much else for you to do. If you're temporarily unable to work because of your injury, you'll also begin receiving checks to cover your wage loss—typically within a week or two after your claim is approved. Your employer will notify the insurance company to stop sending you wage-replacement checks as soon as you recover and return to work.

1. Calculating your benefits

Your workers' compensation benefits may take several forms.

First, the bills for medical care you required because of your workplace injuries will be paid.

Then, if your injury has caused you to lose time from work, you'll receive payments that substitute for the income you would have earned had you not been injured. Typically, you'll be paid two-thirds of your average wages. But since the benefits are tax free, this will usually be roughly equal to your take-home pay.

The states have set minimums and maximums for these payments, so people with unusually low incomes may actually experience an income increase while receiving workers' compensation, and those with very high incomes may experience an income cut.

In most states, workers become eligible for wage loss replacement benefits as soon as they've lost a few days' work because of an injury covered by workers' compensation. The number of days required to qualify varies by state, and some states allow the payments to be paid retroactively to the first day of wage loss if the injury keeps the employee out of work for an extended period.

Finally, you may receive a lump-sum payment. The lump-sum payments that you're eligible to receive under the workers' compensation program will vary greatly with the nature and extent of your injuries. The categories into which the injuries that may qualify you for lump-sum benefits include:

- **Temporary total disability:** You're unable to work at all, but you're expected to recover and return to work.

- **Permanent total disability:** You're unable to work at all, and you're not expected to be able to work again.

- **Permanent partial disability:** Although you're able to perform some types of work, you're not expected to be able to fully regain your ability to earn money. This type of disability is usually divided into two groups, schedule and nonschedule injuries.

Schedule injuries are those for which a set lump-sum payment has been prescribed by law in your state. For example, in New Mexico, an employee who loses a foot in a work-related accident is entitled to $32,626.

Non-schedule injuries are those for which no such lump-sum amount has been specified, so a settlement must be negotiated. In Florida, for example, there is no law specifying the benefit to be paid to an employee who loses a foot in a work-related accident.

If an employee dies from a workplace accident, then the employee's estate receives burial expenses plus the death benefit specified by law in the state where the accident occurred.

A number of states have recently amended their Workers' Compensation laws to restrict or eliminate benefits when an employee's claim is based on injuries caused by non-prescription, illegal drugs. Those states include Alas,a Connecticut, Florida, Georgia, Idaho, Iowa, Kansas, Louisiana, Maryland, Missouri, North Dakota, Ohio, Oklahoma, Oregon, Rhode Island, South Dakota, Virginia and Wyoming.

COMPLEX CASES REQUIRE EXPERTISE

If your workers' compensation claim is denied, you have the right to appeal it at several levels. If your work-related injury is a permanent or long-term one, then pursuing your claim for workers' compensation benefits to its fullest extent will likely be a complicated task.

And there may be added complications: If your workers' compensation claim isn't the first one you've ever filed, the cost of your benefits may have to be distributed between your current employer's insurance carrier and a special state fund that covers workers' compensation injuries beyond the first one.

If your claim falls into any of these categories, you'll probably need to hire a lawyer who specializes in workers' compensation cases to help you. (See Chapter 13, Section D.)

The workers' compensation system is dominated by lawyers, insurance companies and healthcare professionals who specialize in it—and profit highly from it. So even in cases involving simple injuries such as face wounds and minor bone fractures, you'll probably receive substantially higher benefits from the workers' compensation system if you hire a lawyer with workers' compensation experience and connections to help you.

For example, in some states, your workers' compensation benefits will be higher if you can prove that your injury or illness involved a violation of state industrial safety codes. But proving such violations typically requires courtroom expertise and resources that typically only lawyers have.

2. Related lawsuits for work injuries

The workers' compensation system is the normal remedy for work-related injuries and illness. But in a growing number of situations, an injured worker will have the option of filing a lawsuit against another responsible person or company in addition to filing a claim for workers' compensation. For example, an injured worker might sue the manufacturer of a defective machine for negligence.

One such case was decided in favor of the injured worker in 1991 by the Ohio Supreme Court. A man was injured while working on a fertilizer loader that he had known lacked a protective cage when he began working on it. The injured man could sue the company that made the loading machine, the court held, because the tight job market had erased workers' ability to reject dangerous employment (*Cremeans v. Willmar Henderson Mfg. Co.,* 566 N.E. 2d 1203).

A few states have also allowed employees to sue employers who fired them in retaliation for filing a workers' compensation claim. In general, these cases have been pursued under the tort of retaliatory discharge. (For more on illegal firings, see Chapter 4, Section A.)

Employers who fail to maintain the workers' compensation coverage required in their state, or who otherwise violate the laws of the workers' compensation system, generally can be sued over work-related injuries. You'll probably need to hire a lawyer to help you with this type of lawsuit. (See Chapter 13, Section D.)

F. Social Security Disability Insurance

The disability benefits available under the federal Social Security program are intended to prevent people from becoming paupers because an injury or illness has left them completely unable to earn a living.

In contrast to the workers' compensation program, the Social Security disability insurance system doesn't recognize degrees of wage-earning capability. Under Social Security eligibility rules, you're either able to work, in which case you don't qualify for its benefits, or you're not able to work, in which case you may qualify.

1. Employees covered

When you and your employer pay into the Social Security program, you're automatically buying long-term disability insurance coverage. Once you've paid into the program for a period specified by the Social Security program, you're eligible for benefits should you become unable to earn a living.

The formulas for determining eligibility are complex. If you want to determine whether you're covered by Social Security disability insurance, the best place to begin researching is at your local Social Security office. Look in the federal government section of your local telephone directory for contact details.

People who have worked at least a few years as employees, paying into the Social Security fund, generally are covered. In many cases, dependents of those covered are also eligible for benefits.

THE SAD FATE OF ASBESTOS WORKERS

Workers who have been injured or killed by exposure to the mineral asbestos form a special group of injured workers whose rights are being trampled and exploited by the legal system.

Used primarily as a fire retardant, asbestos has been shown to cause cancer and several other types of serious illness, including a general weakening of the immune system. The symptoms of asbestos-caused illness often take decades to appear, so many people were routinely exposed to it until the connection between illness and asbestos was established in recent years.

An estimated 3.5 million American workers have been substantially exposed to asbestos in the workplace, and more than one-quarter million of them are expected to die of asbestos-caused illnesses by the year 2015. On average, more than a thousand asbestos-related personal injury suits are filed each month, but many of the plaintiffs die before their lawsuits conclude.

What's worse, all this litigation has benefited lawyers—and others who make their livings off of lawyers—more than it has the victims of asbestos. For example, in 1991, a committee of federal judges estimated that out of every dollar paid to asbestos victims who successfully sue their former employers and other parties involved in their exposure to asbestos, only 39 cents ever reaches the plaintiffs. The rest goes to lawyers, physicians, other expert witnesses and related costs.

In one case involving only four plaintiffs, the number of lawyers involved reached a high of 58 at one point in the case—and always involved at least 41 lawyers.

Nevertheless, if you are afflicted with an asbestos-related illness, it's better to pursue your rights under this system than to do nothing at all. If you suspect that you've been exposed to asbestos in the course of your work, get more information by contacting the White Lung Association or the Asbestos Victims of America. (See the Appendix.)

2. Disabilities covered

In all but the most unusual cases, the circumstances surrounding your disabling injury or illness are irrelevant to the Social Security system. If you've met the other requirements for coverage, the key issues concerning your disability are simply whether or not it prevents you from earning a living, and whether or not it is expected to keep you out of work for a year or more.

For example, if an injury you suffered in an auto accident while on vacation left you permanently unable to hold any job, you would typically be eligible for Social Security disability benefits. The fact that your injury was not a result of your work wouldn't disqualify you, as it would under workers' compensation insurance.

SPECIAL RULES FOR BLINDNESS

Disability caused by blindness is covered under special rules, so if you become blind you'll need to research the specifics of your eligibility by calling the Social Security Administration office nearest to your home.

G. Filing a Social Security Claim

It is extremely important to file your claim for Social Security disability benefits as soon as you become disabled, because there's a waiting period of five months after filing before you can begin receiving payments. If you wait a long time to file, you may be disappointed to learn that back payments are limited to the 12 months prior to the date on which you file.

The Social Security Administration offices located in most cities are staffed by people who will complete the forms and other paperwork necessary to file a claim. To do so, they will require you to provide documentation such as a copy of your birth certificate and, of course, your Social Security number.

When you visit the Social Security offices for initial help with a claim, you should also bring:

- names, addresses and telephone numbers of doctors, clinics and hospitals—and the dates on which they treated you

- a summary of your work history for the past 15 years

- dates of any military service.

If you have dependents who may be eligible for benefits under your Social Security disability insurance claim, you'll also have to present similar documentation for them when filing a claim. If your disability prevents you from visiting a Social Security office, you can usually file your claim by mail or telephone.

The Social Security Administration will pay for any examinations and reports it requires to verify your claim. The people who staff the office where you file your claim will also help you with the paperwork and procedures required for such payment.

The results of those examinations and reports will usually be sent to your state's vocational rehabilitation agency, which will provide the Social Security Administration with a decision on whether or not you're sufficiently disabled to qualify for benefits. In some cases, the vocational rehabilitation people will call you in so they can conduct their own examinations, tests and interviews, as well.

The Social Security Administration has a program to provide emergency funds for disabled people who need financial help during the long waiting period. The Social Security employees handling your claim can give you details of how to qualify for emergency funds.

1. Calculating your benefits

If your claim for Social Security disability benefits is approved, the five-month waiting period must pass before you'll get any payments. Then, you'll begin receiving monthly checks that are roughly equivalent to those received by a retired person whose wage or salary history was similar to yours in the years just before retirement. Although the amount will be substantial, it alone won't return your income to the level you received before your injury.

If you have dependents, you'll receive extra benefits for each of them in most situations. The dollar amount for which you'll be eligible is calculated by a complex formula that changes frequently with federal budget amendments. The best way to determine your specific benefit level is to file a copy of the Social Security Administration's Form SSA-7004-PC-OP1, entitled Request for Earnings and Benefit Estimate Statement. You can obtain one at your local Social Security Administration office.

You don't need to be planning to file a claim to do this. You can file the form any time you're merely curious. The Social Security staff will calculate benefits to which you're entitled and notify you by mail of its determination.

2. Continuing your claim

Although many people who suffer total disabilities remain disabled for life, that's not always the case. So the Social Security disability insurance program includes various efforts to rehabilitate workers and get them back to work.

If your condition shows any potential for rehabilitation, one or more agencies will probably contact you after you've been collecting benefit checks for a while. They'll typically interview you about your disabling injury or illness, and may suggest various rehabilitation programs.

It's wise to cooperate with any reasonable request these agencies make because your disability benefit could be canceled if you refuse to participate in attempts to get you back into the workforce.

3. Trial runs at returning to work

One factor that makes Social Security disability insurance more friendly than other income-replacement programs is that it allows you to try going back to work without canceling your claim. You can participate in a total of nine months of trial work without losing any benefits, and the nine months needn't be consecutive or in one job. You could, for example, continue to receive Social Security disability checks while trying different jobs for a week or two every few months until you find one that doesn't clash with your disability.

If you succeed in returning to work after qualifying for Social Security disability benefits, the checks will keep coming for two months after your period of disability has ended to allow you a comfortable transition back into the workforce.

4. Appealing a denied claim

If your claim for Social Security disability benefits is denied, there are four levels of appeal available to you. At each step of the appeal process, you have 60 days from the date of the previous decision to take action to move up to the next appeal level.

With the exception of the fourth option, filing a suit in federal court, the staff at the Social Security Administration office will supply you with the proper forms for pursuing an appeal, and will even help you fill them out.[1]

Request for reconsideration. You ask to see the Social Security Administration's files concerning your claim, and then submit corrections or additional information that you hope will cause the agency to reconsider your claim and approve it.

Administrative hearing. You request a hearing by an independent administrative law judge who has never looked at your case before. You can ask to have the judge issue a ruling based on the evidence you've already submitted, or you can ask for a ruling without a hearing but with consideration of additional written evidence. Or you can request a hearing at which new or more detailed evidence can be presented. These hearings are usually run informally and held in the same city where you filed your claim.

Review by appeals council. You ask to have the Social Security Appeals Council, based in Washington, D.C., consider your claim. This council can decide whether or not to hear your appeal. If it decides to hear it, you can submit a written argument in support of your evidence. Or you can elect to go to Washington and appear before the council to argue your case.

Federal court. If you fail to win approval of your claim at all the previous levels, or if the appeals council refuses to hear your appeal, you can file a lawsuit in federal court to try to get the courts to order the Social Security Administration to approve your claim. You'll probably have to hire a lawyer to help you at this appeal level. (See Chapter 13, Section D.)

---

[1]For more detail on filing and appealing Social Security disability insurance claims, see *Social Security, Medicare and Pensions* by Joseph L. Matthews (Nolo Press).

H. Other Income Replacement Options

Although the government insurance programs covering unemployment, workplace injuries and permanent disability are the most substantial sources of replacement income for people who are out of work, there are other options.

1. Private disability insurance

While you were working, you or your employer may have been paying into a private disability insurance program. If you were paying for it through payroll withholdings, or if all the premiums were being paid by your employer, you may have forgotten that you have this coverage.

First, review the employee policy manual or packet that your employer gave you when you took the job to see whether any private disability coverage is described there. If not, the people who handle benefits for your employer should be able. to help you determine whether you have such coverage.

2. State disability programs

A few states offer disability benefits, usually as part of their unemployment insurance programs. Calls to your local unemployment insurance and workers' compensation insurance offices should allow you to determine whether your state is one that maintains this kind of coverage.

3. Withdrawals from pension plans

Some pension programs allow withdrawals prior to retirement for emergency purposes. The administrator of your pension plan can advise you on whether you have this option. (For more on pensions, see Chapter 9, Section B.)

4. Food stamps

Although many people incorrectly think that the federal food stamp program is a form of welfare, it's actually financed by the U.S. Department of Agriculture as a way of increasing the demand for food products. You don't have to be receiving welfare to qualify for food stamps. In fact, the eligibility formula for food stamps makes them available to many people who are not all that poor. If your income is eliminated or significantly reduced for several months because you're not working, it's worth checking on whether you're eligible for food stamps.

To locate the agency in your area that issues food stamps, scan the county government offices listings in the telephone directory. Typically, you'll find a listing for food stamp information under a category such as Human Services. If not, call your local office of the U.S. Department of Agriculture.

5. Veterans' benefits

There are programs that provide income to veterans of the U.S. military who become unable to work because of a disability, even if that disability is not a result of military service. Your local Veterans' Administration office, listed in the federal government agency section of the telephone directory, can give you details.

6. Supplemental Social Security

Usually known as SSI, this program provides money to disabled people who have low incomes and very few assets. Unlike regular Social Security disability insurance, it doesn't require you to have worked under and paid into the Social Security program. If the circumstances surrounding your inability to earn income are so unusual that you've fallen between the cracks of the larger programs, SSI may be the one program that provides you with some income.

You can get details and file a claim at your local Social Security Administration office. Look in the federal government section of your local telephone directory for contact details.

7. Black lung benefits

The Social Security Administration also runs a special federal program that provides money benefits to victims of anthracosilicosis, an occupational disease often suffered by miners. Typically known as black lung, the disease is caused by long exposure to coal particles in the air. It frequently leaves miners unable to work because they can't breath properly.

The benefits under this program are also payable to dependents of black lung victims, so the best way to research your eligibility for those benefits is to investigate details of the program at your local Social Security office.

8. Disaster benefits

When a flood, hurricane or other natural disaster tears through an area, the president or governor will often declare it a disaster area and special unemployment benefits will become available to persons who lost their jobs because of the disaster. These special unemployment benefits are usually handled by the same offices that handle regular unemployment claims.

9. Medicare

Like Social Security, Medicare is usually thought of as being for elderly people. But, in fact, it also covers disabled people, and can be a good way of coping with medical bills when an injury or illness prevents you from working. For more details on this program, call the Medicare information line: 800-234-5772.

However, you should be aware that the federal government has been tightening the restrictions for qualifying for Medicare before you're 65 years old, so qualifying for this type of coverage is extremely difficult.

9

Healthcare Insurance, Pensions and Other Benefits

The logical way to pay someone for work is with money. However, because of a number of motivations such as special tax write-offs, employers developed a tradition of giving employees part of their pay in other forms.

Because they weren't all that important when first invented, these other forms of pay were at first called fringe benefits. In recent years, however, these other forms of pay have become a larger part of the employment scene and their name has been shortened to benefits.

It's an awfully broad term. Benefits can include anything from company-paid insurance coverage against legal expenses, to company-paid membership fees for health clubs, to a company-purchased watermelon for the annual employee picnic. Unless they're part of an employment contract or can be shown to violate anti-discrimination laws (discussed in Chapter 5, Sections A and J), most benefits aren't guaranteed to you by law.

For example, giving employees a turkey for the Thanksgiving holiday is a tradition in many companies—but you and your co-workers have no legal right to get that turkey.

However, there are some laws that grant you rights to some employer-provided benefits. And since those benefits can sometimes be worth a lot of money and peace of mind, it's worth learning about those laws.

A. Healthcare Insurance

Healthcare insurance coverage can be a matter of life and death. For example, a study published in 1991 showed that people who were admitted to American hospitals without healthcare insurance were as much as three times more likely to die there than were those who had insurance coverage.[1]

There are two main categories of employee healthcare insurance: coverage for current employees and coverage for former employees.

---

[1] *Journal of the American Medical Association*, Jan. 16, 1991, pp. 374-378.

1. Coverage for current employees

It is a matter of tradition, not law, for employers to offer healthcare insurance coverage to current employees. This truth flies in the face of many firmly-held beliefs about what people are entitled to at work. But in fact, there is no federal law that requires employers to provide or pay for healthcare insurance coverage for current employees. And no federal law requires employers to provide healthcare coverage to any employee who works full-time.

The belief that such laws exist is probably rooted in the way insurance companies structure their group policies. Most insurers require every one of a company's full-time employees—typically defined as those who work 40 or more hours—to participate in the company's group healthcare plan. The insurance companies do this to prevent getting into what is for them a money-losing proposition: Without such a rule, only unhealthy people would elect to be covered, while those who aren't ill—and have no reason to think they will become ill—would elect not to be covered.

A few states, counties and cities now require some employers to provide healthcare insurance coverage for some employees who work there. For example, Hawaii requires employers to provide coverage to employees earning a certain amount per month or more (Hawaii Rev. Stat. §393-11).

Some states are imposing additional restrictions on workplace healthcare insurance. In Illinois, for example, it is illegal for employers to fire employees because they file a legitimate claim against their company's healthcare insurance (Illinois Pub. Act 85-930).

WHY MANY EMPLOYERS NO LONGER PAY FOR HEALTHCARE INSURANCE

For many people, the greatest shock involved in finding their first job or securing a new one comes from learning that few employers pay all the costs of healthcare insurance anymore—and that a growing number of employers don't pay anything at all.

The sad truth is that America's healthcare costs are so out of control that most companies are no longer willing or able to pay for them. In recent years, U.S. healthcare costs have been rising at nearly three times the rate of inflation. The situation is so bad that in 1990, 26% of the average company's net earnings went to pay for healthcare.

Employers who pay for healthcare insurance as an employee benefit now spend more than $3,500 per year for healthcare coverage for each employee, on average. If healthcare costs continue to rise as they have, the cost of providing healthcare coverage at the start of the 21st century will be a whopping $22,000 per employee per year, according to estimates by the consulting firm of Foster Higgins in New York City. That's about $10.50 for every hour that a typical employee works.

---

2. Coverage for former employees

Ironically, workers have more rights to healthcare insurance coverage after they lose their jobs than while employed. The main reason for this is a 1986 law, the Consolidated Omnibus Budget Reconciliation Act (COBRA). Under COBRA, employers must offer former employees the option of continuing to be covered by the company's group healthcare insurance plan at the workers' own expense for some time after employment ends. Family coverage is included.

COBRA also requires that, as a former employee, your cost of continuing group healthcare coverage be similar to the cost of covering people who are still working for your former employer. However, the formulas for determining what you'll have to pay to continue your coverage are complex, and some employers and insurance companies intentionally manipulate them upward in hopes that you won't want to or be able to pay the premiums.

In general, COBRA gives an employee who quits or is dismissed for reasons other than gross misconduct the right to continue group healthcare coverage for 18 months. In some other circumstances, such as the death of the employee, that employee's dependents can continue coverage for up to 36 months.

WHY HEALTHCARE INSURANCE FOR RETIREES IS FADING FAST

During the booming decades that followed World War II in America, many big corporations promised their employees that the company would pay all the costs of their healthcare insurance—not only while they were on the company payroll, but also after they retired.

The catch was that many of those corporations never put away enough money to pay for their promises. Indeed, some didn't put any money at all away for that purpose. When healthcare costs got out of control in the 1980s, many corporations were hit by enormous medical bills for retired people who used to work for them.

It didn't take long for the investors who buy stock in those corporations to begin complaining about the big healthcare bills and the way they were cutting into the profits that investors are supposed to receive in return for buying a corporation's stock. It's dishonest, the investors argued, for a corporation not to put aside money to cover long-term commitments such as retiree healthcare costs.

The result was a rule from the Financial Standards Accounting Board—the group that governs the art of accounting in the United States—requiring that companies that promise retirement healthcare insurance coverage to employees must put aside money to cover the cost of those promises on a pay-as-you-go basis.

The formula for estimating how much companies have to set aside to pay for retiree healthcare is too complex to be discussed here. However, it's sufficient to know that for a company with 10,000 employees, the amount that would typically have had to be put aside in 1990 alone to pay for future retiree healthcare coverage was $21.5 million, according to the consulting firm of Towers Perrin in New York City.

Faced with such huge bills, most corporations now admit that they really can't afford to pay for retiree healthcare coverage. So they're doing everything they can to cut back on promises of retiree healthcare coverage that they've already made, and to avoid making any more such promises.

---

3. Enforcing COBRA

COBRA provides for a number of fines for employers and healthcare insurance plan administrators who violate its requirements. However, the Act has so many complexities that no one can agree on exactly what circumstances release an employer from its requirements. What's worse, there's no one place you can call to get help if you think your rights under COBRA have been violated. Parts of the law are administered by the Labor Department and other parts fall under the Internal Revenue Service—and the two agencies frequently refer COBRA complaints back and forth to each other.

If you have a COBRA-related question or complaint, you can try calling your local office of either of those agencies, but neither has a track record of actively enforcing COBRA requirements. Your employer is required to provide you with an explanation of your COBRA rights when you're enrolled in a group healthcare plan covering 20 or more employees. However, these materials are seldom well written or easy to understand.

If you need detailed information on when and how COBRA governs your right to continue healthcare insurance coverage, the best source is a well-written report entitled "COBRA Continuation Coverage" available for $10 per copy from the International Foundation of Employee Benefit Plans. (See the Appendix for contact information.)

In general, COBRA can be enforced only through an expensive lawsuit. That means that it typically can be used only by large groups of ex-employees who have been denied their rights to continue group healthcare insurance coverage—and who can share the expense of filing a lawsuit to enforce that right.

4. State healthcare insurance laws

Because COBRA generally cannot be enforced by any means other than a complex and expensive lawsuit, state laws that give ex-employees the right to continue group healthcare insurance coverage after leaving a job are often a better alternative. (See Chart 9-1 at the end of this chapter.) In nearly all instances, any continuation of coverage will be at your expense—just as it would be under COBRA.

However, the specific requirements of these laws and how they are enforced vary tremendously. For more specific information, contact your state's insurance department, or read the statute at a local law library. (See Chapter

13, Section E.) If you can't find the law you need under your state's insurance statutes, try the statutes listed under human rights or labor law.

The plant-closing laws of a few states also may give you the right to continue group healthcare insurance coverage. (See Chart 4-2.)

5. Individual healthcare insurance

Even if your state doesn't have a law that gives you the right to continue group healthcare coverage after employment ends, it may have a law that requires healthcare insurance companies to offer you the option of converting your group policy to individual coverage.

Individual coverage typically is much more expensive than group coverage, and the coverage limits are usually much lower than those offered under group coverage. For example, a group healthcare insurance policy often won't have any limit on total benefits paid during your lifetime, while individual coverage often limits total lifetime benefits to $500,000. However, laws that give you the right to convert to individual healthcare coverage usually don't require you to lose your job to be eligible.

If your employer cancels your group healthcare coverage but continues to employ you—an increasingly common situation—these laws can give you the right to convert to individual coverage until you can find a better insurance deal, or a job with better healthcare insurance benefits. You can usually find the laws guaranteeing you the right to convert group healthcare insurance coverage to individual coverage among the statutes governing your state's insurance industry. Some states have a consumer complaint section in their insurance departments that can help you with this.

6. Utilization review

If your healthcare insurance coverage provider is among the growing number that use a process called utilization review, you may get caught in the crossfire of one of the greatest workplace legal feuds in history if you become ill.

The idea behind utilization review is simple: By having someone other than your doctor take a look at your medical problem and approve or disapprove the things your doctor recommends, insurance companies can cut down on treatments that are unnecessary and expensive. The savings can then be passed along to the employers and employees who are finding it ever more difficult to pay for healthcare insurance coverage.

Most physicians hate utilization review, and the reason for their attitude is simple: Any process that prevents doctors from prescribing unnecessary treatment significantly reduces the charges that they can bill to your insurance company. For example, a study done by Blue Cross of Illinois in the 1980s showed that one-third of all hysterectomies performed in that state—at an average cost of more than $10,000 each—were unnecessary.

But employers like utilization review. So lawyers have found a lucrative place for themselves in the middle of that opinion clash—routinely filing lawsuits on behalf of doctors, employers and their insurance companies. And in 1990, a California appeals court ruling paved the way for employees to file lawsuits over utilization review problems. The court held that the parents of a patient who died 20 days after being discharged from a hospital's drug abuse program may sue a review agency and two insurance companies who were involved in pressuring the patient's doctor to have him discharged (*Wilson v. Blue Cross of Southern California.*, 271 Cal. Rptr. 876 (1990)).

UTILIZATION REVIEW AND INSURANCE COVERAGE

Until and unless the legal feud over utilization review is settled, employees need to be particularly careful in making sure they understand what role the utilization review concept would play in their healthcare if they became ill and needed to file a claim.

Here are some questions you may want to ask about your coverage:

1. Does my healthcare insurance coverage include a provision for utilization review?

2. If so, who will perform the review? Will it be someone on the company's staff, someone on the insurance company's staff, or an outside agency?

3. What kind of professional credentials are required of the people who would review my doctor's recommendations for treating me?

4. What methods does my healthcare insurance coverage use to enforce its utilization review decisions? For example, some healthcare insurance plans merely compile lists of doctors whose charges are habitually high, and then try to talk them into exercising restraint. Others use more aggressive tactics, such as reducing by 25% the fees paid to doctors who fail to obtain permission from the insurance company before performing a treatment on a patient.

5. Do I have the option of electing to participate in a healthcare insurance plan that doesn't include utilization review? If so, will it cost me more to be covered by that plan?

6. If my doctor or I disagree with a decision made by a reviewer, would I have the option of rejecting the utilization reviewers' decision?

Having this information isn't likely to keep you completely out of the utilization review feud, but at least you'll understand what's happening to you and what options you have if you get caught in it.

B. Pensions

Programs that provide income to people after they've left the workforce because of their advancing age have been lumped under one label: pensions.

Originally invented to soothe the fears of early factory workers about what would happen to them after they became too old and weak to tend the machines, pensions have evolved into a huge and complex world unto themselves.

1. Social Security retirement benefits

The government's income system for people 55 and over created by the passage of the Social Security Act in 1935 wasn't meant to be a pension program as much as insurance against extreme poverty in the later years of life. And, although Social Security benefit checks for retirees have become increasingly lucrative in recent years, they still don't provide enough income for most people to maintain their pre-retirement lifestyles. Consequently, many people rely on some form of private pension—however small—to enhance their incomes after they retire.

There are many ins and outs to the Social Security retirement benefit system—most of them dependent on factors such as the type of job you worked, length of time at work and the age at which you retire.[2] If you want to estimate the amount of Social Security benefits you're entitled to receive after you've retired from your job, complete and submit the Social Security Administration's Form SSA-7004-PC-OP1, Request for Earnings and Benefit Estimate Statement. You can obtain one from the Social Security Administration office closest to you. (Disability insurance benefits available under Social Security are discussed in Chapter 8, Section F.)

2. Private pensions

The amount of money tied up in various type of plans is so enormous that even a minor moodswing among private pension managers can send the stock markets zooming upward or crashing downward. And as can be expected

---

[2]For more detailed information on these matters is *Social Security, Medicare and Pensions: The Sourcebook for Older Americans* by Joseph L. Matthews (Nolo Press).

whenever large amounts of other people's money are involved, a huge subculture of lawyers, accountants, actuaries, insurance agents and consultants has developed specifically to shape and control the pension industry through technical and convoluted laws.

This book can't begin to cover all aspects of pension law. But it discusses the most important laws concerning your right to collect the pension benefits for which you've worked.

3. Pension terms defined

Jargon dominates the pension industry. However, these definitions of some of the terms you commonly see in connection with benefits will get you well on the road to understanding your pension rights and wrongs.

Defined benefit plan. A pension program through which the employer promises to pay the employee a fixed amount of money, usually monthly, after the employee retires. Although a defined benefit plan is what usually comes to mind when people think about pensions, this type of plan has been replaced in many cases by the defined contribution type.

Defined contribution plan. A pension program through which the employer promises to pay a certain amount into the employee's retirement account while the employee is working, but doesn't promise a specific amount of income for the employee after retirement. Your employer may promise to pay $50 per month per employee into the company's pension plan, for example, but the size of the pension check you would receive each month after retirement would vary according to the interest rate paid on your pension account and other economic factors.

Defined contribution plans can take several different forms, such as 401(k) plans through which your employer and you can contribute jointly to retirement savings. For the most part, defined contribution pension plans are individual savings accounts that have some tax advantages—but also some limitations on withdrawals and reinvestment—that regular savings accounts don't have.

Distress termination. When a company ends its pension plan because it is filing for protection under the bankruptcy laws or because the rights of the pension plan's participants would be endangered if the plan continued.

Employee Retirement Security Act. The Employee Retirement Security Act of 1974 (ERISA), is the most important federal law governing pensions and other employee benefit programs. Administered by the U.S. Department of Labor, the Internal Revenue Service and the Securities and Exchange Commission, ERISA sets minimum standards for pensions and attempts to guarantee that pension rights cannot be unfairly taken from or denied to workers.

Pension Benefit Guaranty Corporation. An organization that insures many pension plans in the United States, the PBGC is half private and half public. It's supposed to get its money from insurance premiums paid by the pension plans it covers, but it regularly turns to the federal government for money when it runs short.

Plan administrator. The person or organization in charge of managing your pension program. Most of the responsibility for operating your pension plan according to law rests with the plan's administrator.

Standard termination. When a company brings its pension plan to an end voluntarily.

Vesting. This means getting a legal right to collect from a benefit program. For example, some pension plans require you to work a certain number of years for a company before you have any right to a pension. Once you complete the required number of years with that company, you continue to have rights to the pension plan even if you no longer work there. The process of racking up the required number of years is called vesting; a person who has worked the required number of years is said to be vested in the pension plan.

4. Eligibility for pension coverage

There's no law that requires an employer to offer a pension plan. However, if a company chooses to do so, ERISA requires that the pension plan spell out who is eligible for coverage. Pension plans don't have to include all workers, but they cannot legally be structured to benefit only the top executives or otherwise discriminate. The plan administrator for your company's pension program can provide you with details of whether or not you're eligible to participate.

If you're eligible to participate in your employer's pension program, the administrator must provide you with the documents you need to understand the plan. The documents that your plan's administrator is required to provide to you are:

- **A summary plan description:** Usually published as a booklet, this document explains the basics of how your plan operates. ERISA require that you be given the summary plan within 90 days after you begin participating in a pension plan, and that you must be given any updates to it.

  This document will also tell you the formula for vesting in the plan (if it's a plan that includes vesting) the formula for determining your defined benefits or the defined contributions that your employer will make to the plan, and whether or not your pension is insured by the PBGC.

- **A summary annual report:** This document is a yearly accounting of your pension plan's financial condition and operations.

- **Survivor coverage data:** This is a statement of how much your plan would pay to any surviving spouse should you die first.

  Your plan administrator is also required to provide you with a detailed, individual statement of the pension benefits you've earned, but only if you request it in writing or are going to stop participating in the plan because, for example, you change employers. Note, however, that ERISA gives you the right to only one such statement from your plan per year.

5. Early retirement

Each pension plan has its own rules on the age you must reach before filing for benefits. Most private pension plans consider 65 to be the normal retirement age. However, some private pensions also offer the option of retiring early, usually at age 55. If you elect early retirement, however, expect your benefit checks to be much smaller than they would be if you waited until the regular retirement age.

Many corporations now use the early retirement option of their pension plans to cut staff. By making a temporary offer to increase the benefits available to those who opt to retire early, these corporations create an incentive for employees to volunteer to leave the company's payroll before turning age 65. Sometimes companies make the early retirement offer even more attractive by throwing in a few months of extra severance pay.

Some early retirement offers are very lucrative, and some are not. Before accepting one, study the details carefully, keeping in mind that the offer you accept may have to serve as your primary income for the rest of your life. (See Chapter 5, Section G, on the Older Workers Benefit Protection Act.)

Because pension law is so specialized and complex, you may also want to consult a lawyer who specializes in it if the terms of your employer's early retirement offer to you aren't clear.

6. Filing for benefits

The summary plan of your pension program will spell out when you become eligible for benefits, and how to file a claim for them. It will also describe how you can appeal the decision if you are denied benefits under your pension plan.

Under ERISA, the administrator of your pension plan must approve or deny your claim for benefits within 90 days after you file it. If the administrator of your plan fails to respond within 90 days, assume that your claim has been denied. ERISA makes it a crime for an employer to fire, suspend, or otherwise discriminate against or punish employees or their beneficiaries for pursuing their rights to pension benefits.

7. Appealing a denial of benefits

Each pension plan has its own system for appeals. If your pension plan denies you benefits to which you're entitled, its administrator is required to advise you about how to appeal that decision. You'll have 60 days to request such an appeal, and the group that reviews your appeal will, in most cases, have 120 days after you file it to issue its decision. ERISA requires that you be given a plain English explanation of the decision on your appeal.

If your pension plan's internal review system also rules against you, you can further appeal that decision by contacting the Pension and Welfare Benefits Programs Office of the Department of Labor. (See the Appendix for contact information.) If your claim to pension benefits continues to be denied, and you believe that you are being unfairly denied those benefits, ERISA also gives you the right to file a federal suit against your pension plan. You'll probably need the help of a lawyer to file that type of lawsuit. (See Chapter 13, Section D.)

8. Terminated plans

If your employer terminates your pension plan, your plan administrator is required to notify you in writing of the approaching termination at least 60 days before the plan ends. This is true whether it's a standard termination or a distress termination.

If the termination is a standard one, that means that your plan has enough assets to cover its obligations. Your plan's administrator is required to notify you in such cases of how the plan's money will be paid out, and what your options are during the pay-out period.

If the termination is being done under distress, the PBGC may become responsible for paying your pension benefits. If your plan isn't insured by the PBGC and it is terminated under distress, your pension rights may be reduced—or you may lose them.

9. Mismanaged plans

If you think you can prove that the people managing your pension plan are not handling your pension money for your best interests—for example, making questionable investments—ERISA gives you the right to file a lawsuit against them in federal court. You'll probably need to hire a lawyer to help you with this type of lawsuit. (See Chapter 13, Section D.)

If you want more detail on your rights to receive benefits from a private pension plan, a good source is a booklet entitled "A Guide to Understanding Your Pension Plan," which you can get free from the American Association of Retired Persons (AARP). Or contact the Pension Rights Center, which offers a number of publications relating to pensions. (Contact specifics for both organizations are listed in the Appendix of this book.)

C. Other Employee Benefits

Companies have invented so many types of employee benefit programs that it's impractical to list them all. Many companies have a person or department that has been given responsibility for managing all benefits programs. Larger companies usually have an employee handbook that gives details about them. If your company has neither of these, a little asking around at work will usually lead you to the central point for obtaining all the benefits to which you're entitled.

Here's a rundown of three benefit programs that companies commonly offer in addition to healthcare insurance and pensions.

1. Life insurance

One of the least expensive benefits that a company can offer to its employees is term life insurance; that is, life insurance that pays off only if you die during the policy term—usually 5, 10 or 20 years. If you die during this period, your survivors will be paid whatever value the policy specifies, typically $10,000 to $50,000. However, if you live longer, there is no pay-off as the policy has no cash value.

Many employers automatically purchase a term life insurance policy for each employee who has completed enough time on the job to qualify for the company's benefit program. In some cases, your employer will pay for the first $10,000 of term life coverage or so—and you'll have the option of purchasing additional coverage under the same plan.

You can buy term life insurance yourself, but there are a lot of high-priced bad deals waiting out there for individuals shopping for their own term life insurance. In most cases, you'll do better by purchasing life insurance coverage through your employer's group plan. Even if you eventually leave that job, you'll usually have the option of converting the company life insurance coverage to an individual policy with premiums less expensive than you can find by shopping around on your own.

2. Disability insurance

If an illness or injury not covered by workers' compensation (discussed in Chapter 8, Section D) keeps you out of work so long that you use up all the paid sick leave that your company provides, disability insurance is the most likely source of replacement income. There are two types of disability insurance, public and private.

Public disability coverage provided by the Social Security system (discussed in Chapter 8, Section F) is valuable. However, it typically leaves you with large gaps in your income while you're waiting to qualify, and a level of income far below that which you need to maintain your pre-disability lifestyle.

To bridge these gaps, there is private disability insurance. There are short-term versions, which give you a few months of income if you become disabled, and long-term versions to give you income for many years—or even for life. The costs of these policies vary, of course, with the amount and length of coverage provided.

Some employers pay all the costs of disability insurance but some require you to pay part of the cost if you decide to be covered. You can shop for your own disability coverage, but group plans offered by your employer are usually a better deal and may offer you the option of continuing coverage on your own should you leave your job.

LEARNING WHILE YOU'RE EARNING THROUGH INDEPENDENT STUDY

For many working people, the subject of continuing education has become a stress point. They know that increased knowledge is the surest route to greater success, but their families and job responsibilities and, in some areas, growing traffic jams make it nearly impossible to get to a formal campus after the workday ends or on weekends.

Even in companies that offer very generous tuition reimbursement programs, many employees can't find time to take advantage of those benefits.

Two very good ways to relieve that stress are often overlooked: learning by computer and learning by mail. If you own or have access to a personal computer, you can plug into college-level courses through The Electronic University Network. If you don't have access to a computer, you can still further your education from the comfort of your home by using *The Independent Study Catalog*, published by Peterson's Guides. It lists dozens of accredited colleges and universities throughout the United States that offer courses through the mail. (Contacts for both of these resources are listed in the Appendix.)

If you have not accumulated many college credits and the thought of taking many years to earn a conventional degree part-time discourages you, look into the certificate options offered by some independent study programs. You may be able to earn a certificate in business administration, for example, by taking a dozen courses directly related to running a business—while skipping all those elective courses in such subjects as Ancient Art and the History of Philosophy that are typically required to earn a traditional degree.

3. Company-paid tuition

Many employers recognize that continuing education can make their employees more productive, so they offer to pay all or part of the cost of certain types of schooling that employees pursue outside working hours.

You can expect your employer to set some guidelines for the type of continuing education it will finance, how many dollars it is willing to spend on your education and at what point in the educational process it will issue tuition reimbursement to you. For example, your company's tuition program may limit the amount it will pay for up to 12 credit hours per year at an accredited college or university if you successfully complete courses with a grade point average of 2.0 or better. In some companies, tuition reimbursement is limited to courses that are connected with your job.

So before you commit to a continuing education program, check with the person or department that administers your company's benefit program to make sure when and how much of the tuition the company will pay.

Chart 9-1

STATE HEALTH INSURANCE CONTINUATION LAWS

This is a synopsis of state laws that give you the right to continue group health insurance after leaving the employment of the company sponsoring the insurance.

Arkansas

Ex-employees and their spouses have the right to continue group insurance coverage for 120 days after the coverage would have ended because of a change in employment status. Ark. Stat. Ann. §23-86-114 (1987)

Colorado

Ex-employees who were terminated and had been covered for at least three months by group healthcare insurance have the right to continue that coverage 90 days or until re-employed, whichever comes first. Colo. Rev. Stat. §10-8-116 (1989)

Connecticut

Ex-employees have the right to continue group health insurance for 78 weeks after the coverage would have ended, or until they are covered by another group plan, whichever comes first. Conn. Gen. Stat. §38-262d (1988)

Florida

Ex-employees who were terminated and had been covered by group health insurance for at least three months have the right to covert the coverage to an individual policy. Fla. Stat. §627.6675 (1989)

Illinois

Ex-employees who were terminated and had been covered by group health insurance for at least three months have the right to continue group coverage unless they are covered by another group plan. Ill. Ann. Stat. Ch. 73 §979.2 (1987)

Iowa

Ex-employees who were terminated have the right to continue group health insurance, but some types of coverage such as prescription drug benefits are excluded. Iowa Code Ann. §509B.3 (1988)

Kentucky

Ex-employees who had been covered by group health insurance for at least three months have the right to continue that coverage. Ky. Rev. Stat. Ann. §304.18-110 (1988)

Maryland

Ex-employees who were terminated and had been covered by group health insurance for at least three months have the right to continue that coverage. Md. Ann. Code Art. 48A, §§354FF, 477K and 490G (1986)

Massachusetts

Group healthcare insurance plans must cover involuntarily laid-off employees for 39 weeks after the layoff. Mass. Gen. Laws Ann. Ch. 175 §110G (1987)

Minnesota

Ex-employees who quit or were terminated for reasons other than gross misconduct have the right to continue group healthcare coverage for 18 months after it would otherwise end or until they become covered by another group plan, whichever comes first. Minn. Stat. Ann. §62A.17 (1989)

Missouri

Ex-employees have the right to continue group healthcare insurance for up to nine months after it would otherwise end. Mo. Ann. Stat. §376.428 (1989)

Nevada

Employers must give employees upon termination written notice of how to obtain a replacement policy from the insurer that provides the company's group healthcare insurance. Nev. Rev. Stat. §608.1585 (1986)

New Mexico

Ex-employees have the right to continue group healthcare insurance coverage for up to six months after it would otherwise end. N.M. Stat. Ann. §59-18-16(a) (1988)

North Dakota

Ex-employees who had been covered by group healthcare insurance for at least three months have the right to continue that coverage. N.D. Cent. Code §26.1-36-23 (1987)

Ohio

Ex-employees who were terminated have the right to continue group healthcare insurance coverage. Ohio Rev. Code. Ann. §1737.30 (1985)

Rhode Island

Ex-employees who were terminated have the right to continue group healthcare insurance coverage for up to 18 months after it would otherwise end. R.I. Gen. Laws §27-19.1-1 (1988)

South Dakota

Ex-employees have the right to continue group healthcare insurance coverage for up to 18 months after it would otherwise end. S.D. Codified Laws Ann. §58-18-7.5 (1989)

Tennessee

Ex-employees who had been covered by group healthcare insurance for at least three months have the right to continue that coverage for up to three months after it would otherwise end. Tenn. Code Ann. §56-7-1501 (1988)

Utah

Ex-employees have the right to covert group healthcare insurance coverage to an individual policy. Utah Code Ann. §§ 31A-22-501 to 715 (1986)

Wisconsin

Ex-employees who had been covered by group healthcare insurance for at least three months have the right to continue coverage or convert it to an individual policy, unless they were fired for misconduct. Wis. Stat. §632.897 (1988)

10

Parents' Workplace Rights

As recently as the 1950s, the majority of American families were rigidly organized around a wage-earning father and a housekeeping mother who typically bore nearly all of the responsibility for raising the family's children.

But the structure of the typical American household has changed dramatically in the decades since. Today, neither men nor women have a monopoly on—or all the responsibility for—working outside the home or raising children.

A. The Income Flip-Flop

It would be nice to say that this change in parental roles was due to an intentional effort to give equal responsibilities to men and women at work and at home. But, in fact, it is often the result of workplace flip-flops that few people anticipated just a few years ago.

For example, it is becoming increasingly common for the income potential of the partners in a household to become the reverse of what their parents regarded as normal.

Example: When Harry and Janet met, he was a highly paid corporate manager and she a poorly paid licensed practical nurse. During their first five years together, Janet attended weekend college and moved up to being a physical therapist. Harry, meanwhile, was dismissed from his managerial job as part of a corporate downsizing, and the only other acceptable job he's been able to find is as a store manager with an auto parts retailing chain. Harry's income potential is now about half of Janet's, so when they had their first child, the logical decision was to have Janet return to work as soon as possible. Harry took a three-month parental leave to care for their baby until it was old enough to be placed in a daycare program.

Today's responsibilities of being a good parent and at the same time earning a living are likely to compete energetically for any parent's time. And a new set of workplace rights is slowly emerging from that competition between work and family responsibilities.

PARENTS WILL GAIN MORE RIGHTS IN COMING YEARS

Although there are now only a few laws guaranteeing the rights of parents in the workplace, expect to see many more of them.

Working peoples' need to merge their careers and family responsibilities comfortably has grown so compelling that politicians won't be able to ignore it much longer.

This prediction is bolstered by the results of two recent surveys.

The first was conducted by a workplace advocacy group, Formerly Employed Mothers At Loose Ends (FEMALE). Fully 48% of the stay-at-home mothers who responded to that survey said they would be working outside the home if they could find a job that accommodated their family responsibilities by allowing them to use flexible scheduling. And 96% said they had definite plans to return to work outside their homes once their children are grown and gone. (See the Appendix for details on how to contact FEMALE.)

The second survey was conducted by the law firm of Jackson, Lewis, Schnitzler & Krupman, headquartered in New York City. It found that, within a year after New Jersey enacted a family leave law in 1990, 70% of the 120 companies surveyed in that state had received requests for such leaves.

B. Federal Law and Parents

There is no federal law that specifically grants parents a right to take leaves from their jobs. But the most sweeping workplace rights for parents come from Title VII of the Civil Rights Act of 1964—which was amended in 1978 by the Pregnancy Discrimination Act (PDA) to clearly outlaw discrimination against women on the basis of pregnancy, childbirth or any related medical condition.

1. What is covered by Title VII

Title VII specifies that:

- Pregnant women employees who need time off from work must be treated the same as employees who take time off because of other medical conditions. This protection includes women who must take time off from work to recover from an abortion.

Example: A company that allows employees to return to work with full seniority and benefit rights after taking time off for a surgical operation and recovery must similarly reinstate women who take time off because of a pregnancy.

- A pregnant woman cannot be required to take a leave from work during her pregnancy if she remains able to do her job.

Example: Judy's pregnancy is proceeding without problems, and she has no difficulty performing her job as an office manager. Even though she is a week overdue to deliver, according to her doctor's calculations, her employer can't force her to take off work in anticipation of labor.

- An employer cannot refuse to hire or promote a woman solely because she is pregnant.

Example: Rachel is the most qualified applicant for a job, but is six months pregnant. The company cannot choose another applicant simply because it doesn't want to have to find a replacement for Rachel when she takes a leave to give birth.

- An employer cannot refuse to provide healthcare insurance benefits that cover pregnancy if it provides such benefits to cover other medical conditions.

Example: The Dumont Company provides complete hospitalization insurance to spouses of female employees, but has a $500 cap on childbirth coverage for spouses of male employees. This policy is illegal under the PDA.

- A woman cannot be forced to take a minimum amount of time off from work after giving birth.

Example: Elizabeth and George have decided that she will continue her career while he takes primary responsibility for raising their children and taking care of their home. Two weeks after their baby is born, Elizabeth is physically able to resume her work. It would probably be illegal gender discrimination if her employer required Elizabeth to stay away from work an additional month to recover from childbirth.

WORKPLACE BENEFITS FOR MOTHERS AREN'T A NEW IDEA

Although current controversies may make it seem new, the idea that motherhood should be given special treatment in the workplace has been endorsed around the world since the early 20th century.

One of the oldest official recognitions of the special workplace needs of mothers is a resolution passed in 1919 by the International Labor Organization or ILO—an organization of workplace rights advocates that in 1946 became an agency of the United Nations. Known as Convention No. 3, the resolution called for maternity leaves during which the female industrial workers would be given financial support and medical care—both paid for by the government or some form of publicly financed insurance.

In 1952, the ILO went two steps further. Its proposal extended maternity leaves to women working in agriculture, and stated that maternity income benefits should equal at least two-thirds of a woman's normal earnings (Convention No. 103).

However, despite the passing of many decades, neither of the ILO's resolutions endorsing maternity rights in the workplace have been turned into U.S. law.

2. Men's rights to leaves

Under Title VII, an employer must grant men the same options for taking leave from their jobs to care for a child as it grants to women. To do otherwise would constitute illegal discrimination based on gender.

> **Example:** Steven works for a company whose employment policies include a 12-week unpaid leave for women who give birth to or adopt a child. If his employer refuses to allow Steven to take such a leave to adopt a child, he can file a complaint against his employer under Title VII, alleging gender discrimination.

However, a study released by the U.S. Small Business Association in 1991 showed that this is one area where Title VII is routinely violated: Most companies offer some type of leave for childbirth to female workers, the study found, but less than 8% offer the same option to their male employees.

For details about who is covered by Title VII and how to file a complaint under it, see Chapter 5, Section C. But first read Section C of this chapter to see if your state offers a more direct approach.

C. State Laws and Parents' Rights

Several states have laws that specifically grant employees the right to take leaves for childbirth or other parental responsibilities. Although the rights they guarantee differ greatly from state to state, these laws can be divided into two basic categories:

- new-parent laws, which deal with pregnancy, childbirth and adoption; and

- parental responsibility laws, which cover such events as a child having disciplinary trouble at school. (See Charts 10-1 and 10-2 at the end of this chapter.)

Anti-discrimination laws often can be applied to such leaves only through slow-moving complaints to the Equal Employment Opportunity Commission, or through complex and expensive lawsuits. But, in general, state laws that grant new-parent and parental-responsibility leaves offer a clear basis for enforcing your right to take such a leave.

For example, in Oregon, you can file a complaint with the state labor department against an employer who refuses to allow you to take a leave for childbirth. And in New Jersey, you can ask the state attorney general's office to file a lawsuit against an employer who violates your rights to take a parental leave.

Each state has different rules. State laws governing new-parent and parental-responsibility leaves vary greatly in such aspects as the length of notice that an employee must give before taking a leave, whether or not benefits must be continued and at whose expense, how rights to parental leaves are divided when both parents are employed by the same company and how the laws can be enforced.

A few states also include in these laws the right to take an unpaid leave from work to care for a sick spouse, parent or in-law. But these provisions vary greatly from state to state as well.

If you need more detail on your state's leave laws than is contained in Charts 10-1 and 10-2, read the actual laws at a local library. (See Chapter 13, Section E.)

1. Most leaves are unpaid

In general, state new-parent and parental-responsibility leave laws require employers to grant an employee only a leave without pay.

Paid leaves are uncommon, but some companies—typically very large ones or very small ones that regard their employees as family members—do have them. Check with your supervisor well before you anticipate needing a leave to determine whether your workplace has such a policy. Make sure that you fulfill all the requirements for receiving your regular pay during the time that you're away from work—such as giving your employer adequate notice of your need to take such a leave.

2. Comply with time restrictions

Most state laws granting new-parent and parental-responsibility leaves specify time limits, such as how long in advance you must advise your employer of your intent to take such a leave or how many weeks you can take.

Complying with those limits will, of course, safeguard your legal right to take a leave. Respecting the time limits will also lessen the possibility of your employer becoming inconvenienced by your absence from work and then searching for some other reason to dismiss you from your job. Your employer's needs may seem insignificant when you're needed at home, but this is one situation where a little mutual respect goes a long way toward peaceful relations.

Unpredictable developments such as a baby's illness can require you to extend a leave. If you've been fair with your employer in taking your leave, then the employer is more likely to be fair with you if you need to extend it.

3. Check for pay-back clauses

A common sore point with employers is that some employees officially state that they're taking a parental leave of only a few months, but then decide to become full-time parents and quit their jobs outright.

This strategy is particularly popular among employees who are having their first baby because, at the very least, it seems to allow the option of going back to a job after experimenting with a few months of stay-at-home parenting.

But this strategy isn't new, and most employers have seen it before. Many companies now require employees who take paid parental leaves and then decide to leave their jobs permanently to pay back all compensation received during the leave.

To enforce this type of policy, employers usually need you to sign an agreement in which you agree to make such a repayment, so be careful to read and understand anything you sign in connection with any paid leave that's granted to you.

The law in at least one state, Vermont, requires employees who decide not to return to their jobs after a new-parent leave to pay back the money they were paid during the leave even if there is no written agreement to do so.

4. State anti-discrimination laws

Some state laws also forbid workplace discrimination on the basis of gender. In states that have no specific new-parent or parental-responsibility leave laws, anti-discrimination laws often can be used to establish a right for parents to take time off from work for pregnancy and childbirth.

Example: Jim is a salesperson for a trucking company in Nebraska that expects its salespeople to entertain clients by taking them out for dinner and to sporting events. Because of all of the after-hours socializing that the job requires, most of the company's salespeople have never married or are divorced. However, Jim is married and has three young children at home. Because he believes in sharing the responsibilities of parenthood as much as is possible with his wife, Jim tries to avoid spending more than one evening per week entertaining his employer's clients.

One day, Jim's boss told him he was fired because he was spending too much time at home instead of with clients. "Being married is something that we frown upon here," the boss said. But because Nebraska's laws forbid workplace discrimination on the basis of marital status, Jim may be able to win a wrongful-discharge lawsuit against his former employer.

The anti-discrimination laws of at least 21 states include marital status among the factors that may not be used as the basis for work-related discrimination. Alaska goes a step further, protecting even unmarried couples by specifically listing parenthood as an illegal basis for discrimination. (See Chart 5-1 for a listing of state anti-discrimination laws.)

5. How to enforce your rights

The most direct and constructive way to exercise your right to take a new parent or other parental leave is to know your rights and to make sure your employer is aware of them as long before you need to take a leave as possible. Nearly all state new-parent and parental-responsibility leave laws have been enacted recently and your employer may be sincerely unaware of them. So this is one area of law in which you're likely to know much more than your employer.

If you've made your employer aware of your right to take such a leave and the employer refuses to comply, the options available to you will vary with the situation.

- If your problem seems to be merely a matter of disagreement over interpretation of the law, you can suggest to your employer that a mediator or arbitrator be used to help settle the dispute. (See Chapter 13, Section A.)

- If your state is listed in Chart 10-1 or 10-2 as having a specific parental leave law, you may be able to have a state agency intervene in your case. The best way to determine where state help is available is to research you state's law in detail. (See Chapter 13, Section E.)

- If your case involves a violation of Title VII, you can file a complaint with the EEOC; if the EEOC fails to take action, you may be able to file a federal lawsuit on your own. (See Chapter 5, Section D.)

- If your case involves a violation of a state anti-discrimination law, your state may have an agency with which you can file a complaint. (See Chart 5-1.)

- If your state has no agency to enforce its law, you may be able to file a lawsuit on your own behalf. In some states, those who sue under new-parent and parental-responsibility leave laws are allowed to collect punitive damages, court fees and the cost of hiring a lawyer to help.

D. Balancing Work and Family: Other Ways to Cope

Some companies are trying to help employees cope with the conflict between work and family responsibilities by allowing them to put in some of their work hours at home.

1. Work-at-home agreements

These programs often involve a written agreement between the worker and the company that details who is responsible for any legal liabilities that arise from the work-at-home arrangement and how on-the-job time will be measured.

For example, a work-at-home agreement may specify that you are respon-sible for any damage that occurs to a company-owned laptop computer while it's being used in your home. If you're considering working under such an agreement, discuss it with your insurance agent to make sure that you're cov-ered for any losses that could become your responsibility under it. Most homeowners' and renters' insurance policies don't automatically cover busi-ness equipment, so you may have to purchase additional coverage.

Also, check the agreement against the wage-and-hour laws (discussed in Chapter 2) to make sure that neither you nor your employer would be break-ing the Fair Labor Standards Act through your work-at-home plan. In general, if you're not an exempt employee, the Act still applies even when you're working at home.

2. Help if you can't work

For an increasing number of people, the pressures of juggling work and family responsibilities are becoming virtually impossible. If you're one of these people, and none of the other alternatives discussed in this chapter can provide you the kind of relief you need to keep working, consider filing claims for unemployment insurance and workers' compensation.

Although neither of these programs was intended to deal with the conflict between work and family, the restrictions on who can collect from these pro-grams are being loosened rapidly.

If the responsibilities of caring for an ill child prevent you from going to work, for example, you may be eligible for unemployment insurance benefits. Or you may be able to qualify for workers' compensation payments if keeping up with your employer's expectations in the face of family problems has caused you to develop symptoms of work-related stress.

In most states, it's illegal to collect both unemployment insurance and workers' compensation payments at the same time. But you can file a claim for both, and then accept benefits from whichever program offers you the best support. (For details on these programs, see Chapter 8, Sections B through E.)

Chart 10-1

STATE LAWS REQUIRING NEW-PARENT LEAVES

Fourteen states and the District of Columbia have laws that specifically guarantee people employed in private industry the right to take work leaves because of pregnancy, childbirth or the adoption of a child.

Here is a synopsis of the basic rights granted to employees by state laws.

California

Female employees must be allowed to take up to four months unpaid leave for pregnancy or childbirth. Cal. Gov't. Code §12945 (1980)

Colorado

Employer policies applying to leaves for biological parents must also be extended to adoptive parents. Colo. Rev. Stat. §19-5-211 (1.5) (1988)

Connecticut

Employees must be allowed to take up to 24 weeks of unpaid leave within any two-year period upon the birth or adoption of a child. Employees who take such leaves must be allowed to return to their original job, or an equivalent job. Ct. Public Act No. 89-382 (1989)

District of Columbia

An employee who has worked with a company for at least one year, and who has worked at least 1,000 hours during the previous 12-month period, must be granted up to 16 weeks of unpaid leave during any 24-month period in connection with the birth or adoption of a child. Employees who take such leaves must be restored to their original jobs, or equivalents. D.C. Law 8-181 (1990)

Iowa

Female employees who are disabled by pregnancy, childbirth or related medical conditions must be granted an unpaid leave for the duration of their disability, up to a maximum of eight weeks. Iowa Code Ann. §601.a.6(2)(e) (1988)

Maine

An employee who has worked at least 12 consecutive months with a company employing at least 25 people must be granted up to eight consecutive weeks of unpaid leave for the birth of a child or the adoption of a child 16 years old or younger. Employees who take such leaves must be restored to their original jobs, or equivalent jobs. Me. Rev. Stat. Ann. §844 (1988)

Minnesota

A company employing 21 or more people must grant employees up to six weeks of leave for the birth or adoption of a child. However, only employees who have worked for the company an average of at least 20 hours per week for at least 12 months before the request for leave is made are covered. During the leave, the employer must offer the employee the option of continuing group healthcare insurance coverage. However, the employer is not required to pay for that coverage during the leave. Employees who take such leave must be returned to their original jobs, or equivalent jobs. Minn. Stat. Ann. §181.941 (1989)

Montana

An employer may not dismiss a woman because she becomes pregnant, or refuse to allow her to take a reasonable unpaid leave for pregnancy, or refuse to allow her to use accrued disability or other leave benefits for a pregnancy leave. Women also cannot be required to take pregnancy leave for an unreasonable period of time. A woman who takes a pregnancy-related leave must be returned to her original job, or its equivalent. Mont. Code Ann §49-2-310 and §49-2-311 (1987)

Nevada

The same leave policies that apply to other medical conditions must be extended to female employees before and after childbirth, or after a miscarriage. Nev. Rev. Stat. §608.159 (1988)

New Jersey

An employee who has worked for a company for at least 12 months, and who has worked at least 1,000 hours in the preceding 12 months, must be granted up to 12 weeks of unpaid leave in any 24-month period for the birth or adoption of a child under 18 years old, or one older than 18 who is incapable of self-care. Employees who take such leaves must be restored to their original jobs, or equivalents. N.J. Stat. Ann. 34:11B (1989)

Oregon

Employees who have worked with a company at least 90 days must be granted up to 12 weeks of unpaid leave for childbirth or the adoption of a child less than six years old. The employer may require employees to give 30 days notice of intent to take such a leave, and employees returning from such a leave must be returned to their original jobs, or equivalent jobs. Pregnant employees must also be given the right to transfer to a less strenuous job. Or. Rev. Stat. §659.360 (1987)

Rhode Island

Employers must grant employees who have worked for them for at least 12 consecutive months up to 13 weeks of unpaid leave for the birth or adoption of a child. Employees who take such leave must be restored to their original jobs, or equivalent jobs. R.I. Gen. Laws §§28-48-2-3 (1988)

Tennessee

Companies with 100 or more employees must grant up to four months of unpaid leave to any female employee for pregnancy or childbirth. If the employee gives the employer at least three months advance notice of her intent to take such a leave, or if a medical emergency makes the leave necessary, she must be restored to her original job or its equivalent upon returning to work. The employer must allow an employee who takes such a leave to continue benefits such as healthcare insurance, but the employer is not required to pay for the benefits during the leave period. Tenn. Code Ann. §4-21-408 (1988)

Vermont

Companies must allow female employees who have worked with them an average of at least 30 hours per week, for at least one year, to take up to 12 weeks of unpaid leave for pregnancy or childbirth, but the employee must provide the employer with written notice of her intent to take such a leave and of its anticipated duration. The employee must be allowed to use accrued vacation or sickness leave for up to six weeks of the maternity leave. The employee must also be given the option of continuing benefit programs at her own expense. After returning from such a leave, the employee must be restored to her original job or its equivalent. If the employee fails to return to the job after taking such a leave, she must refund to the employer any compensation paid to her during the leave, except payments for accrued vacation or sickness leave. Vt. Stat. Ann. 21 §472 (1989)

Washington

Companies grant employees up to 12 weeks of unpaid leave during any two-year period in connection with the birth or adoption of a child. The employee must provide the employer with at least 30 days advance notice in most situations. Employees who take such leaves must be restored to their original jobs or equivalent jobs. Wash. Rev. Code §49.78 (1989)

Chart 10-2

STATE PARENTAL-RESPONSIBILITY LAWS

Nine states and the District of Columbia have laws that give employees in private industry the right to take time off from work to deal with specific parental responsibilities such as caring for a child who is ill or attending school conferences concerning a child's behavior.

Here is a synopsis of the basic rights granted to employees by those laws.

California

An employer may not discriminate in any way against an employee who takes time off to attend a child's school conference scheduled under §48900.1 of the Education Code, provided that the employee gives the employer reasonable notice of the need to attend such a conference. Cal. Lab. Code §230.7 (1989)

Companies that employ 25 or more workers may not fire or otherwise discriminate against an employee who is a parent or guardian of any child in kindergarten, or in grades 1 through 12, for taking one four-hour leave from work each school year, per child, to visit the child's school. The employee must give the employer reasonable prior notice of the need for such a leave. Cal. Lab. Code §230.8 (1990)

Connecticut

Parents may take up to 24 weeks of unpaid leave within any two-year period to care for an ill child. Employees who take such leaves must be restored to their original jobs, or equivalent jobs. Ct. Public Act No. 89-382 (1989)

District of Columbia

An employee who has worked with a company for at least one year, and who has worked at least 1,000 hours in the preceding 12 months, must be granted up to 16 weeks of unpaid leave in any 24-month period in connection with the serious illness of a child. Employees who take such leaves must be restored to their original jobs, or equivalent jobs. D.C. Act 8-249 (1990)

Maine

An employee who has worked for more than 12 consecutive months for a company that employs at least 25 workers at a given site may take up to eight consecutive weeks of unpaid leave in any two-year period to care for an ill child who is 16 years old or younger. Employees who take such a leaves must be restored to their original jobs, or equivalent jobs. Me. Rev. Stat. Ann. § 844 (1988)

Minnesota

An employee may take up to 16 hours of unpaid leave per year to attend school conferences or classroom activities if those conferences or activities cannot be scheduled during nonwork hours. An employee may also use accrued paid vacation leave for these purposes. Minn. Stat. Ann. §181.9412 (1990)

An employee may use employer-provided paid sick leave to care for a sick child. Minn. Stat. Ann. §181.9413 (1990)

Nevada

An employee may take an unpaid leave to attend a conference with school officials concerning a child, or in connection with court action involving a child. Nev. Rev. Stat. Ch. 392 and Ch. 418 (1989)

New Jersey

An employee who has worked with a company for at least 12 months, and has worked at least 1,000 hours in the preceding 12 months, must be granted up 12 weeks of unpaid leave in any 24-month period in connection with a serious health condition of a child. Employees who take such leaves must be restored to their original jobs, or equivalent jobs. N.J. Stat. Ann. 34:11B (1989)

Rhode Island

A worker who has been employed by a company for 12 consecutive months must be granted up to 13 consecutive weeks of unpaid leave to care for a child who is seriously ill. Employees who take such leaves must be restored to their original jobs, or equivalent jobs. R.I. Gen. Laws §28-48-2 (1988)

Washington

An employee may use accrued sick leave to care for an ill child under age 18. An employee also may take up to 12 weeks of unpaid leave within any 24-month period to care for a child under 18 years old who is terminally ill. Employees who take such leaves must be restored to their original jobs, or equivalent jobs. If circumstances have changed to the point that no equivalent job is available, the employee must be given any vacant job for which he or she is qualified. Wash. Rev. Code §49.12.270 (1988) and §49.78 (1989)

Wisconsin

An employee may take up to two weeks of unpaid leave within any 12-month period to care for an ill child. This leave, when combined with any other family-related leave, may not exceed a total of eight weeks within a 12-month period. Wis. Stat. §103.10 (1988)

11

Keeping Your Workplace Safe

Although people are increasingly concerned about their health and physical well-being, safety on the job still isn't automatic—or even predictable. Workplace safety laws rely for their effectiveness on employees who are willing to report hazards in their work environments.

A. The Occupational Safety and Health Act

The federal law covering threats to workplace safety is the Occupations Safety and Health Act of 1970. That law created the Occupational Safety and Health Administration (OSHA) to enforce workplace safety, and the National Institute for Occupational Safety and Health (NIOSH) to research ways to increase workplace safety.

1. Employers covered by OSHA

Unlike many other laws which cover only companies with a minimum number of employees, OSHA covers nearly all private employers engaged in interstate commerce. By today's standards, that includes nearly every employer that uses the U.S. Postal Service to send messages to other states, or makes telephone calls to other states.

Farms owned and operated by a family are the only significant private employers exempted from OSHA coverage.

2. OSHA requirements

The Occupational Safety and Health Act requires all private employers to maintain a workplace that is as free of dangers to employees as is reasonably possible. The Act doesn't limit the types of dangers covered, so hazards ranging from things that cause simple cuts and bruises to the unhealthy effects of long-term exposure to some types of radiation are covered.

Under OSHA, the definition of a workplace isn't limited to the inside of an office or factory. The Act requires that work conditions be safe no matter where the work is performed—even when the workplace is an open field or a moving vehicle.

Depending on the types of hazards and workplaces involved, the employer's responsibility for creating and maintaining a safe workplace can include such diverse things as labeling potentially hazardous substances, upgrading or removing machinery that poses a danger, providing employees with special breathing apparatus to keep dust created by a manufacturing process from entering workers' lungs, improving lighting above work areas, vaccinating against diseases that can be contracted at work, or even tracking the effects of workplace conditions on employees' health through periodic medical examinations.

Employers are required to meet OSHA's safety standards for their specific industry. OSHA also requires employers to post a poster explaining workers' rights to a safe workplace in a conspicuous spot. If the workplace is outdoors, the poster must be displayed where employees are most likely to see it—such as a trailer where workers use a timeclock to punch in and out at a construction site.

These posters are supplied to employers by OSHA and commercial publishers. An employer's failure to display such posters is in itself a violation of OSHA rules that you can report to your local OSHA office if you wish.

3. Injury and illness reports

Within 48 hours of any workplace accident that results in the death of a worker or requires hospitalization of four or more workers, employers are required to report the accident to OSHA. Companies employing 10 or more people must also keep records of work-related injuries and illness among workers, and post a report on those injuries and illnesses for at least 30 days per year.

4. Retaliation is prohibited

Under OSHA, it is illegal for an employer to fire or otherwise discriminate against you for filing an OSHA complaint or participating in an OSHA investigation. OSHA can order an employer who violates this rule to return you to your job and to reimburse you for damages such as lost wages, the value of lost benefit coverages and the cost of searching for a new job.

B. Enforcing Your OSHA Rights

If you believe that your workplace is unsafe, your first action should be to make your supervisor at work aware of the danger as soon as possible. If your employer has an employee manual that designates a particular person or department as responsible for workplace safety, inform them of the danger.

In general, you will increase the chances of a complaint getting a quick and effective response if it's presented on behalf of a group of employees who all see the situation as a safety threat. And an employer who becomes angry over a safety complaint is much less likely to retaliate against a group of employees than against an individual.

Sometimes, workplace dangers are caught and corrected during unannounced inspections by OSHA. But these cover only a tiny percentage of all work situations. All but a very few of OSHA's actions against workplace hazards are initiated by complaints from employees or labor unions representing them.

1. Filing a complaint

If you've tried to take action inside your company to correct a workplace safety hazard but the danger continues, you can file a complaint by contacting the nearest OSHA office. Look under the Labor Department in the federal government section of your local telephone directory.

Your complaint should be filed on OSHA Form 7. You can request one from any OSHA office. You also have the option of telephoning your complaint to your nearest OSHA office, where a compliance officer will fill out a Form 7 for you and then send you the completed version for your approval and signature.

If requested to do so, OSHA must keep confidential your identity and that of any other employees involved in the complaint. Section 11 on Form 7 asks whether you want your identity to be kept secret, so be sure to check the section in that box that says "Do not reveal my name to the employer" if that's what you want.

Once you've completed your complaint form, file it with the nearest OSHA office. You can do this in person, but if you send it in by certified mail, you'll have proof that OSHA received it should it get mislaid in OSHA's offices. Keep a photocopy of your completed complaint form for your own files.

Upon receiving your complaint, OSHA will assign a compliance officer to investigate your case. The compliance officer will likely talk with you and your employer and inspect the work conditions that you have reported.

2. How complaints are resolved

A compliance officer who finds that the condition about which you complained poses an immediate danger to you and your co-workers can order the employer to immediately remove the danger from the workplace—or the workers from the dangerous environment.

Where the danger is particularly urgent or the employer has a record of violations, OSHA may get tough by asking the courts to issue an injunction—a court order requiring the employer to eliminate workplace hazards.

> **Example:** A group of pipeline workers complained to OSHA that the earth walls of the excavation in which they were working weren't well supported and could collapse on them. The OSHA compliance officer tried unsuccessfully to talk the employer into improving the safety of the situation.
>
> OSHA went into court and obtained an injunction forbidding work to continue within the excavation until the walls were shored up with steel supports.

If the danger is less immediate, the compliance officer will file a formal report on your complaint with the director of OSHA for your region. If the facts gathered by the compliance officer support your complaint, the regional director may issue a citation to your employer.

The citation will specify what work conditions must be changed to ensure safety of the employees, the timetable that OSHA is allowing for those changes to be made—usually known as an abatement plan—and any fines that have been levied against your employer.

> **Example:** Terri is a machine operator in an old woodworking shop that is still using lathes that throw a large quantity of wood dust into the air inside the shop. The wood dust appeared to be a hazard to the employees who breath it, and Terri was unsuccessful in resolving the problem with the shop's owner. She filed a complaint with OSHA.
>
> OSHA studied the air pollution in the shop and agreed that it was a threat to workers' health. It ordered the shop's owner to install enclosures on the lathes to cut down on the amount of dust put into the air, and filter-equipped fans throughout the shop to capture any wood dust that escapes from the enclosures. But because the lathe enclosures and fans needed to be custom-designed and installed, OSHA allowed the shop's owner six months to correct the situation.

In the meantime, OSHA ordered the shop's owner to immediately provide Terri and all the other people employed there with dust-filtering masks to wear over their mouths and noses. However, since OSHA regulations generally require employers to make the workplace safe and not just protect workers from an unsafe work situation, the masks are considered merely a temporary part of the long-term abatement plan.

3. Walking off the job

OSHA gives you the right to refuse to continue doing your job in extreme circumstances that represent an immediate and substantial danger to your personal safety.

You can't walk off the job and be protected by OSHA in just any workplace safety dispute, and this right cannot be used to protest general working conditions. But OSHA rules give you the right to walk off the job without being later discriminated against by your employer if the situation fits these definitions of a true workplace safety emergency:

- You asked your employer to eliminate the hazard and your request was ignored or denied. To protect your rights, it would be best to tell more than one supervisor about the hazard, or to call the danger to the attention of the same supervisor at least twice—preferably in front of witnesses.

- You didn't have time to pursue normal OSHA enforcement channels. In most cases, this means that the danger must be something that came up suddenly, and isn't a safety threat that you allowed to go unchallenged for days, weeks or months.

- Staying on the job would make a reasonable person believe that he or she faced a threat of serious personal injury or death because of the workplace hazard. If the hazard is something that you can simply stay away from—such as a malfunctioning machine in a work area that you don't have to enter—it probably wouldn't qualify as creating an emergency.

- You had no other reasonable choice but to walk off the job to avoid injury.

Example: Mike is a welder in a truck building plant. Shortly after starting work one day, he noticed that a large electrical cable running along the plant's ceiling had broken overnight, was coming loose from the hardware attaching it to the ceiling, and was dangling closer and closer to the plant floor. He and several of his co-workers immediately told their supervisor about the broken cable, but the supervisor did nothing about it. The group also told the supervisor's boss about the danger, but still nothing was done to correct it.

By about 11 a.m., the broken cable had dropped to the point where it was brushing against the truck body that Mike was welding. Sparks flew each time the cable and the truck body touched. Because he had a reasonable fear that an electrical shock transmitted from the broken cable could seriously injure or kill him, Mike walked off the job. His supervisor fired him for leaving work without permission. But because the danger fit OSHA's definitions of an emergency, OSHA ordered the company to reinstate Mike to his job with back wages—after first repairing the broken and dangling cable.

If you use the extreme option of walking off a job because of a safety hazard, be sure to contact your nearest OSHA office as soon as you're out of danger. Make a note of the name of the OSHA officer you spoke with, and the time that you reported the hazard. That way, you'll protect your right to be paid back wages and other losses from the time that the hazard forced you to walk away from work.

4. Tracking OSHA actions

Any citation issued by OSHA must be posted in a conspicuous place within the workplace it affects for at least three days. If the hazard specified in the citation is not corrected within three days after the citation is issued, then the citation must remain posted until it is corrected.

Compliance officers are required to advise those who originally filed a complaint of the action taken on it. If you need more information about the outcome of an OSHA investigation that affects your workplace, call, write or visit your local OSHA office.

THE IMPORTANCE OF BEING SPECIFIC

Like many other government agencies, OSHA is a huge bureaucracy that operates on computerized file numbers. So the best way to get prompt service and accurate information from OSHA is to be as specific as possible. In your dealings with OSHA, always mention the name of the company, the department of that company, the number assigned to the complaint that you're tracking and the date on which it was filed.

If OSHA has given your employer an extended time to remedy a workplace hazard, then you also have a right to request a copy of that abatement plan from your employer. Your other recourse is to obtain a copy from the OSHA compliance officer who handled your complaint.

5. Contesting an abatement plan

You have the right to contest an abatement plan granted to your employer by OSHA to correct a workplace hazard. To do so, send a letter expressing your intent to contest the plan to your local OSHA director within 15 days after the OSHA citation and announcement of the plan is posted in your workplace. You needn't list specific reasons for contesting the plan in this letter; all you need to make clear is that you think the plan is unreasonable.

Example:

                                    April 10, 1992

Ms. Mary Official
Regional Director
Occupation Safety and Health Administration
321 Main Street
Anycity, USA 55555

Dear Ms. Official:

As allowed by 29 U.S.C. Section 659(e), I wish to contest
the abatement plan agreed to by your agency and my employer, the Oldtime Mousetrap Company. This abatement
program resulted from a complaint that I filed with your
office on April 3, 1992. That complaint was assigned
number A-123456 by your office.

I contest this agreement because I believe that it is
unreasonable.

                        Sincerely,

                        Elmer Springmaker
                        456 Central Road
                        Anycity, USA 55550
                        123/555-5555

After it receives your letter, OSHA will refer the case to the Occupational Safety and Health Review Commission in Washington, D.C., an agency independent of OSHA. That commission will then send your employer a notice that the abatement plan is being contested.

This notice also will order the employer to post in the workplace affected an announcement that the plan is being contested. It will also require the employer to send a form that certifies the date on which that announcement was made back to the commission—with copies to OSHA, to you and to other employees who have contested the plan.

Then, everyone involved in the case has 10 days from the date the employer posted the contest notice to file an explanation of their viewpoints on the abatement plan with the commission. Copies must also be sent to all others involved in the case.

6. Presenting your views

The explanation you file need not be fancy; it should be as clear, brief and precise as possible. For example, if you've made a list of employee injuries that have already resulted from the hazard in your workplace, list the date, time, location and identity of the worker injured for each incident in your explanation.[1]

Your explanation need not be typewritten, but your odds of communicating your viewpoint effectively will be increased if it is. If you don't have access to a typewriter or computerized word processor, consider having your explanation typed by a commercial typing service. You can usually find them in the Yellow Pages of your local telephone directory.

---

[1]If you want to make your explanation as formal as possible, see Appendix II of *Legal Research: How To Find and Understand the Law* by Stephen Elias (Nolo Press) for guidance on how to write a legal memorandum.

Send your explanation by certified mail to:

Executive Secretary
Occupational Safety and Health Review Commission
1825 K Street, NW; Room 413
Washington, DC 20006

Be sure to include a cover letter—and to specify in it the name of the company involved, the number assigned to the case by the review commission and OSHA, your mailing address and telephone number. Send a copy to the OSHA office where you filed your original complaint, to your employer and to any people identified in the paperwork the commission sent to you as parties in the case. Also, be sure to save a copy of your cover letter, your explanation and any supporting documents that you send with it for your personal files.

After it has gathered all the statements on the case, the commission will typically turn them over to Labor Department lawyers who will attempt to meet with everyone who submitted statements and negotiate a resolution that is agreeable to all. The commission tries to negotiate settlements whenever possible, and by this point everyone involved will have had an opportunity to read and think about everyone else's viewpoints. So the odds are that your complaint will be resolved at this stage.

7. If negotiations don't work

When negotiations to reach a resolution are unsuccessful, the commission submits the case to an administrative law judge. These proceedings usually take at least a number of months—and sometimes years—depending upon the complexity of the workplace hazards involved.

Hearings before administrative law judges are very much like any other trial. Much time and money can be consumed in gathering evidence, and the hearings are usually scheduled during daytime hours when most employees are at work. You'll probably have to hire a lawyer to help if you decide to pursue your safety complaint successfully at this level. (See Chapter 13, Section D.)

You also have the right to appeal a decision by an administrative law judge for the Occupational Health and Safety Review Commission to the full commission or in federal court, but you'll probably have to hire a lawyer to help you at these levels, as well.

8. If you're punished for complaining

It is illegal for an employer to fire you or otherwise discriminate against you because you filed an OSHA complaint or assisted in investigating such a complaint. However, the Act doesn't authorize you to enforce this restriction by going directly into court; you must ask OSHA to intercede.

If you suspect illegal retaliation, you have 30 days from the time the illegal action took place to file a complaint about it with your local OSHA office.

The best way to file such a complaint is by using OSHA's Form 7. If you submit it to your local OSHA office by certified mail, you'll be able to prove when it was submitted should it get mislaid in OSHA's offices. Keep a photocopy of the completed complaint form for your personal files.

The outcome of illegal discrimination complaints filed under OSHA often turns on whether an employee can prove that interacting with OSHA was the reason for firing or other retaliation by the employer. So be sure to back up your complaint with as much documentation for your employer's action as possible. (For details on how to document a dismissal, see Chapter 4, Section C.)

Once you've filed a complaint about illegal job discrimination, OSHA has 90 days to respond. If you've shown that you were fired or otherwise punished because of complaining to OSHA, the compliance officer handling your complaint will attempt to convince your employer to reinstate you to your job with back pay, or whatever other remedy is appropriate.

For example, if you were demoted in retaliation for your OSHA complaint, the OSHA compliance officer would probably ask your employer to reinstate you to your original position. If OSHA is unsuccessful in talking your employer into reversing the effects of the illegal discrimination, it can sue your employer in federal court on your behalf.

9. Additional legal claims

Even though you have filed an OSHA complaint, you may still be able to file other types of lawsuits for the same legal wrong. For example, if OSHA fails to reverse illegal workplace discrimination prompted by your participation in an OSHA complaint, you may be able to file a lawsuit based on a tort such as intentional infliction of emotional harm. You'll probably need the help of an attorney to do so. (See Chapter 13, Section D.)

EMPLOYERS ARE RARELY CONVICTED IN WORKPLACE DEATH CASES

Although employers can be prosecuted for criminal negligence when an employee dies as a result of violations of OSHA regulations, such convictions are rare. In fact, from 1970 to 1990, only one employer was convicted and sent to jail for such a death.

The main reason for this low conviction rate is that, under OSHA, prosecutors must prove that an employer's violation of workplace safety rules was willful—a subjective standard.

For example, in 1985, a 23-year-old Massachusetts college student who was working a construction job when not in class died from electrocution when he grabbed a chain to steer a piece of pipe into a trench. The arm of the backhoe that was holding the chain and pipe aloft had come into contact with a high voltage electrical cable.

OSHA requires that construction equipment such as that backhoe be operated no less than 10 feet from live electrical lines. What's more, other workers at the construction site told police investigators that they had warned the employer earlier on the day of the accident to keep the backhoe arm away from the overhead wires. So the employer, who had been operating the backhoe at the time of the electrocution, was charged with criminal negligence.

Nevertheless, the employer was acquitted by a federal jury after a two-day trial because the jury decided that his actions leading to the electrocution were not, in fact, willful.

---

10.   Criminal prosecutions for workplace hazards

As noted, OSHA has the power in some situations to pursue criminal prosecutions against employers who fail to maintain a safe workplace, but it rarely does.

However, state prosecutors increasingly are bringing criminal charges such as reckless endangerment and even murder against employers whose behavior seriously endangers workers. This trend was given a boost in 1990 when the New York Court of Appeals ruled that complaints under the Occupational Safety and Health Act do not take the place of criminal actions against employers whose actions cause workers to be injured or killed. Other state courts have ruled differently, however, so the issue may need to be resolved ultimately by the U.S. Supreme Court.

In the meantime, you may want to contact your state's attorney general to inquire about the possibility of criminal action if your employer subjects you to work conditions that you consider to be a serious threat of injury or death to you or your co-workers and you aren't able to resolve your concerns through OSHA or other civil actions.

C. Pesticides in the Workplace

For people who work on farms, in other parts of the food industry and in gardening and lawn care companies to name just a few, misused and overused pesticides are one of the greatest threats to workplace safety. Heavy exposure to some of these chemicals can cause serious health problems and even death. For people with certain types of allergies, even small doses of some pesticides can cause severe illness.

However, in 1975, a federal court ruled that the U.S. Environmental Protection Agency (EPA)—not OSHA—is responsible for making sure that workers aren't injured by exposure to pesticides at work (*Organized Migrants in Community Action, Inc. v. Brennan*, 520 F. 2d 1161).

There have been some disputes between the EPA and OSHA over this ruling in recent years, and the situation remains legally unsettled. So if you believe that you or your co-workers are being exposed to dangerous doses of pesticides at work, the best thing to do is to file complaints with both OSHA and the EPA—and let them decide which agency controls your workplace.

WORKERS' GREATEST HEALTH THREAT: STRESS

All the evidence points to stress as the most widespread threat to physical well-being in the modern workplace. For example, the Bureau of National Affairs—a business research organization in Washington, D.C.—has estimated that as many as one million Americans are absent from work on any given day as a result of stress related to their jobs.

The National Safe Workplace Institute (listed in the Appendix) says that long-term exposure to work-related stress can cause heart attacks, migraine headaches, decreased immunity to viruses, depression, sleep and appetite disorders, high blood pressure and various muscle pains. The job factors most likely to cause such stress, according to the Institute, are repetitive and boring work, excessive monitoring by management, fear of death or injury on the job, sexual harassment, insufficient control over your work situation, lack of recognition for work accomplished, an overly large workload, fear of losing your job or being demoted, insufficient use of your workplace skills and lack of support from supervisors and co-workers.

The courts have been inconsistent in deciding whether employees can file lawsuits for personal injury caused by workplace stress. But in many states, illness caused by work-related stress can be the basis for a workers' compensation claim. (See Chapter 8, Section D.)

D. State and Local Safety Laws

Many states and municipalities have laws that can help to ensure a certain level of safety in the workplace. In 1991, California began enforcing the most powerful of these laws: It requires every employer in the state to have a written plan to prevent workplace injuries.

Safety laws vary greatly in what they require, how they are enforced and even which employers they cover. In some states, the amount you receive from a workers' compensation claim will be larger if a violation of a state workplace safety law contributed to your injury. (See Chapter 8, Section E.) You can research the details of the state and local safety laws that cover your workplace at a local law library or at the city hall of the community in which you work. (See Chapter 13, Section E.)

Often, the state and local laws you can use most quickly and easily to keep your workplace safe weren't intended specifically to ensure workplace safety, but are part of programs designed to ensure sanitation and public safety in general. Typically, these laws are part of health or building codes—which you can usually research at the local city hall.

For example, the health department of the city in which you work probably has the power to order an employer to improve restroom facilities that are leaking and causing unsanitary workplace conditions. And your local building inspector typically can order an employer to straighten out faulty electrical wiring that presents a shock or fire hazard to people working near that wiring.

1. Detecting hazardous substances

At least 38 states have laws that restrict or regulate the use, storage and handling of hazardous substances used in the workplace. These laws vary greatly from state to state, and the identification of toxic and otherwise hazardous substances is a very technical matter that most often is the responsibility of the state's labor department.

In some cases, workers detect that they're being exposed to hazardous substance when one or more of them notices that a health problem—a skin rash or eye irritation are common examples—coincides with work hours.

If you think that you're being subjected to hazardous substances in your workplace, follow your complaint to OSHA with a call to your state's labor department, which you can typically locate in the government section of your local telephone directory.

Example: Hanchung took a job as a forklift driver in a metal plating plant. After his first few hours at work, his eyes began to water and became badly reddened. On the way home from work, Hanchung visited a walk-in medical clinic, where the doctor used a cotton swab to take samples of skin residues from his face.

A few days later, the doctor told Hanchung that his problem with his eyes was a reaction to sulfuric acid that apparently was in the air where he worked, and had settled on his skin and eyes.

Hanchung filed a complaint with OSHA and his state's labor department. As a result of the joint investigation, OSHA ordered his employer to construct an enclosure around processing areas that use sulfuric acid, and to provide Hanchung and his co-workers with protective clothing to wear at work while the enclosures were being built.

2. Preventing additional injuries

Workplace hazards often become obvious only after someone has been injured by them. For example, an unguarded machine part that spins at high speed may not seem dangerous until someone's clothing or hair becomes caught in it. But even after a worker has been injured, employers sometimes fail—or even refuse—to recognize that something that hurt one person is likely to hurt another.

If you've been injured at work by a hazard that should be eliminated before it injures someone else, take these steps as quickly as possible after obtaining the proper medical treatment:

- File a claim for workers' compensation benefits so that your medical bills will be paid and you'll be compensated for your lost wages and injury. (See Chapter 8, Section E.) Workers' compensation claims can cost a company a lot of money, so they tend to focus an employer's attention on safety problems.

- Point out to your employer the continuing hazard created by the cause of your injury. As with most workplace safety complaints, the odds of getting action will be greater if you can organize a group of employees to do this.

- If your employer fails to eliminate the hazard promptly, file a complaint with OSHA and any state or local agency that you think may be able to help.

Always involve OSHA. Even if you opt to use a state or local law to remedy a safety hazard in your workplace, file a complaint with OSHA over the hazard at the same time. That way, you'll be able to claim OSHA's anti-discrimination protection if your employer decides to retaliate against you because you filed a safety complaint. (See the discussion of OSHA's anti-discrimination rules in Section A.)

E. Tobacco Smoke and the Workplace

OSHA rules apply to tobacco smoke only in the most rare and extreme circumstances, such as when contaminants created by a manufacturing process combine with tobacco smoke to create a workplace air supply so soupy and dangerous that it fails OSHA standards. Those standards, and the methods for comparing workplace air quality to them, are so technical that typically only OSHA agents or consultants who specialize in environmental testing are able to determine when the air quality falls below allowable limits.

But the bad effects of tobacco smoke on human health have been clearly established and even certified by the government. A recent report by the Environmental Protection Agency, for example, estimated that tobacco smoke generated by other people kills 53,000 Americans per year. So people who smoke cigarettes, cigars or pipes at work are increasingly finding themselves to be an unwelcomed minority—and many employers already take actions to control when and where they do it.

For example, a recent survey by *Industry Week* magazine found that nearly three-fourths of the 6,000 companies questioned had established a policy that either prohibits smoking in the workplace or restricts it to designated areas that nonsmokers can avoid. What's more, about 15% of the companies that participated in that survey but still didn't have a smoking policy were considering one.

1. Unsettled legal issues

The legal issues surrounding tobacco smoke in the workplace are unsettled. Airline flight attendants have secured some indirect protection from secondhand smoke in their workplace from Federal Aviation Administration restrictions on in-flight smoking by passengers. And although there is no federal law that directly controls smoking at work, at least 15 states and many municipalities have laws restricting smoking in privately owned workplaces.

In contrast, at least 15 states have laws that make it illegal to discriminate against employees or potential employees because they smoke during nonworking hours. And because it has much encouragement and financial support from the tobacco industry, this smokers' rights movement appears to be gaining strength.

So this ongoing legal battle boils down to a question of what's more important: one person's right to preserve health by avoiding co-workers' tobacco smoke, or another's right to smoke without the interference of others.

2. Taking individual action

If your health problems are severely aggravated, you may not be able to wait for a legal battle over workplace smoke to play out. Your best solution may be to work with your employer to find a way for you to avoid your co-workers' smoke.

> **Example:** Carmelita's sinus problems were made almost unbearable by the smoke created by the people who work with her in an insurance claims processing office. Since her job involves primarily individual work on a computer terminal and no contact with people outside the company, Carmelita convinced her employer to allow her to start her workday at 4 p.m., just an hour before her co-workers leave for home.
>
> When Carmelita needs to discuss something with co-workers or her supervisor, she does so via electronic mail or at occasional one-hour staff meetings that begin at 4 p.m.—and at which smoking is not allowed.

If you're unable to work out a plan that will solve a serious problem with workplace smoke, you may be able to qualify for workers' compensation or unemployment insurance benefits.

> **Example:** Albert has suffered various problems with breathing since birth. The insurance agency where he has worked for five years has no policy on smoking, and his state has no law restricting smoking in the workplace. Albert has complained repeatedly to the management that the smoke-filled air in the office has often caused him to suffer spells of coughing and dizziness.
>
> One day several of his co-workers puffed up a virtual storm of cigarette smoke, reducing visibility in the office to less than 20 feet, and Albert suffered a particularly bad bout of coughing and dizziness. An ambulance had to be called to take him for emergency medical attention.

Albert's physician advised him that he would be risking serious, permanent damage to his health if he returned to the smoky environment of his job. Albert was able to qualify for unemployment insurance benefits while he looked for a new job, because the cause of his unemployment was beyond his control. (For details on unemployment insurance and workers' compensation benefits, see Chapter 8, Sections B and D.)

3. Nonsmoking policies

Because of the potentially higher costs of healthcare insurance, absenteeism, unemployment insurance and workers' compensation insurance associated with employees who smoke, many companies now refuse to hire anyone who admits to being a smoker on a job application or in pre-hiring interviews.

The sentiment against smoking in the workplace and any other space shared with others has grown so strong that many companies now increase their attractiveness to job-seekers by mentioning that they maintain a smoke-free workplace in help-wanted advertising.

Except in the 15 states that forbid work-related discrimination against smokers and the five states where it is illegal for employers to discriminate against employers on the basis of any legal activities during nonwork time (see Chart 11-1 below), there's nothing to prevent employers from establishing a policy of hiring and employing only non-smokers.

Chart 11-1

SMOKERS' RIGHTS LAWS

Fifteen states have laws that specifically prohibit employers from discriminating against people who smoke tobacco during nonwork time. They are: Arizona, Connecticut, Indiana, Kentucky, Louisiana, Maine, Mississippi, New Hampshire, New Jersey, New Mexico, Oklahoma, Oregon, Rhode Island, South Carolina and South Dakota.

Five other states have laws that prohibit employers from discriminating against people on the basis of any legal activity, including smoking, during nonwork time. They are: Colorado, Nevada, New York, North Dakota and Tennessee.

CHAPTER

12

Other Workplace Rights

Some workplace laws affect only a tiny percentage of the workforce. Others are in the process of becoming obsolete. Still others are just now developing. And some other controversial aspects of workplace law are destined for legal battles and can't yet be regarded as clear workplace rights.

This chapter is a rundown of these workplace legal issues.

A. Personal Privacy

There are few legal controls on what an employer or prospective employer can find out about you. But there are some subtle limits on the extent to which your personal privacy can be invaded in connection with employment. In general, employers are entitled to intrude on your personal life no more than necessary for legitimate business interests.

In most cases, the most powerful weapon you can use against a company that has tread too deeply into your personal life or otherwise abused its power to check up on you is to file a lawsuit claiming invasion of privacy. And the most likely way to win such a case is to show that in the process of collecting information on you, the employer was guilty of one or more of the following:

Deception. Your employer asked you to submit to a routine medical examination, for example, but mentioned nothing about a drug test. However, the urine sample that you gave to the examining physician was analyzed for drug traces, and because drugs were found in your urine, you were fired.

Violation of confidentiality. For instance, your employer asked you to fill in a health questionnaire and assured you that the information would be held in confidence for the company's use only. But you later found out that the health information was divulged to a mortgage company that inquired about you.

Secret, intrusive monitoring. Installing visible video cameras above a supermarket's cash registers would usually be considered a legitimate method of ensuring that employees aren't stealing from the company. But installing hidden video cameras above the stalls in an employee restroom would probably qualify as an invasion of privacy in all but the most high-security jobs.

Intrusion on your private life. Your employer hired a private detective, for example, to monitor where you go in the evening when you're not at work. When the company discovered that you are active in a gay rights organization, you were told to resign from that group or risk losing your job.

1. Workplace searches

In general, it is legal for employers to monitor business-related telephone calls to and from their own premises. Employers may also search through items owned by an employee but kept at work—unless the employee logically expects that the spot in which those items are stored is completely private:

Example: Maryellen sold household appliances for a department store that provides each employee with a storage cabinet for personal belongings in a room adjacent to the employee lounge. The store's employee manual states that although the company doesn't provide locks for the cabinets and doesn't take responsibility for any thefts from the storage area, employees may bring in a lock of their own to secure their individual cabinet.

One day while at work, Maryellen was called to the manager's office, where she was confronted with a letter that had been written to her from her drug rehabilitation counselor. The manager said the letter had been found in her storage cabinet during a routine search by the company's security force, and that she was being fired because she had a history of drug abuse.

Maryellen could likely win an invasion of privacy lawsuit against her ex-employer because, by allowing her to use her own lock to secure her cabinet, the department store had given her a logical expectation of privacy for anything kept in that cabinet.

At least five states—Connecticut, Georgia, Ohio, Virginia and Wisconsin—have laws that specifically restrict searches and surveillance of employees, and some of them are quite powerful.

In Connecticut, for example, an employer who repeatedly uses electronic devices such as video cameras or audio tape recorders to monitor employees in restrooms, locker rooms or lounges can be charged criminally and sentenced to jail for 30 days (Conn. Gen. Stat. §31-48b (1987)).

2. How to check your personnel files

The best way to find out just how much a company knows about you, or what it is saying about you to businesses and people from outside the company who inquire, is to obtain a copy of the contents of the files that your employer or ex-employer maintains on you.

In many cases, the only way you'd get to see those files is while collecting evidence after filing a lawsuit against the employer or ex-employer. And even then you might be in for a big legal fight over what portions of the files are relevant to the case. But in at least 17 states, you have the right to see the contents of your personnel file without filing a lawsuit. (See Chart 12-1 at the end of this chapter.)

Each of these laws includes technical rules covering such matters as when your request must be made and how long the employer has to respond.

Before you request your file, it would be wisest to read the law on procedures for your state. The reference librarians at your local law library will help you find it. But, in general, you must make your request to see your personnel files in writing to your employer or ex-employer as soon as possible after you decide that you want to see them. If you send your request by certified mail, you'll be able to prove when the request was submitted, should you need that evidence later.

3. Criminal records

Since criminal court proceedings are matters of public record, there is little a job applicant or employee can do in most cases to stop an employer from discovering criminal records.[1] In fact, some credit reporting companies also do routine checks of criminal court records throughout the country and then use those records to create reports on individuals—reports which they then sell to employers who inquire about those individuals.

However, the anti-discrimination laws of at least three states—California, Colorado and Oregon—have laws that restrict using criminal records in making employment-related decisions.

B. Polygraph Tests

For decades, polygraphs—or lie detectors—that purport to measure the truthfulness of a person's statements by measuring such bodily functions as blood pressure and perspiration—were routinely used on employees and job applicants.

Employers could—and often did—ask employees and prospective employees questions about extremely private matters such as sexual preferences, toilet habits and family finances while a polygraph machine passed judgment

---

[1]For details on how you may be able to keep employers and potential employers from getting access to your criminal records, see *The Criminal Records Book* by Warren Siegel (Nolo Press).

on the truthfulness of the employee's answers. Push the machine's needle too far by reacting to an offensive question and you might be labeled a liar and, therefore, denied employment.

However, in 1988, the federal Employee Polygraph Protection Act (29 U.S.C. §2001) virtually outlawed using lie detectors in connection with employment. That law covers all private employers in interstate commerce, which includes just about every private company that uses the U.S. mail or the telephone system to send messages to another state.

Under the Act, it is illegal for all private companies to:

- directly or indirectly require, request, suggest, or cause any employee or job applicant to submit to a lie detector test

- use, accept, refer to or inquire about the results of any lie detector test conducted on an employee or job applicant

- dismiss, discipline, discriminate against or even threaten to take action against any employee or job applicant who refuses to take a lie detector test.

The law also prohibits employers from discriminating against or firing those who use its protections.

1. When polygraph tests can be used

The Employee Polygraph Protection Act allows polygraph tests to be used in connection with jobs in security and handling drugs, or in investigating a theft or other suspected crime. However, before you can be required to take such a test as part of an investigation of an employment-related crime, you must be given a written notice stating that you are a suspect.

The Act does not apply to employees of federal, state or local government, nor to certain jobs that handle sensitive work relating to national defense.

2. How to take action

The Employee Polygraph Protection Act is enforced by the U.S. Department of Labor. If you have questions about whether the Act applies to your job or if you suspect that you have been illegally subjected to polygraph testing, call the office of the Labor Department's Wage-and-Hour Division nearest you. It's listed in the federal government section of the telephone directories of most cities under Labor Department.

There's no official form for filing a polygraph-related complaint. If, after discussing your situation with a Wage-and-Hour Division investigator, you decide to file a complaint, do so as soon as possible by writing a letter addressed to your local Wage-and-Hour Division office. Include such details as the name and address of the employer, when the incident occurred and the address and telephone number where an investigator can reach you. And keep a copy for your records.

Example:

October 31, 1992

Wage-and-Hour Division
U.S. Department of Labor
1234 Main Street
Anycity, USA 34567

Dear Sir or Madam:

As authorized by 29 U.S.C. §2001, the Employee Polygraph
Protection Act, I am filing a complaint against the Dine
and Dash Restaurant, located at 732 South Street,
Anycity, USA.

I had been employed as a cook at Dine and Dash for four
and one-half years. But two days ago, I was told by the
restaurant's owner, Henry Hash, that all my co-workers
and I would have to agree to take a lie detector test
because he wants to make sure than none of us eat into
his profits by snacking on the job and taking home food.

Because I refused to take the test, I was fired. I will
be glad to cooperate in your investigation of this
complaint.

Sincerely,

Joe Chef
1244 Linton Lane
Anycity, USA 34567

If the Labor Department finds that your rights under the Act were violated, it can fine the employer up to $10,000 and issue an injunction ordering the employer to reinstate you to your job, promote you, compensate you for back wages, hire you or take other logical action to correct the violation.

If the Labor Department's action on your complaint doesn't satisfy you, you can file a lawsuit against the employer to obtain whatever compensation or other remedy would be appropriate. Move quickly, because the lawsuit must be filed within three years.

You'll probably need to hire an attorney to help you if you decide to file a lawsuit under this Act. (See Chapter 13, Section D.) But the law allows the court to grant you attorneys' fees and other costs if you win.

3. State polygraph laws

Some states have laws prohibiting or restricting employers from using lie detectors in connection with employment, but most have been made obsolete by the federal anti-polygraph statute.

However, a few states enforce stricter penalties against employers who illegally use polygraphs than are available under federal law. In New York, for example, an employer who uses polygraph tests illegally may be convicted of a misdemeanor and sentenced to up to one year in jail (N.Y. Lab. Law 189 §§733-39 (1988)).

Some states have also expanded anti-polygraph laws to cover other types of tests that probe bodily functions in connection with employment. For example, it is illegal for employers in Oregon to require employees to submit to brainwave testing (Or. Rev. Stat. §659.227).

4. Integrity testing

Several publishers claim they've developed series of written questions that can predict whether a person would lie, steal or be unreliable if hired for a particular job. And since lie detector tests are now generally illegal in the workplace, many employers use these questionnaires—which are usually called integrity tests—as a substitute in the process of screening applicants for job openings.

If a potential employer asks to you take an integrity test, you have few options other than to take it or drop out as a job applicant.

C. Credit Checks

This era of the computer is also the era of the ever-present personal credit rating. Credit bureaus—profit-making companies that gather and sell information about a person's credit history—have become a booming business. And the growing power and popularity of the computerized credit rating has found its way into the workplace, as well.

Many employers now use the same credit bureaus used by companies that issue credit cards and make loans to do routine credit checks on employees and job applicants. Unfortunately, there's very little you can do to prevent employers from using your personal credit bureau files in deciding whether to hire, promote or even continue to employ you.

1. Employers' access to your record

The Fair Credit Reporting Act of 1970 requires credit agencies to share their data only with those who have a legitimate business need for the information, and employers generally qualify. In short, as far as your employer or prospective employer is concerned, your credit rating is an open book.

Credit bureaus typically track not only your bill-paying habits, but also the companies that have asked to see your credit rating as part of their job applicant screening process. The result is that credit bureaus are increasingly being used by employers to find out which employees are actively seeking new jobs with other companies.

2. How to take action

There's nothing you can do to stop an employer from checking your credit, or to stop the credit bureaus from telling one employer whether other employers have checked up on you.

But you do have the right to correct any errors in credit reports compiled about you, and most experts recommend that you check and correct your file every couple years.

Call the nearest office of the Federal Trade Commission, which you can locate in the federal government section of most telephone directories, for instructions on how to correct your credit report.[2]

D. Drug Testing

Even though the abuse of drugs such as alcohol and cocaine has been widely publicized for many years, the laws regulating drug abuse in the workplace—and testing employees for such abuse—are relatively new and are still being shaped by the courts.

---

[2]For more detailed information about how credit bureaus operate and how to deal with them, see *Money Troubles* by Robin Leonard (Nolo Press).

Work-related drug tests can take a number of forms. Although analyzing urine samples is the method most commonly used, samples of worker's blood, hair and breath can also be tested for the presence of alcohol or other drugs in the body.

In general, employers have the right to test new job applicants for traces of drugs in their systems as long as the applicant knows that such testing will be part of the screening process for new employees and agrees to it in writing. Today, virtually any company that intends to conduct drug testing on job candidates includes in its job application an agreement to submit to such testing. The applicant approves that agreement by signing the application. If, in the process of applying for a job, you are asked to agree to drug testing, you have little choice but to agree to the tests or drop out as an applicant.

1. Testing existing employees

Many employers connected with the federal government are specifically authorized to test existing employees for drug abuse periodically. The Department of Defense authorizes employers with which it does business to do drug testing in certain circumstances, for example, and the Department of Transportation requires drug testing for some critical positions, such as airline pilots.

There are some legal constraints on testing existing employees in private employment for drug usage. Companies can't conduct blanket drug tests of all employees or random drug tests just because they feel like doing so without taking big legal risks. In some cases where employers have tested for drugs without good reason, the employees affected have sued successfully for invasion of privacy and infliction of emotional harm.

However, the courts have generally ruled that companies may test for drugs among employees whose actions could clearly cause human injury or property damage if their performance was impaired by drugs, and in cases where there is good reason to think that the employee is abusing drugs. For example, a bulldozer operator who swerved the machine illogically through a field could probably be the legal target of drug testing.

2. State and local drug testing laws

At least 14 states and a few municipalities have laws that regulate work-related testing for substance abuse. Many of these laws provide ways of dealing with abusive workplace drug testing that is simpler, quicker and less expensive than filing a lawsuit. Some states also require companies to distribute to employees written policies on drug testing and rehabilitation.

These laws vary tremendously and are changing rapidly. The best way to get up-to-date details on any drug testing laws in your state is to research them at a library near you. (See Chapter 13, Section E.)

E. AIDS in the Workplace

The disease of Acquired Immune Deficiency Syndrome (AIDS) did not become a workplace controversy until the 1980s. And to make the issue even more complicated and elusive, the disease itself is surrounded by misunderstanding, misinformation and often unreasonable fears.

Government polls indicate that as many as one in every 100 American workers already have been infected by HIV, the virus that causes AIDS—and that as many as 50,000 more people are being infected by the virus each year. However, not everyone who is infected by HIV develops AIDS.

More importantly, the virus is not spread through the kind of casual contact with other human beings that typically takes place at work.

1. How the virus is spread

Extensive medical research has shown that the HIV virus is spread primarily through sexual intercourse and the exchange of blood by intravenous drug users, not by everyday workplace interactions such as:

- sharing a work environment with someone who is infected
- shaking hands, hugging, or using the same furniture as an infected person

* sharing bathroom facilities with people who are infected with HIV.

Nevertheless, some employers and employees have reacted to the spread of AIDS with panic—and a strong prejudice against working with people who are infected with the HIV virus. Some insurance companies have made that panic worse by restricting healthcare coverage or dramatically raising premiums for those infected.

2. Rights of infected workers

In recent years, the courts have generally—but not always—held that being infected with the HIV virus or having AIDS is a type of physical handicap, and that the Federal Rehabilitation Act and many state and local anti-discrimination laws make it illegal to discriminate in employment-related matters on the basis of HIV infection or AIDS.

A number of states and municipalities have also passed AIDS-specific laws in recent years in attempts to deal with injustices arising from panicked reactions to AIDS in the workplace. For the most part, these laws limit the testing of employees and job applicants for the HIV virus to positions such as those in hospital laboratories, where the virus might conceivably be passed accidentally from an employee to a patient.

These inconsistent, piecemeal approaches to dealing with AIDS in the workplace have been expensive, time-consuming and often frustrating for those infected with the HIV virus. But the legal picture for workers with HIV and AIDS is becoming much clearer as the Americans with Disabilities Act (ADA) is being phased into effect.

Under the ADA, it is clearly illegal for any company employing 15 or more people to discriminate against workers because they are HIV infected or suffering from AIDS.

Employers covered by ADA must also make reasonable accommodations to allow employees with AIDS to continue working. Such accommodations include extended leave policies, re-assignment to vacant positions within the companies that are less physically strenuous and flexible work schedules.

For more details on ADA, the timetable by which it is taking effect and how to use it to enforce your workplace rights, see Chapter 5, Section H. For more information on the HIV virus, AIDS and resources on AIDS in the workplace, contact the National Leadership Coalition on AIDS. (See the Appendix for contact details.)

F. Grooming and Clothing Codes

In general, employers have the right to dictate on-the-job standards for clothing and grooming as a condition of employment. There is nothing inherently illegal, for example, about a company requiring all employees to wear navy blue slacks during working hours.

Codes governing employees' appearance may be illegal, however, if they result in a pattern of illegal discrimination against a particular group of employees or potential employees. This type of violation has most often arisen in companies with grossly different codes for male and female employees. Also, several successful lawsuits have been waged by black men against companies that refuse to hire men with beards or that fire men who don't comply with no-beard rules.

> **Example:** Nelson, a black man, was advised by his physician not to shave his facial hair too closely because that would cause his very curly whiskers to become ingrown and infected. Although Nelson took with him to a job interview a note from his doctor attesting to this problem, he was turned down for employment because the company where he had applied had a no-beard policy.
>
> Nelson filed a complaint against the company under his state's anti-discrimination laws on the basis of racial discrimination. Medical experts testified in his case that the condition which prevented Nelson from shaving usually affected only black men.
>
> The court ruled in Nelson's favor, saying that the company's failure to lift its ban on beards despite Nelson's well-documented medical problem resulted in illegal workplace discrimination against black men. (For details on anti-discrimination laws, see Chapter 5.)

For the sake of creating a uniform company-wide appearance, many employers provide workers with some or all of the clothing that they are required to wear on the job. A few companies even rent suits for their employees to assure that they will be similarly dressed. Although generally legal, such systems can violate your rights if the cost of the clothing is deducted from your pay in violation of the Fair Labor Standards Act (FLSA).

For example, it is illegal under the FLSA for an employer to deduct the cost of work-related clothing from your pay so that your wages dip below the minimum wage standard, or so that the employer profits on the clothing. (For details on the FLSA and how to file a complaint under it, see Chapter 2.)

G. Noncompete Agreements

Noncompete agreements are contracts in which an employee agrees not to compete with an employer during the course of employment or for a time after that employment has ended. Typically, these contracts specify that the employee won't compete against the employer by working in the same industry—or starting a business similar to the employer's—within a certain geographic region for a specified number of years.

There is no federal law controlling noncompete agreements. But at least four states—Montana, Nevada, North Dakota and Oklahoma—have outlawed all noncompete agreements governing employees. And at least seven others—Colorado, Florida, Hawaii, Louisiana, Oregon, South Dakota and Wisconsin—have laws that limit the situations in which noncompete agreements can be used by employers. In Hawaii, for example, noncompete contracts may be used only to protect trade secrets such as lists of customers and a company's strategy for pricing its products.

In general, the courts regard noncompete contracts as being contrary to the American tradition of free competition, and support such contracts only where necessary to protect a company's confidential information. Even then, the courts usually require noncompete contracts to be very specific and reasonable about the region and timespan covered. In general, a noncompete contract can't restrict your career any more than is absolutely necessary to the basic business interests of your employer or ex-employer.

Example: Karl was an account executive at the Promo-Plus advertising agency in Dallas, Texas. When he took the job, his employer required him to sign a noncompete agreement prohibiting him from soliciting clients anywhere in Texas for 10 years after he had left that agency. Two years later, Karl left Promo-Plus to start an agency of his own in Houston. When Karl began prospecting for clients, Promo-Plus filed a lawsuit against him, relying on the noncompete agreement that Karl had signed.

The court found the agreement to be invalid, however, because both the geographic area and the number of years it stipulated were unreasonable.

If your employer asks you to sign a noncompete agreement, you probably won't have much choice but to agree to that request—although you may be able to negotiate on some points. Try pointing out to the employer that the more fair and specific such an agreement is, the more likely it is to be enforceable.

If you're already working under such an agreement, don't let it intimidate you away from pursuing other career opportunities. If your next job or business venture is an honest one that doesn't unfairly exploit customer contacts or information that you gained in your current job, your current employer isn't likely to go to court to prevent you from carrying on a similar business.

This is particularly true if your new job or business offers products or services that are in some way different from those of the company with which you have a noncompete contract. For example, a shop that does alterations on clothing purchased in stores would probably not be considered competition for one that creates custom designed garments—even though both require sewing skills.

H. Immigration and the Workplace

Since the 1920s, America has worked hard at restricting the inward flow of people from other countries. That effort began to be targeted in the workplace, however, when the Immigration Reform and Control Act (IRCA) was passed in 1986.

With IRCA, the responsibility for detecting and rejecting foreign-born workers who lack the documents such as permanent resident visas that are required to legally be employed in America shifted from the federal government to employers.

1. Who is covered

IRCA covers all employers and all employees hired since November 6, 1986, except employees who provide occasional, irregular domestic services in private homes. Independent contractors aren't covered. (See Chapter 1, Section B for details on independent contractor status.)

Employers may continue to employ workers who were on their payrolls before November 6, 1986—regardless of their immigration status—as long as those workers continue in essentially the same jobs they had before the law went into effect.

Your employer is not required under IRCA to fire you if you lack authorization from the U.S. Immigration and Naturalization Service (INS) to be employed but have been in the same job since before IRCA went into effect. Note, however, that this provision does not exempt the employee from complying with other requirements of U.S. immigration law.

2. Restrictions on employers

Under IRCA, it is illegal for an employer to:

- hire a worker who the employer knows has not been granted permission by the INS to be employed in the United States

- hire any worker who has not completed an INS Form I-9, the Employment Eligibility Verification Form

- continue to employ an unauthorized worker—often called an illegal alien or undocumented alien—hired after November 6, 1986.

A LAW WITH CONFLICTING GOALS

The Immigration Reform and Control Act of 1986 (IRCA) is fraught with conflict. It tries to soothe the fears common among some American workers of losing their jobs to newly arrived immigrants, while continuing to respect the American standard for racial and ethnic equality established by the Civil Rights Act of 1964.

To try to accomplish those conflicting goals, IRCA requires even native-born Americans to prove that they have the right to work in this country. Yet it includes provisions designed to prevent workplace discrimination against people who are American citizens—or who are otherwise legally working in America—but who look or sound different from the status quo.

This law is commonly ignored by employers, employees and the government in areas of the country where immigration has been low in recent decades. But it is aggressively enforced in Arizona, California, Florida, New York City, Texas and other areas where recent immigrants have tended to settle.

3. Filing INS Form I-9

When you take a new job, you are required to fill out the employee's section of Form I-9 by the end of your first day on the job. You then have three business days to present your new employer with documents that prove:

- that you are who you say you are, and
- that you are legally authorized to work in the United States.

a.   Proof of identity

The INS considers a current U.S. passport sufficient to prove both your identity and your eligibility to be employed in the United States.

If you don't have a passport, a current driver's license or photo identification card issued by the state in which you reside will typically prove your legal identity. If your appearance or speech differs from the Anglo standard, you may have to provide a second form of verification such as a military ID card, a draft record, a voter registration card or Native American tribal documents. For young workers, the INS considers a school report card or a hospital record such as a birth certificate acceptable as proof of identity.

b.   Proof of employment eligibility

Native-born Anglo adults can typically prove employment eligibility by producing a Social Security card or a birth certificate issued by the state of birth. If you look or sound as though you might be an immigrant, you may have to produce both a Social Security card and a birth certificate.

When pulling together the documents required to prove these two things may take some time—such as when you have to obtain a certified copy of a birth certificate from another state—your employer can give an additional 18 business days to produce your documents if you can prove that you've applied for them by producing, for example, a receipt for fees charged for the documents.

The INS standard for the acceptable documents for verification frequently changes, partly because a substantial industry has grown around producing and selling counterfeit documents.

If you're an immigrant legally authorized to work in the United States, obtain up-to-date information on documentation by calling the nearest office of the INS. Look in the federal government section of your telephone directory.

Your new employer is required to note the type of documents you produce and any expiration dates on your Form I-9. Although employers are not required to photocopy such documents, they have the right to do so. If they do, the copies must be kept on file with your Form I-9.

4. Illegal discrimination under IRCA

IRCA makes it illegal for an employer with three or more employees to:

- discriminate in hiring and firing anyone—other than an unauthorized immigrant worker, of course—on the basis of what country they were born in or the fact that they became or are in the process of becoming U.S. citizens through the naturalization process

- retaliate against an employee for exercising any rights under IRCA.

5. How to take action

If your rights under IRCA have been violated, you have 180 days from when the violation occurred to file a complaint with the Office of the Special Counsel for Unfair Immigration-Related Employment Practices. The most common violation of IRCA's anti-discrimination section occurs when employers refuse to hire someone because they suspect—incorrectly—that the person is legally authorized to work in America.

You can file your complaint on the special counsel's Form CRT-37, or you can simply write a letter summarizing the situation. If you need legal advice, call the special counsel offices to discuss your situation with a staff attorney.

The special counsel has 120 days from the day it received your complaint to investigate and decide whether it will pursue a charge of violating IRCA against the employer before an administrative law judge.

If the special counsel does not bring a charge against the employer within the 120 days, or notifies you that it has not found sufficient evidence to support your charges, you have the right to plead your case directly before an administrative law judge. But you must request your hearing within 90 days of the end of the original 120-day period allowed for the special counsel to take action.

Immigration law is a world all its own, so you'll probably need the help of an attorney with experience in immigration law if you decide to pursue an anti-discrimination complaint under IRCA after the special counsel has failed to do so. (See Chapter 13, Section D.)

Since IRCA specifically outlaws immigration-related discrimination only in hiring and firing decisions but not in other employment-related actions such as promotions and wage increases, you may want to file your immigration-related complaint under Title VII of the Civil Rights Act or your state's anti-discrimination laws. (For details on those laws and how to take action under them, see Chapter 5, Sections A and J.)

6. English-only rules

People who resent or fear workers from other countries and cultures also frequently complain about immigrant workers who talk in their native languages at work.

The use of languages other than English, these people usually argue, is part of a conspiracy against or secret mockery of native-born Americans by the immigrants. These allegations have caused some employers to establish policies that require employees to use only the English language in the workplace.

In general, the Equal Employment Opportunity Commission and the courts regard English-only rules in the workplace to be illegal discrimination on the basis of national origin under the Civil Rights Act of 1964. Exceptions are allowed only in cases where there is a clear and compelling reason for uniformity of language, such as for air traffic controllers.

Chart 12-1

STATE LAWS ON EMPLOYEE ACCESS TO PERSONNEL RECORDS

This is a synopsis of state laws that give you the right to inspect the files that your employer or ex-employer keeps on you.

Alaska

Employees have the right to see their personnel files. Alaska Stat. §23.10.430 (1989)

Arkansas

Employees may demand to see their own personnel and workplace evaluation records. Ark. Stat. Ann. §§25-19-104 and 25-19-105 (1987)

California

Employees have the right to see their personnel files and to demand a copy of any document relating to employment that they have signed. Employers must maintain a copy of the employee's personnel file where the employee reports to work, or must make the file available at that location within a reasonable time after the employee asks to see it. Cal. Lab. Code §§432 (1971), 1198.5 (1989)

Connecticut

Employees have the right to see their personnel files and to insert rebuttals of information with which they disagree. Conn. Gen. Stat. §31-128 (1987)

Delaware

Employees have the right to see their personnel files and to insert rebuttals of information with which they disagree. Del. Code Ann. tit. 19 §730-735 (1988)

Illinois

Companies employing five or more people must allow employees to see their personnel files, and to insert rebuttals of any information with which they disagree. Ill. Rev. Stat. Ch. 48 §2010(c) (1989)

Maine

Employees have the right to see their personnel files and workplace evaluations. Me. Rev. Stat. tit. 26 §631 (1988)

Massachusetts

Employees have the right to see their personnel files and to insert rebuttals of any information with which they disagree. Employees may take court action to expunge from personnel records any information that the employer knew, or should have known, was incorrect. Mass. Gen. Laws Ann. Ch. 149 §52C (1989)

Michigan

Employees have the right to see their personnel files and to insert rebuttals of any information with which they disagree. Mich. Comp. Laws Ann. §423.501-512 (1988)

Minnesota

Employees have the right to see their personnel files and to insert rebuttals of any information with which they disagree. Minn. Stat. Ann. §181.960 (1988)

Nevada

Employees have the right to see any records that the employer used to confirm the employee's qualifications, or as the basis for any disciplinary action. If those records contain incorrect information, the employee may notify the employer of the errors in writing. But the employer is required to correct the challenged information only if the employer decides it is false. Nev. Rev. Stat. §613.075 (1988)

New Hampshire

Employees have the right to see their personnel files and to insert rebuttals of any information with which they disagree. N.H. Rev. Stat. §275:56 (1987)

Oregon

Employees have the right to see any documents used by the employer in making work-related decisions, such as promotions, wage increases, or termination. Or. Rev. Stat. §652.750 (1985)

Pennsylvania

Employees and persons who they designate in writing as their agents have the right to see their personnel files. 43 Pa. Cons. Stat. Ann. §§1321-1324 (1990)

Rhode Island

Employees have the right to see their personnel files. R.I. Gen. Laws §§28-6.4-1, -2 (1988)

Washington

Employees have the right to see their personnel files, and to insert rebuttals of any information with which they disagree. Wash. Rev. Code §49.12.240 (1985)

Wisconsin

Employees have the right to see their personnel files, and to insert rebuttals of any information with which they disagree. Wis. Stat. §103.13 (1988)

CHAPTER

13

Lawyers and
Legal Research

There are several established agencies with staffs to advise and assist you with legal problems in the workplace.

If your problem is a matter of wage-and-hour law, for example, you can call the Labor Department's investigators directly to ask for their assistance. If your problem involves illegal discrimination, you can call the Equal Employment Opportunity Commission and talk over your case with a compliance officer or staff attorney.

With some types of workplace problems, however, you're on your own. If you need help getting your former employer to continue your healthcare benefits after you've lost your job, for example, no one's quite sure where to call. In some unsettled legal areas, you may need to decide the best course of action: an alternative to court such as mediation, a small claims court claim, hiring a lawyer to help you through or doing some of your own legal research.

A. Mediation and Arbitration

At least partly because of how the legal world is portrayed on television and in movies, some people think that a courtroom is the best place to resolve any dispute. In fact, mediation or arbitration can be faster, less expensive, more satisfying alternatives to going into court in someb matters involving workplace law.

Although mediation and arbitration are often lumped together under the general heading of alternative dispute resolution, there are significant differences between the two.

Mediation: Two or more people or groups get a third person they trust to help them communicate. The mediator does not represent either side, but assists both. The mediator does not impose a decision, but helps the disagreeing parties to formulate their own resolution of their dispute.

Arbitration: Both sides agree on the issue but cannot resolve it themselves. They agree to pick an arbitrator who will come up with a solution. Essentially, the arbitrator acts as an informal judge, but at far less cost and expense than most legal proceedings require.

Mediation or arbitration are not realistic alternatives in serious workplace disputes such as a wrongful-discharge claim (discussed in Chapter 4, Section A) where the parties involved have no mutual interest in continuing their relationship. But either may be ideal where the parties have a continuing relationship and want to find a mutually acceptable way to work together.

Leading sources of professional arbitrators and mediators—and of information on how to use these approaches to resolve disputes—are the American Arbitration Association and the American Bar Association's Standing Committee on Dispute Resolution. (See the Appendix for contact details.)

B. Small Claims Court

Some disputes over workplace law, such as wages owed to you by a former employer, involve only relatively small amounts of money. In many of those cases, you can file your own lawsuit to collect the money that's owed to you in small claims court.

The hallmark of small claims court is that it's inexpensive and easy to file a case there, and court procedures have been simplified. You do not need to hire a lawyer to help represent you, and in some states, lawyers are not even allowed. The small claims hearing will be held before a judge, magistrate, commissioner or volunteer attorney, who will usually decide the case on the spot or within a few days.

The amount you can sue for is limited—usually to between $2,000 and $5,000. But these limits increase regularly, so check first with the local court clerk if you decide to use small claims court.[1]

C. Class Action Lawsuits

The federal courts sometimes allow lawsuits to be filed jointly by groups of people who have all been injured by the same or similar conduct of an employer. These are called class actions, and because they spread the cost of bringing the lawsuit among many people who are injured, class actions can make it feasible to take legal action against an employer or former employer where the expense would be too great for an individual.

The requirements that the courts have set for a lawsuit to be pursued as a class action are complex. It's almost always necessary to get help from a lawyer to file a class action suit. But this option is one to keep in mind if your case is one in which a number of other workers were injured.

D. Hiring a Lawyer

If your workplace problem involves a complex or ambiguous area of law—a Title VII lawsuit, claim of blacklisting or a violation of public policy, or an abusive layoff—you will probably need to hire a lawyer.

---

[1]For details on using small claims courts, see *Everybody's Guide to Small Claims Court* by Ralph Warner (Nolo Press).

If you do decide to hire a lawyer, the first task you face is finding one who best suits your needs. The best place to start the process may be to check with your personal network of family, friends and co-workers to see if anyone has gotten legal help with a workplace problem. No two cases are the same, but try to get referrals from people whose work-related legal problems are at least similar to yours.

Other possible sources of referrals to lawyers with special expertise in work-related law include:

- Legal aid clinics. In some cases, local legal clinics only make referrals to lawyers with appropriate knowledge and experience. And some may have lawyers on staff who will handle your case for a low cost or free of charge. Locate your community's legal aid clinics by looking in the telephone directory under Legal Aid Society or Legal Services—or check with the nearest law school.

- Organizations in your area that serve as advocates for the legal rights of minority groups, such as gay rights coalitions and local chapters of the National Association for the Advancement of Colored People (NAACP).

- National organizations that deal with specific types of workplace rights, such as the National Safe Workplace Institute or the National Coalition Against Sexual Assault. These and several others are listed in the Appendix.

BEWARE OF LEGAL SKIMMING

The huge volume of legal advertising that appears on billboards, bus shelters and television—and in telephone directories and brochures—might lead you to think that there are thousands of lawyers out there just panting to help you fight your case to the end.

In fact, many of the most aggressive legal advertising campaigns are part of a process of skimming the community for easy personal injury cases likely to end in huge settlements or jury awards. By spending large amounts of money on advertising, some lawyers hope to ensure a flow of calls to their offices by injured people seeking legal help.

Take notice, however, that the ads make no commitment to take your case; most promise only a free or low-cost consultation. When you call a law firm in response to aggressive advertising, you're likely to be connected with a lawyer or legal assistant who screens cases for potential. Although you may be warmly welcomed at first, you can expect the firm's interest and concern to evaporate rapidly if it determines that your case is unlikely to bring in big dollars for the firm. In general, you're better off choosing a lawyer based on others' recommendations than on the basis of advertising hype.

---

1. Comparison shopping for a lawyer

Take detailed notes on each lawyer mentioned during your research, and hopefully you'll soon have your own small directory of lawyers with employment-related expertise from which to choose.

Be careful that people don't merely give you the names of lawyers they've heard of—or one who handled an entirely different kind of case, such as a divorce or a house closing. Any lawyer can become known as being prominent just by buying a lot of advertising time on television, hogging the shot when the TV cameras scan a well-publicized celebrity event or running repeatedly for election to public office.

Here are a few questions you may also want to ask a person who refers a lawyer who is experienced in employment law:

- Did this lawyer respond to all your telephone calls and other communications promptly?

- Did the lawyer take the time to listen to your explanation and understand your situation fully?

- Were all the bills you received properly itemized and in line with the costs projections you got at the start of your case?

- Did this lawyer personally handle your case, or was it handed off to a younger, less experienced lawyer in the same firm?

- Did the lawyer deliver what he or she promised?

BUY THE STEAK, NOT THE SIZZLE

Despite all the glamor attributed to the legal profession by television in recent years, the truth is that the honest practice of law is still very much a tedious pursuit. In general, the best lawyers are still those who can and will pull together all the law that favors you and then present that law cogently to the court and your opponents.

So as you look over the list of lawyers with expertise in employment law and decide which of them to approach with your case, don't be distracted by prestigious addresses or long-winded law firm names; they're likely to come with big price tags. You should also not be swayed by friends advising that only lawyers of a certain gender or ethnic background are good for your kind of case. The key is to find a lawyer with the expertise you need and with whom you're comfortable.

---

2. The initial interview

Once you've selected about three lawyers that you feel may be right, telephone each of them and ask for an appointment to discuss your situation. Ask them to specify in advance whether you'll be charged for the first meeting. Some may offer not to charge for the first consultation, and that's good. But don't decide against discussing your case with a lawyer who appears to have the type of expertise you need just because he or she wants to be paid for time spent meeting.

A charge of between $75 and $150 for a one-hour consultation is typical for the type of lawyer who handles work-related cases on behalf of employees. If you organize the facts in your case well before going to your consultation, one hour should be more than enough to explain your case and obtain at least a basic opinion on how it might be approached and what it is likely to cost.

CONTINGENCY FEES

The average person can't afford to pay the hourly fees that a lawyer would charge to handle a complicated case involving employment law. So the legal profession has developed a system called contingency fees, under which the lawyer handles a case in exchange for a large percentage of any money judgment that results.

Although there is no set percentage for contingency fees in most types of cases, the standard amount demanded by lawyers in most areas is about 35% if the case is settled before the lawsuit is filed with the courts—and 40% if the case has to be filed and tried.

However, most states set lower contingency fee levels for certain parts of workers' compensation insurance cases. A call to the agency in your state that operates the workers' compensation system should enable you to determine what the allowable rates are in those situations. (See Chapter 8 Section E.)

Typically, a lawyer working for you under a contingency agreement will require that you pay all out-of-pocket expenses, such as filing fees charged by the courts and the cost of transcribing witness depositions. In most cases, the lawyer will want you to keep a substantial amount of money—a thousand dollars or more—on deposit with his or her firm to cover these expenses.

However, the terms of a contingency fee agreement may be negotiable—and you can try to get the lawyer you select to help with your case to agree to a lower percentage or to pay some of the costs. In all cases, the terms under which the lawyer is working on your behalf should be spelled out in detail, in writing.

3. Evaluating a lawyer

After meeting with the lawyers you've selected and discussing your situation with them, ask yourself these questions:

- Does this lawyer have the type of expertise and experience needed to handle my case? In many states, lawyers can advertise any area of specialization they choose—even if they've never handled a similar case. Recheck your notes to see whether any of the lawyers recommended to you is known to have successfully handled a case similar to yours.

- Will my case be important to this lawyer even if the fight gets rough? In complex cases such as a class action alleging illegal discrimination, you may need the expertise and resources of a large law firm. But if you consider only big law firms with lots of other things to do, you're likely to find yourself surrounded by a whole team of lawyers trying to talk you into dropping your case as soon as anything happens to diminish the chance of your lawsuit bringing in a big money award.

Small law firms and lawyers practicing alone, on the other hand, often see even settlements involving less than $25,000 as significant, and will pursue both your case and the collection of any judgment you win with the resolve of the proverbial junkyard dog for years, if necessary.

- Is this lawyer someone with whom you would feel comfortable discussing intimate details of your life? A lawyer can represent you best if you are willing and able to speak candidly about your case. And lawsuits can get dirty; the other side may try to probe deeply into your private life to try to gain the upper edge. So it's important that you like and trust your lawyer.

FEE ARRANGEMENTS—GET IT IN WRITING

After you've interviewed a few lawyers and decided which one can best handle your case, don't just turn the case over to the lawyer of your choice. Most disagreements between lawyers and clients involve fees, so be sure to get all the details involving money in writing—including the per-hour billing rate or the contingency fee arrangement, the frequency of billing and how any funds you're required to deposit in advance to cover expenses will be handled.

---

4. Managing your lawyer

Keep in mind that the lawyer you hire works for you, not the other way around. Your lawyer may be the one with the expertise and the expensive briefcase, but the rights that are being pursued are yours—and you are the most important person involved in your case.

Lawyers can be a frisky and devious breed. So if you hire a lawyer to help with your case, you need to be a strong, alert manager. Here are some ways that you can fill that role well:

- Carefully check every bill you get from your lawyer. If a bill lacks sufficient detail for you to verify that it complies with your written fee agreement, call your lawyer and politely demand that a new, more detailed version be sent before you pay it. Don't feel as though you're being too pushy by demanding more detail: The laws in many states actually require thorough detail in lawyers' bills.

- Challenge any charge that looks suspicious. If a charge for a two-hour consultation with another attorney appears on your bill, for example, demand to know what was discussed, who the other lawyer is, and why he or she was contacted. Don't pay for anything that isn't included in the written fee agreement with your lawyer, any charge that hasn't been explained to your satisfaction, or any charge with which you don't agree.

- Learn as much as you can about the laws and decisions involved in your case. By doing so, you'll be able to monitor your lawyer's work and may even be able to move your case along faster. If your case is being handled on an hourly fee basis, you may even cut your costs by doing some of the legal legwork yourself.

- Keep your own calendar of dates and deadlines in your case, such as when papers and appearances are due in court. If you rely on your lawyer to keep your case on schedule, you may be unpleasantly surprised to find that an important deadline has been missed. Many a good case has been thrown out simply because of a lawyer's forgetfulness. Call or write to your lawyer at least a week before any important deadline in your case to inquire about plans to meet it.

- Maintain your own file on your case. By having a well-organized file of your own, you'll be able to discuss your case with your lawyer intelligently and efficiently—even over the telephone. Being well-informed will help keep your lawyer's effectiveness up and your costs down. Be aware that if your lawyer is working on an hourly basis, you'll probably be charged for telephone consultations. But they're likely to be less expensive than office visits.

- Change lawyers if you feel that's necessary. If the relationship between you and the lawyer you chose doesn't seem to be working out, or if you feel that your case isn't progressing as it should, think about asking your second or third choice among the lawyers you considered to take over.

Be clear with the first lawyer that you are taking your business else-where, putting your decision in writing. Otherwise, you could end up receiving bills from both lawyers—both of whom believe they are han-dling your case. You may have to pay for a few extra hours of consul-tation time to bring the switch about, but that's better than living with a bad choice.

- Take prompt action against any behavior by a lawyer that appears to be deceptive, unethical or otherwise illegal. A call to a bar association in your area, which you can typically locate in the telephone directory, should provide you with guidance on what types of lawyer behavior are prohibited and how to file a complaint. The systems that are sup-posed to police lawyers' behavior are controlled by lawyers in most states, and they rarely take action against their own kind. But by filing a formal complaint, you may create a document that you'll need should you end up filing a lawsuit against a lawyer for malpractice.

E. Doing Your Own Legal Research

This book gives you a general understanding of the legal principles involved in common workplace disputes. However, in negotiating with your employer, presenting your workplace problem to government investigators, preparing for mediation or arbitration, or working with a lawyer you hire, you may gain additional power and speed the resolution of your dispute by having detailed and specific legal knowledge.

In those situations, you may want to do some legal research of your own.[2] If you intend to do legal research on your own, be aware that interpreting statutes and cases can sometimes be difficult without legal training and a spe-cific background in the area being researched.

---

[2]If you want to learn how to do your own legal research in depth, see the comprehensive consumer guide *Legal Research: How to Find and Understand the Law* by Stephen Elias (Nolo Press).

1. Public libraries

The reference section in most public libraries contains a set of local and state laws as well as a set of the federal statutes and the Code of Federal Regulations. The librarians there can help you look up any laws you are interested in that might affect your case.

2. Law libraries

If you want to look up a case (court decision) or a ruling by agencies such as the Occupational Safety and Health Administration or the Equal Employment Opportunity Commission, you'll probably have to visit a law library.

Most counties have one supported by public funds that is open to the public. You can also try the library of the law school nearest you, particularly if it's one that's affiliated with a public university funded by tax dollars. The librarians there are more likely to be friendly and enthusiastic about helping you through the mazes of citations. And law school libraries are usually open from very early in the morning until very late at night, even on weekends and some holidays.

Organizations to Contact for Additional Help with Workplace Problems

AFL-CIO
815 16th Street, NW
Washington, DC 20005
202/637-5000

American Arbitration Association
149 West 51st Street
New York, NY 10020
212/484-4000

American Association of Retired Persons
1909 K Street, NW
Washington, DC 20049
202/872-4700

American Bar Association
750 North Lakeshore Drive
Chicago, IL 60611
312/988-5000

American Civil Liberties Union
National Task Force on Civil Liberties in
the Workplace
132 West 43rd Street
New York, NY 10036
212/944-9800

American Psychological Association
1200 17th Street, NW
Washington, DC 20036
202/955-7600

Asbestos Victims of America
P.O. Box 559
Capitola, CA 95010
408/476-3646

Communications Workers of America
Research Department
1925 K Street, NW
Washington, DC 20006
202/728-2300

Electronic University Network
385 Eighth Street
San Francisco, CA 94103
800/225-3276

Equal Employment Opportunity
Commission
2401 E Street, NW
Washington, DC 20506
800/872-3362
TDD number for the hearing disabled:
202/634-7057

Formerly Employed Mothers At Loose
Ends (FEMALE)
P.O. Box 31
Elmhurst, IL 60126
708/941-3553

International Foundation of Employee
Benefit Plans
18700 West Bluemound Road
P.O. Box 69
Brookfield, WI 53008-0069
414/786-6700

International Resource Network on
Disabilities
2232 SW 15th Street
Fort Lauderdale, FL 33312
305/583-0645

Job Seekers
c/o Pastor Robert Messner
The Chapel
135 Fir Hill
Akron, Ohio 44304
216/376-6400

National Association of
Temporary Services
119 South Asaph Street
Alexandria, VA 22314
703/549-6287

NOW Legal Defense & Education Fund
99 Hudson Street
New York, NY 10013
212/925-6635

National Coalition Against Sexual Assault
2023 Vale Road, Suite 2
San Pablo, CA 94806
415/237-0113

National Employment Lawyers
Association
414 Walnut Street, Suite 911
Cincinnati, OH 45202
513/241-4504

National Leadership Coalition on AIDS
1150 17th Street, NW, Suite 202
Washington, DC 20036
202/429-0930

National Right To Work Committee
8001 Braddock Road
Suite 500
Springfield, VA 22160
703/321-9820

National Safe Workplace Institute
122 S. Michigan Avenue, Suite 1450
Chicago, IL 60603
312/939-0690

9 to 5, National Association of
Working Women
614 Superior Avenue, NW
Cleveland, Ohio 44113
216/566-9308

Pension Benefit Guaranty Corporation
Coverage & Inquiries Branch
2020 K Street, NW
Washington, DC 20006
202/778-8800
TTY/TDD number for the hearing
disabled: 202/778-8859

Pension Rights Center
1346 Connecticut Avenue, NW
Washington, DC 20036
202/296-3778

President's Committee on Employment
of People With Disabilities
1111 20th Street, NW
Washington, DC 20036
202/653-5044

Pension and Welfare Benefits Program
Labor-Management Services
Administration
Room N-5658, 200 Constitution Avenue, NW
Washington, DC 20216
202/523-8776

White Lung Association
P.O. Box 1483
Baltimore, MD 21203
301/243-5864

Women's Legal Defense Fund
1875 Connecticut Avenue NW, Suite 710
Washington, DC 20009
202/986-2600

INDEX

RECYCLE YOUR OUT-OF-DATE BOOKS
AND GET 25% OFF YOUR NEXT PURCHASE

OUT - O F - DATE = DANGEROUS

Using an old edition can be dangerous if information in it is wrong. Unfortunately, laws and legal procedures change often. Generally speaking, any book more than two years old is of questionable value. Books more than four or five years old are a menace.

To help you keep up-to-date, we extend this offer:

If you cut out and deliver to us the title portion of the cover of any old Nolo book, we'll give you a 25% discount off the retail price of any new Nolo book. For example, if you have a copy of *Tenant's Rights,* 4th edition, and want to trade it for the latest *California Marriage and Divorce Law,* send us the *Tenant' Rights* cover and a check for the current price of *California Marriage and Divorce,* less a 25% discount.

Information on current prices and editions is listed in the back of this book and in the catalog in the *Nolo News* (see offer at the back of this book).

This offer is to individuals only.

CATALOG

Everybody's Guide to Municipal Court

Judge Roderic Duncan
California 1st Edition
Everybody's Guide to Municipal Court explains how to prepare and defend the most common types of contract and personal injury lawsuits in California Municipal Court. Written by a California judge, the book provides step-by-step instructions for preparing and filing all necessary forms, gathering evidence and appearing in court.
$29.95/MUNI

Fight Your Ticket
National $15.95/NSCC
California $15.95/ CSCC
Fight Your Ticket
Attorney David Brown
California 5th Edition
This book shows you how to fight an unfair traffic ticket—when you're stopped, at arraignment, at trial and on appeal.
$17.95/FYT

The Criminal Records Book
Attorney Warren Siegel
California 3rd Edition
This book shows you step-by-step how to seal criminal records, dismiss convictions, destroy marijuana records and reduce felony convictions.
$19.95/CRIM

Collect Your Court Judgment
Gini Graham Scott, Attorney Stephen Elias &
Lisa Goldoftas
California 2nd Edition
This book contains step-by-step instructions and all the forms you need to collect a court judgment from the debtor's bank accounts, wages, business receipts, real estate or other assets.
$19.95/JUDG

How to Change Your Name
Attorneys David Loeb & David Brown
California 5th Edition
This book explains how to change your name legally and provides all the necessary court forms with detailed instructions on how to fill them out.
$19.95/NAME

LEGAL REFORM

Legal Breakdown: 40 Ways to Fix Our Legal System
Nolo Press Editors and Staff
National 1st Edition
Legal Breakdown presents 40 common sense proposals to make our legal system fairer, faster, cheaper and more accessible. It explains such things as why we should abolish probate, take divorce out of court, treat jurors better and give them more power, and make a host of other fundamental changes.
$8.95/LEG

MONEY MATTERS

Barbara Kaufman's Consumer Action Guide
Barbara Kaufman
California 1st Edition
This practical handbook is filled with information on hundreds of consumer topics. Barbara Kaufman, the Bay Area's award-winning consumer reporter and producer of KCBS Radio's *Call for Action*, gives consumers access to their legal rights, providing addresses and phone numbers of where to complain where things go wrong, and providing resources if more help is necessary.
$14.95/CAG

Money Troubles: Legal Strategies ' Cope With Your Debts
Attorney Robin Leonard
National 1st Edition
Are you behind on your credit card bills or loan payments? If you are, then *Money Troubles* is exactly wha you need. Covering everything fror knowing what your rights are and asserting them, to helping you evaluate your individual situation, this practical, straightforward book for anyone who needs help understanding and dealing with the complex and often scary topic of debts.
$16.95/MT

How to File for Bankruptcy
Attorneys Stephen Elias, Albin Renauer & Robin Leonard
National 3rd Edition
Trying to decide whether or not filing for bankruptcy makes sense? *How to File for Bankruptcy* contains an overview of the process and all t forms plus step-by-step instructions on the procedures to follow.
$24.95/HFB

Simple Contracts for Personal Use
Attorney Stephen Elias & Marcia Stewart
National 2nd Edition
This book contains clearly written legal form contracts to buy and sell property, borrow and lend money, store and lend personal property, release others from personal liability or pay a contractor to do home repairs. Includes agreements to arrange child care and other household help.
$16.95/CONT

rce & Money

et Woodhouse & Victoria Felton-
ins with M.C. Blakeman
onal 1st Edition
rce & Money explains how to
uate such major assets as family
es and businesses, investments,
sions, and how to arrive at a
sion of property that is fair to
sides. The book emphasizes the
erence between legal reality—
the court evaluates assets, and
ncial reality—what the assets are
ly worth.
.95/DIMO

Guardianship Book

Goldoftas & Attorney
id Brown
fornia 1st Edition
Guardianship Book provides step-
step instructions and the forms
ded to obtain a legal guardianship
hout a lawyer.
.95/GB

ctical Divorce Solutions

orney Charles Sherman
ifornia 2nd Edition
s book is a valuable guide to the
otional aspects of divorce as well
n overview of the legal and
ancial decisions that must be
de.
.95/PDS

w to Do Your Own Divorce

orney Charles Sherman
xas 4th Ed. by Sherman & Simons
ifornia 17th Edition & Texas 2nd
tion
ese books contain all the forms
instructions you need to do your
contested divorce without a
yer.
lifornia $18.95/CDIV
xas $17.95/TDIV

The Living Together Kit

Attorneys Toni Ihara & Ralph Warner
National 6th Edition
The Living Together Kit is a detailed
guide designed to help the increasing
number of unmarried couples living
together understand the laws that
affect them. Sample agreements and
instructions are included.
$17.95/LTK

A Legal Guide for Lesbian and Gay Couples

Attorneys Hayden Curry &
Denis Clifford
National 6th Edition
Laws designed to regulate and protect
unmarried couples don't apply to
lesbian and gay couples. This book
shows you step-by-step how to write a
living-together contract, plan for
medical emergencies, and plan your
estates. Includes forms, sample
agreements and lists of both national
lesbian and gay legal organizations,
and AIDS organizations.
$17.95/LG

How to Adopt Your Stepchild in California

Frank Zagone &
Attorney Mary Randolph
California 3rd Edition
There are many emotional, financial
and legal reasons to adopt a
stepchild, but among the most
pressing legal reasons is the need to
avoid confusion over inheritance or
guardianship. This book provides
sample forms and step-by-step
instructions for completing a simple
uncontested adoption by a
stepparent.
$19.95/ADOP

California Marriage & Divorce Law

Attorneys Ralph Warner, Toni Ihara
& Stephen Elias
California 11th Edition
This book explains community
property, pre-nuptial contracts,
foreign marriages, buying a house,
getting a divorce, dividing property,
and more.
$19.95/MARR

PATENT, COPYRIGHT & TRADEMARK

Patent It Yourself

Attorney David Pressman
National 3rdEdition
From the patent search to the actual
application, this book covers
everything from use and licensing,
successful marketing and how to deal
with infringement.
$34.95/PAT

The Copyright Handbook

Attorney Stephen Fishman
National 1st Edition
Writers, editors, publishers, scholars,
educators, librarians and others who
work with words all need to know
about copyright laws. This book
provides forms and step-by-step
instructions for protecting all types of
written expression under U.S. and
international copyright law. It
contains detailed reference chapters
on such major copyright-related
topics as copyright infringement, fair
use, works for hire and transfers of
copyright ownership.
$24.95/COHA

The Inventor's Notebook

Fred Grissom & Attorney David Pressman
National 1st Edition
This book helps you document the process of successful independent inventing by providing forms, instructions, references to relevant areas of patent law, a bibliography of legal and non-legal aids and more.
$19.95/INOT

How to Copyright Software

Attorney M.J. Salone
National 3rd Edition
This book tells you how to register your copyright for maximum protection and discusses who owns a copyright on software developed by more than one person.
$39.95/COPY

BUSINESS/ WORKPLACE

How to Write a Business Plan

Mike McKeever
National 3rd Edition
If you're thinking of starting a business or raising money to expand an existing one, this book will show you how to write the business plan and loan package necessary to finance your business and make it work.
$17.95/SBS

Sexual Harassment on the Job

Attorneys William Petrocelli & Barbara Kate Repa
National 1st Edition
This is the first comprehensive book dealing with sexual harassment in the workplace. It describes what harassment is, what the laws are that make it illegal and how to put a stop to it. This guide is invaluable both for employees experiencing harassment and for employers interested in creating a policy against sexual harassment and a procedure for handling complaints.
$14.95/HARS

Your Rights in the Workplace

Dan Lacey
National 1st Edition
Your Rights in the Workplace, the first comprehensive guide to workplace rights—from hiring to firing—explains the latest sweeping changes in laws passed to protect workers. Learning about these legal protections can help all workers be sure they're paid fairly and on time, get all employment benefits, and know how to take action if fired or laid off illegally.
$15.95/YRW

Marketing Without Advertising

Michael Phillips & Salli Rasberry
National 1st Edition
This book outlines practical steps for building and expanding a small business without spending a lot of money on advertising.
$14.00/MWAD

How to Form Your Own Corporat⃨

Attorney Anthony Mancuso
California 7th Edition
New York 2nd Edition
Florida 3rd Edition
Texas 4th Edition
These books contain the forms, instructions and tax information need to incorporate a small busin⃨ yourself and save hundreds of do⃨ in lawyers' fees.
California $29.95/CCOR
New York $24.95/NYCO
Florida $24.95/FLCO
Texas $29.95/TCOR

The Partnership Book

Attorneys Denis Clifford & Ralph Warner
National 4th Edition
This book shows you step-by-step how to write a solid partnership agreement that meets your needs. covers initial contributions to the business, wages, profit-sharing, bu⃨ outs, death or retirement of a par⃨ and disputes.
$24.95/PART

How to Form Your Own Nonprofit Corporation

Attorney Anthony Mancuso
National 1st Edition
This book explains the legal formalities involved and provides detailed information on the differences in the law among 50 states. It also contains forms for t⃨ Articles, Bylaws and Minutes you need, along with complete instructions for obtaining federal 501 (c) (3) tax exemptions and qualifying for public charity status
$24.95/NNP

California Nonprofit Corporation
book

ney Anthony Mancuso
ornia 6th Edition
book shows you step-by-step
to form and operate a nonprofit
oration in California. It includes
atest corporate and tax law
ges, and the forms for the
les, Bylaws and Minutes.
95/NON

California Professional
oration Handbook

ney Anthony Mancuso
ornia 4th Edition
th care professionals, lawyers,
untants and members of certain
r professions must fulfill special
rements when forming a
oration in California. This book
ains up-to-date tax information
all the forms and instructions
ssary to form a California
ssional corporation.
95/PROF

ndependent
egal's Handbook

ney Ralph Warner
nal 2nd Edition
ndependent Paralegal's Handbook
des legal and business guidelines
ose who want to take routine
work out of the law office and
it for a reasonable fee in an
endent business.
95/ PARA

Getting Started as an Independent Paralegal
(Two Audio Tapes)
Attorney Ralph Warner
National 2nd Edition
If you are interested in going into
business as an Independent
Paralegal—helping consumers
prepare their own legal paperwork in
uncontested proceedings such as
bankruptcy, divorce, small business
incorporation, landlord-tenant
actions and probate—you'll want to
listen to these tapes. Approximately
two hours in length, the tapes will
tell you everything you need to know
about what legal tasks to handle, how
much to charge and how to run a
profitable business.
$44.95/GSIP

HOMEOWNERS

How to Buy a House in California
Attorney Ralph Warner, Ira Serkes &
George Devine
California 1st Edition
This book shows you how to find a
house, work with a real estate agent,
make an offer and negotiate
intelligently. Includes information on
all types of mortgages as well as
private financing options.
$18.95/BHCA

For Sale By Owner
George Devine
California 2nd Edition
For Sale By Owner provides essential
information about pricing your
house, marketing it, writing a
contract and going through escrow.
$24.95/FSBO

The Deeds Book
Attorney Mary Randolph
California 1st Edition
If you own real estate, you'll need to
sign a new deed when you transfer the
property or put it in trust as part of
your estate planning. This book shows
you how to find the right kind of deed,
complete the tear-out forms and
record them in the county recorder's
public records.
$15.95/DEED

Homestead Your House
Attorneys Ralph Warner, Charles
Sherman & Toni Ihara
California 8th Edition
This book shows you how to file a
Declaration of Homestead and
includes complete instructions and
tear-out forms.
$9.95/HOME

THE NEIGHBORHOOD

Neighbor Law: Fences, Trees, Boundaries & Noise
Attorney Cora Jordan
National 1st Edition
Neighbor Law answers common
questions about the subjects that
most often trigger disputes between
neighbors: fences, trees, boundaries
and noise. It explains how to find the
law and resolve disputes without a
nasty lawsuit.
$14.95/NEI

Dog Law
Attorney Mary Randolph
National 1st Edition
Dog Law is a practical guide to the
laws that affect dog owners and their
neighbors. You'll find answers to
common questions on such topics as
biting, barking, veterinarians and
more.
$12.95/DOG

LANDLORDS & TENANTS

The Landlord's Law Book: Vol. 1, Rights & Responsibilities
Attorneys David Brown & Ralph Warner
California 3rd Edition
This book contains information on deposits, leases and rental agreements, inspections (tenants' privacy rights), habitability (rent withholding), ending a tenancy, liability and rent control.
$29.95/LBRT

The Landlord's Law Book: Vol. 2, Evictions
Attorney David Brown
California 3rd Edition
Updated for 1992, this book will show you step-by-step how to go to court and get an eviction for a tenant who won't pay rent—and won't leave. Contains all the tear-out forms and necessary instructions.
$29.95/LBEV

Tenants' Rights
Attorneys Myron Moskovitz & Ralph Warner
California 11th Edition
This book explains how to handle your relationship with your landlord and understand your legal rights when you find yourself in disagreement. A special section on rent control cities is included.
$15.95/CTEN

OLDER AMERICANS

Social Security, Medicare & Pensions
Attorney Joseph Matthews with Dorothy Matthews Berman
National 5th Edition
This book contains invaluable guidance through the current maze of rights and benefits for those 55 and over, including Medicare, Medicaid and Social Security retirement and disability benefits and age discrimination protections.
$15.95/SOA

Elder Care: Choosing & Financing Long-Term Care
Attorney Joseph Matthews
National 1st Edition
This book will guide you in choosing and paying for long-term care, alerting you to practical concerns and explaining laws that may affect your decisions.
$16.95/ELD

JUST FOR FUN

29 Reasons Not to Go to Law School
Attorneys Ralph Warner & Toni Ihara
National 3rd Edition
Filled with humor and piercing observations, this book can save you three years, $70,000 and your sanity.
$9.95/29R

Devil's Advocates: The Unnatural History of Lawyers
by Andrew & Jonathan Roth
National 1st Edition
This book is a painless and hilarious education, tracing the legal profession. Careful attention is given to the world's worst lawyers, most preposterous cases and most ludicrous courtroom strategies.
$12.95/DA

Poetic Justice: The Funniest, Meanest Things Ever Said About Lawyers
Edited by Jonathan & Andrew Roth
National 1st Edition
A great gift for anyone in the legal profession who has managed to maintain a sense of humor.
$8.95/PJ

RESEARCH & REFERENCE

Legal Research: How to Find and Understand the Law
Attorney Stephen Elias
National 3rd Edition
A valuable tool on its own or as companion to just about every other Nolo book. This book gives easy to use, step-by-step instructions on to find legal information.
$16.95/LRES

Family Law Dictionary
Attorneys Robin Leonard & Stephen Elias
National 2nd Edition
Finally, a legal dictionary that's written in plain English, not "legalese"! *The Family Law Dictionary* is designed to help the nonlawyer who has a question or problem involving family law—marriage, divorce, adoption or living together.
$13.95/FLD

al Research Made Easy:
oadmap Through the Law
rary Maze
/2 hr. videotape and 40-page manual
ional 1st Edition
o Press/Legal Star Communications
ou're a law student, paralegal or
arian—or just want to look up the
for yourself—this video is for you.
iversity of California law professor
Berring explains how to use all
basic legal research tools in your
al law library.
.95/LRME

) F T W A R E

Maker
o Press
sion 4.0
s easy-to-use software program
you prepare and update a legal
—safely, privately and without
expense of a lawyer. Leading you
-by-step in a question-and-answer
nat, *WillMaker* builds a will
und your answers, taking into
ount your state of residence.
lMaker comes with a 200-page
al manual which provides the legal
kground necessary to make sound
ices. Good in all states except
isiana.
PC
/2 & 5-1/4 disks included)
.95/WI4
CINTOSH $69.95/WM4

For the Record
Carol Pladsen & Attorney Ralph Warner
Version 2.0
For the Record provides a single place
to keep a complete inventory of all
your important legal, financial,
personal and family records. It can
compute your net worth and also
create inventories of all insured
property to protect your assets in the
event of fire or theft. Includes a 200-
page manual filled with practical and
legal advice.
IBM PC
(3-1/2 & 5-1/4 disks included)
$59.95/FRI2
MACINTOSH $59.95/FRM2

California Incorporator
Attorney Anthony Mancuso
Version 1.0 (good only in CA)
Answer the questions on the screen
and this software program will print
out the 35-40 pages of documents you
need to make your California corporation legal. Comes with a 200-page
manual which explains the
incorporation process.
IBM PC
(3-1/2 & 5-1/4 disks included)
$129.00/INCI

The California Nonprofit Corporation Handbook
(computer edition)
Attorney Anthony Mancuso
Version 1.0 (good only in CA)
This book/software package shows
you step-by-step how to form and
operate a nonprofit corporation in
California. Included on disk are the
forms for the Articles, Bylaws and
Minutes.
IBM PC 5-1/4 $69.95/ NPI
IBM PC 3-1/2 $69.95/ NP3I
MACINTOSH $69.95/ NPM

Nolo's Living Trust
Attorney Mary Randolph
Version 1.0
A will is an indispensable part of any
estate plan, but many people need a
living trust as well. By putting
certain assets into a trust, you save
your heirs the headache, time and
expense of probate. *Nolo's Living
Trust* lets you set up an individual or
shared marital trust, make your trust
document legal, transfer your
property to the trust, and change or
revoke the trust at any time. The 380
page manual guides you through the
process step-by-step , and over 100
legal help screens and an on-line
glossary explain key legal terms and
concepts.
MACINTOSH $79.95/LTM1

How to Form Your Own New York Corporation
&
How to Form Your Own Texas Corporation
Computer Editions
Attorney Anthony Mancuso
These book/software packages
contain the instructions and tax
information and forms you need to
incorporate a small business and save
hundreds of dollars in lawyers' fees.
All organizational forms are on disk.
Both come with a 250-page manual.

New York 1st Edition
IBM PC 5-1/4 $69.95/ NYCI
IBM PC 3-1/2 $69.95/ NYC3I
MACINTOSH $69.95/ NYCM

Texas 1st Edition
IBM PC 5-1/4 $69.95/ TCI
IBM PC 3-1/2 $69.95/ TC3I
MACINTOSH $69.95/ TCM

IT OUR STORE

live in the Bay Area, be sure to visit the Nolo Press
store on the corner of 9th & Parker Streets in West
ley. You'll find our complete line of books and
are—new and "damaged"—all at a discount. We
ave t-shirts, posters and a selection of business and
self-help books from other publishers.

Hours

Monday to Friday	10 a.m. to 5 p.m.
Thursdays	Until 6 p.m
Saturdays	10 a.m. to 4:30 p.m.
Sundays	10 a.m. to 3 p.m.

950 Parker Street, Berkeley, California

DER FORM

ss (UPS to street address, Priority Mail to P.O. boxes)

g Code	Quantity	Item		Unit price	Total
			Subtotal		
			Sales tax (California residents only)		
			Shipping & handling		
			2nd day UPS		
			TOTAL		

TAX

rnia residents add your local tax.

ING & HANDLING

   1 item
   2-3 items
   each additional item
2-3 weeks for delivery

URRY?

nd day delivery is available:
5.00 (contiguous states) or
(Alaska & Hawaii) to your regular shipping and handling
s

**FOR FASTER SERVICE, USE YOUR CREDIT CARD AND OUR
TOLL-FREE NUMBERS:**
Monday-Friday, 7 a.m. to 5 p.m. Pacific Time

Order line	1 (800) 992-6656
General Information	1 (510) 549-1976
Fax us your order	1 (800) 645-0895

METHOD OF PAYMENT
☐ Check enclosed
☐ VISA ☐ Mastercard ☐ Discover Card
☐ American Express

Account #   Expiration Date

Signature

Phone

YRW

S SUBJECT TO CHANGE

OLO PRESS / 950 PARKER STREET / BERKELEY CA 94710